THE PERSISTENT VOICE OF DIETRICH BONHOEFFER

Also by Edwin Robertson

Paul Schneider: the Pastor of Buchenwald
Man's Estimate of Man
Tomorrow is a Holiday: A South American Journey
New Translations of the Bible
Take and Read: A Guide to Group Bible Study
Light in Darkness
Mini-Commentaries 8 & 9 (The Old Testament Prophets)
Corinthians One and Two
Local Broadcasting
Breakthrough
Chiara Lubich
Igino Giordani
The Wounded Healer (with Vera Phillips)
Wycliffe: Morning Star of the Reformation
Christians against Hitler

THE PERSISTENT VOICE OF DIETRICH BONHOEFFER

The life and teaching of Dietrich Bonhoeffer

Edwin Robertson

Eagle Publishing
Bath

This edition published by Eagle Publishing Ltd, Unit 2, Atworth Industrial Estate, Atworth, Wiltshire, SN12 8SB.

British Library Cataloguing in Publication Data. A catalogue record for this book is available from the British Library.

Typeset by Eagle Publishing Ltd
Printed by Bookmarque Ltd
ISBN No: 0 86347 621 X

'To punish sin and to forgiveness you are moved,
God, this people I have loved.
That I bore its shame and sacrifices
And saw its salvation – that suffices'

(From, *The Death of Moses* by Dietrich Bonhoeffer)

Writings by Dietrich Bonhoeffer in English Translation:

Sanctorum Communio, Collins, 1963 (American title, *The Communion of Saints*, Harper & Row, 1963)
Act and Being, Collins 1962 (Harper & Row, 1962)
The Cost of Discipleship, SCM Press, 1959 (Macmillan, New York, 1959)
Ethics, SCM Press, 1964 (Macmillan, 1964)
Letters, Lectures and Notes from the *Collected Works*, introduced and selected by Edwin Robertson:
1. *No Rusty Swords* (1928 – 36) Collins & Harper & Row, 1965
2. *The Way to Freedom* (1935 – 39) Collins & Harper & Row, 1966
3. *True Patriotism* (1939 – 45) Collins & Harper & Row, 1973
'Christology' – reconstructed lectures – Collins & Harper & Row, 1966 & 1978 (translated by John Bowden and Edwin Robertson)
Letters and Papers from Prison, SCM Press & Macmillan, 1971
Prayers from Prison, edited by J. C. Hampe, Collins 1977
(containing the text of *The Death of Moses*)

Biographies

Edwin Robertson, Lutterworth, 1966; Mary Bosanquet, Hodder & Stoughton, 1968.
Eberhard Bethge, Collins, translated from the German under the Editorship of Edwin Robertson, 1970.
I Knew Dietrich Bonhoeffer, edited by Wolf-Dieter Zimmermann & Ronald Gregor Smith, 1973 edition with Introduction by Edwin Robertson.

Contents

Acknowledgements

Anyone who writes about Dietrich Bonhoeffer owes a debt to Eberhard Bethge, who has devoted his life to protecting and communicating the words of his close friend and colleague. I had the privilege of editing and, with the help of John Bowden as translator, preparing Bethge's carefully garnered *Gesammelte Schriften* (*Collected Writings*) for publication in the separate volumes of *No Rusty Swords, The Way to Freedom* and *True Patriotism.* Together with Ronald Gregor Smith, I had also the privilege of editing Bethge's formative biography and supervising its translation.

All these and others who worked with me gave me an insight into Dietrich Bonhoeffer which I value. But there was another extraordinary man of the theatre who lit up the humanity of Bonhoeffer in a remarkable way. He is Wilfred Harrison, who over long years has interviewed more people who knew Bonhoeffer than anyone else. He has long been preparing a play about him and when that is accomplished, it will bring before our eyes on stage and screen the authentic portrait of Dietrich Bonhoeffer.

At an Anglo-Dutch Conference held in 1985 he presented his picture of the humanness of Dietrich Bonhoeffer and it so brought him alive before us all that I asked him to give us a version of that presentation to open my own biography of the man. He graciously decided to let me use a large part of it.

Over the years, at Bonhoeffer conferences or in the course of German Kirchentage, in homes, lecture rooms and wine cellars, I have met Bonhoeffer's students. Some have written their own stories in German and I have made good use of their books. Zimmermann collected impressions from those who knew him in *I Knew Dietrich Bonhoeffer* and that is of constant help to those who want to paint a rounded portrait. Werner Koch, in his books about the Third Reich and his own brilliant conversations, gave me a close view. There was one part of the Bonhoeffer family which escaped into England – the Leibholzs.

Sabine Leibholz is Dietrich's twin sister; Gerhard, her husband, was part Jewish and therefore the family had to escape early. He was a brilliant and successful lawyer, who wrote clearly from Oxford. Their daughter was brought up in England and has been a great source of help to me. Marianne has shown a lively interest in the progress of this book through the press and has been most helpful in her comments.

For the rest there are too many to record them all – Dudzus who gave us two volumes of Bonhoeffer's sermons; Geff Kelly who has kept the Bonhoeffer Society alive in America; Mary Bosanquet who came to me as Mary Derby when she was preparing her penetrating account of the life and death of Dietrich Bonhoeffer; Terence Tiller who produced my two imaginary conversations for the Third Programme and made me write my first sketch biography of the man he had not met till then – and so many others. All have played their part, however unwittingly, in this book.

The Memory of a Child: Bonhoeffer's Family

RENATE BETHGE

I was seven years old when Hitler came to power and nineteen when the war ended. Bonhoeffer was just twenty years older than me. My parents' house was quite near the Bonhoeffer grandparents in Berlin.

I remember how disturbed all the members of that big family were when Hitler became Reich Chancellor. Quite early they had seen the danger of the Nazis.

I knew about the brutality of the Nazis, their lying propaganda, their scurrilous stories of the Jews. Everyone knew about such things; but many people were in despair, without work and food, so that they just wanted someone to rescue them. They believed Hitler's promises and hoped that he would drop the less attractive part of his image when he came to power. Some didn't even notice the less attractive side. Our family was not in such a bad situation and therefore we could keep our eyes open. We knew quite early of Hitler's concentration camps for his opponents, especially the Jews. But we also knew that outside the family we must not speak in any way about what the family thought or said.

That became particularly clear to me in connection with the Röhm Putsch. Röhm, who was an old friend of Hitler's, chief of the SA and secretly contending for leadership, did not see eye to eye with Hitler about the tempo of the revolution. Thereupon, Hitler on 30 June 1934 had him and many others, including a former Reich Chancellor, General von Schleicher, and his wife, shot without trial, together with other political opponents. On that 30 June day, I visited my aunt, youngest sister to my mother and Dietrich, in Lichterfelde. From the nearby barracks we heard shots, and my aunt said that with every shot someone whom Hitler did not like was being destroyed. I remember the anxiety of those days at the house of my grandparents, the waiting for a reliable word, and the great disappointment when this word did not come. My grandparents' house was the accepted meeting place for the family. I can remember that there was always deep concern or even fury when politics was discussed. Sometimes there was whispering, sometimes one would go to the door to see if anyone was listening. Sometimes a cushion was put over the telephone, because it was rumoured that the Secret Police (Gestapo) could hear even when the receiver was replaced. Later, we children were sent outside to look out, particularly when my grandparents were listening to the BBC News. My grandmother never missed it. If she was with us, she would stand up shortly before ten o'clock – the time of the BBC News in German – and say, 'We must now go to our *prayers*!' Such code words were quickly introduced into our family conversations. They were spontaneously invented and understood. In this way, the family could always telephone and quickly be understood, even though the Gestapo was listening to our calls.

It was a very close family. Apart from the parents, four of the children lived in Berlin: Dietrich always had his room in the parents' house, and was often with them. During the Nazi period, that was important for him, if only for political information and discussion. The oldest brother, Karl-Friedrich, who was Professor of Physical Chemistry in Leipzig and Dietrich's twin sister, Sabine, who was in Göttingen, came often to visit their parents in Berlin.

I think the size of the family was a help. All were politically in harmony and strengthened one another. The father's ability to observe carefully and objectively (he was Professor of Neurology and Psychiatry in the University of Berlin), enabled him to see through Hitler and his followers from the beginning, and from the letters of the brothers and sisters, written already in the early twenties, it is noticeable how negatively the family felt towards the Nazis. The family carried so much weight that it would have been much more difficult for any single member of it to become a Nazi, or even a 'fellow-traveller', than to take part in the resistance. The principal source of information in the family was Hans von Dohnanyi, the husband of Dietrich's sister, Christine. He was at that time the first and most fully involved in the 'conspiracy'. He worked in the Ministry of Justice under Gürtner, and had already started to compile a dossier of Nazi crimes in 1934, with the intention of bringing charges against Hitler if there was a rising of the people. But for such a rising, the people would have to have their illusions about Hitler shattered.

From 1939, Dohnanyi was in the Foreign Office of the *Abwehr* (military intelligence), under Admiral Canaris, where quite early many threads of the resistance groups were woven together. He worked there, protected by Admiral Canaris and Colonel Oster, for the overthrow of the regime. From that time on, Oster and Dohnanyi worked together on several plans for the overthrow, which again and again came to nothing because the generals, in view of Hitler's victories, could not bring themselves to act. (I remember, through those years, the repeated groans of doubt and disappointment in 'the generals' which I heard in the family, largely from Klaus Bonhoeffer and Christine Dohnanyi.)

Dietrich Bonhoeffer himself was admitted to the political resistance in 1940 through Dohnanyi. He was appointed to the staff of Admiral Canaris and thus exempted from military service. Dohnanyi was also successful in freeing some of Bonhoeffer's former seminary students from the threat of conscription, but he expected no service in return. On the other hand, he did want to make use of Dietrich Bonhoeffer's wide-ranging international contacts for the resistance. Dohnanyi could also protect him from Gestapo investigations, because they had no access to the 'military secrets' of the *Abwehr*.

Klaus Bonhoeffer too, who was also a lawyer, employed by Lufthansa, worked with his whole heart for the resistance. He had sought and found connections with opposition groups and individuals, whom he linked up with one another. Among his contacts were the cousins of his wife, Ernst and Arvid von Harnack, also Wilhelm Leuschner, Julius Leber, Johannes Popitz, Joseph Wirmer, Carlo Mierendorff, Jakob Kaiser, Prinz Louis Ferdinand, Karl-Ludwig Freiherr von und zu Guttenberg and his wife's brother, Justus Delbruck. Klaus was frequently with these men in their homes and therefore came back home late at night. He would return, sometimes full of hope, sometimes cast down, but always excited, to my parents or grandparents. But unfortunately, I knew no more than that, because he was very careful not to give any of his news in the presence of the 'youngsters'. This care was of course necessary. It was seldom possible to write down anything clearly. It is therefore very difficult to reconstruct the details of the resistance, especially as the Nazis left very few of the main participants alive.

Christine von Dohnanyi, who was herself very active as a resistance worker – she lived until 1965 – was very well informed about the procedures in the foreign office of the Abwehr. Unfortunately, she withdrew into herself soon after the war, full of disappointment that survivors in their publications had enlarged and embellished their own images at the cost of those put to death for their principal roles in the resistance. She feared that representation of the events by the survivors would determine the picture of the resistance. My father, Dr Rüdiger Schleicher also suffered. He helped the resistance, when in the National Ministry for Air Traffic, whose legal department he headed until 1939, with information. When he became honorary professor in the University of Berlin and head of the Institute for Air Traffic Law, he worked closely with Dr Hans John (brother of Klaus Bonhoeffer's colleague, Dr Otto John), who was deeply involved with the resistance. My father made possible and covered up his conspiratorial journeys.

In the early period after Hitler came to power, conversations at home were mainly concentrated on the Church. Even those for whom the Church, until then, had not been very important, began to interest themselves in it. The Church was the only institution which took definite steps and set itself against the ideologies of the Nazis, and also publicly formulated words of protest and circulated them through groups in the Church: in particular, that group which was formed as the Confessing Church in 1934. All other independent or hostile associations and institutions were simply dissolved by the Nazis or taken over by them. So one no longer saw the Church as concerned only with its own interests. When one supported the Confessing Church, it was hoped that it would encourage the non-Nazis in the government, the authorities and public servants. Anyone who wanted to show opposition to the Hitler regime could do so by an ostentatious visit to a church service where the pastor was a member of the Confessing Church.

Dietrich and his friend, Franz Hildebrandt, a Lutheran theologian of Jewish parentage, discussed the situation constantly during the first years of the Nazis – and worked out plans for the Confessing Church – in the family. In these matters, my grandmother, Dietrich's mother, was deeply involved. She made contacts with people who had been in the government before Hitler's seizure of power and still remained, smoothing the way here and there for the conspirators. I can see her always telephoning, calling upon friends to get things moving. On Sundays, she often went to Niemöller's church in Dahlem to attend service there; she took several of us children with her, so as to fill up even more a church which was already well attended. My grandmother was, of course, enrolled in the membership list of the 'confessing' congregation, and had the famous 'red card'. Susanne Dress, the youngest of Dietrich's sisters had the 'red card' even earlier, on 23 July 1934. (The red card, as a mark of personal commitment, was first introduced as a result of the 'Barmen Declaration' of 31 May 1934.)

As Dietrich was in England from the end of 1933 until 1935, his mother kept him informed by means of frequent telephone conversations.

Naturally the family was always talking about church events and making plans, for example in 1936, whether Dietrich should accept the invitation to speak in Berlin during the Olympic Games or, by his refusal, leave the Nazis alone to present Germany in their own favourable light.

Unfortunately, I was often quite uninterested in the conversations of the grown-ups, but I was very aware of the highly charged atmosphere. But I do remember Niemoller's arrest, then his acquittal, followed by his admission to the concentration camp. That disturbed everyone dreadfully, and Niemöller's health was a constant concern.

In later years, the subject of the Confessing Church did not retain its central place in the conversation of the family. Whether it was because not so much was expected of it, or – what is naturally related to this - that the family began now to be far more involved in the political field, or simply that what happened politically was so outrageous and deadly that it left no room for further discussion, I do not know.

The Jewish question took precedence over all other subjects, and all political questions were related to it. Already two months after Hitler came to power, there came together with other laws 'The Law for the Restructuring of the Civil Service'. It contained the Aryan clauses, which deprived Jews of their office. In 1935, there followed the infamous 'Nüremberg Laws', which classified and denigrated Jews, and imposed penalties upon their children even when they were partially 'Aryan'. Later, we had to study, in school, the details of 'National Socialist State Structures'. Long before Auschwitz, there was the daily harassment of Jews with minor and major irritations, which began with notices on park benches, 'Jews not wanted here!' – also on public buildings and restaurants. There was the boycott of Jewish shops and then later what came to be known as 'Kristallnacht', which was nationwide, smashing the windows of Jewish shops and burning the synagogues. Jews were attacked and sometimes killed, always humiliated.

Earlier in Berlin, liberal Christians and liberal Jews had lived quite happily together. In the Grunewald where the Bonhoeffers lived there were many Jews. Thus, the Bonhoeffers had many close friends who were Jews; Karl Bonhoeffer, the father, had Jewish assistants; Dietrich's twin sister, Sabine, married a man of Jewish parentage. Although Gerhard Leibholz was held in high regard in the family, there was some hesitation about the proposed marriage to Sabine at first. Each marriage in the family, which would have introduced a partner with a different, for instance Catholic, background, would have been looked upon in the same hesitant way. In 1933, the point at issue in the family discussion was how Jews would continue to live in Germany. Most of our Jewish friends had left Germany already in the first years after Hitler came to power. I can well remember the many considerations over the years on whether to emigrate, brought forward with serious concern. Every tiny indication that the regime might come to an end was seized upon. Every political movement was followed with great interest. Moreover, there were many people in the government itself, with whom the family had contact, who were hostile to the regime. It was hoped that such people might intervene in an emergency – only, one never knew whether they would be dismissed suddenly or become victims of the regime themselves. The decisive factor for the emigration was the secret information that passports of Jews would soon be marked with an 'Israel' for a man, and 'Sarah' for a woman, so that travel would be controlled for Jews and could be stopped all together.

From the beginning the family knew about the deportations and of the atrocities and killings by the Nazis. How soon they knew about the mass extermination I cannot say. The first news of torture and cases of killing aroused the family to high indignation and anger. The fury could hardly be increased. And yet we still heard of more and more terrible things. We never

ever got to know about the whole dimension of the crimes. I myself – and I think most of the family – did not regard the mass murders as something qualitatively new, but as a horrible crescendo of that which had been carried out and planned from the beginning, a nightmare in fact, which made plans for the assassination of Hitler ever more urgent. But these plans ran into more and more hitches and hindrances. Despite all, one went on living and managing one's days. We children were in the Hitler Youth Movement. I acquired a certificate to say that I had a 'weak heart' and was soon forgotten, so that I took no part in the organisation after I turned fourteen. My brother with his cello became a member of the Hitler Jugend broadcasting group, and instead of doing the customary service was able to play good music. My very athletic younger sister should have been appointed leader of a team of girls, but my parents knew how to withdraw her on 'medical grounds', but not to the pleasure of my sister!

The schools, of course, were pressurised by Nazi demands. You could soon tell who the real Nazis were. If the teacher hurriedly made the obligatory Nazi salute at the beginning and end of each lesson, he was no real Nazi. The same would be true if he said 'Hitler' instead of 'Führer'. In this way we picked out the non-Nazis – and not only among the teachers. A clear indication was also the size of the flag that you were required to hang out on special occasions. You could write off those with big flags. My parents had a somewhat small flag, but my grandparents had one that was so small that I was nervous for them – perhaps also a little proud, thinking of those terrible Nazis disturbed by it.

It is astonishing that through all these years we never lost hope, even when the five men of the family – the fifth was my husband, who alone survived and came out – even when they sat in prison and both my father and Klaus Bonhoeffer were sentenced to death. The activities of the family for the rescue of their men never stopped, even when the possibilities of success grew more and more slender. You can have no idea what went on in the minds of the family when Hans von Dohnanyi and Dietrich were arrested on 5 April 1943 – Christine von Dohnanyi was also in prison for five weeks – consultations, decoding messages out of books, direct intervention by my grandfather, who as a scientist enjoyed a great reputation. And there were constant private discussions with people who were well informed. Many of these discussions were about contact men who had unobtrusive access to people in key positions and could approach them without arousing suspicion. My father had also been used in this before he was put in prison. The pressures on my aunt, Dohnanyi – who at his request sent food with diphtheria bacillus into his prison so as to make him unfit for interrogation – were intolerable. Escape plans for Dietrich and for Dohnanyi were ultimately smuggled in, but they fell through. My parents and I brought the boiler suit in which Dietrich was to escape, and gave it to the warder who had conceived this plan. When Klaus and my father were arrested a few days later, Dietrich would not proceed with the plan.

Then came 2 February 1945, the day on which my father and Klaus were sentenced to death. Before then, there had been innumerable discussions and attempts at bribery, then more interventions and deep concern about the whereabouts of Dietrich and Hans, who had been moved out of Berlin. The end was a hard blow. But one had the feeling that, for our family, who had known so much, there was no other way, we were given no choice. Thus my grandfather after the war wrote to his former assistant, who now lived in America:

> I hear you know that we have been through a lot and lost two sons and two sons-in-law through the Gestapo. You can imagine that that has not been without its effect on us old folk. For years we had the tension caused by anxiety for those arrested and for those not yet arrested but in danger. But since we were all agreed on the need to act, and my sons were also fully aware of what they had to expect if the plot miscarried and had resolved if necessary to lay down their lives, we are sad, but also proud of their attitude, which has been consistent.

Introduction

To be born into a family with a distinguished liberal tradition in 1906 in Germany more or less guaranteed a life of upheaval and drama. But few of the scenarios that came out of the struggle with the Nazis can match the life and death of Dietrich Bonhoeffer, the Lutheran theologian.

He grew up in Berlin during the First World War, too young to fight, but old enough to know what was going on. At the end of that war he felt the shame of defeat and, as a teenager, the anger of a humiliating Versailles Treaty. He did not suffer the worst effects of Germany's currency devaluation because his father, a psychiatrist, could collect foreign currency from many of his clients. He had the best education a young German could have in Berlin and Tübingen. He surprised his family by choosing the Church as his career, but pleased them with his academic success. He travelled at a time when few Germans could afford that luxury, studying in America, working in Spain, holidaying in Italy and North Africa.

He was involved, although critically, in the growing ecumenical movement and met friends in many countries. With his whole family he was deeply concerned at the rise of the National Socialist Party (the Nazis) and broadcast the earliest attack on the principle of 'Dictatorship' within a few days of Hitler being elected. His voice was among the first Christian voices to be raised against the persecution of the Jews. From a safe pastorate in London, he joined with those who tried to keep the Church from being too influenced by Nazi teaching and found a friend in Bishop Bell of Chichester.

He returned to Germany to lead an illegal seminary for the training of ministers to serve the Confessing Church. He helped draft the Barmen Declaration which gave that Church a charter for theological resistance. In evident danger, he was invited to lecture in America for his own safety. After a very short stay he insisted upon returning to the dangers of Nazi Germany in order to share the 'shame and the sacrifice' with his own people. After much agonising, he joined the resistance movement and acted as a double agent. He conspired in the attempted assassination of Hitler, he travelled on a Nazi passport to neutral countries during the war and offered peace proposals to the enemy and a promise of a government to overthrow the Nazis. He was arrested and imprisoned for two years. In prison he wrote works that have rocked the world of theology ever since. As the war was drawing to a close, he was summarily tried, accused and hanged.

As a man he enjoyed life, accepting very reluctantly the role of double agent or leader of resistance. He would rather have made music with his friends, enjoyed their company at good meals and married to bring up a family. As a theologian, he was wholly Lutheran, but original in his interpretation of the master. In his thirty-nine years, he contributed much to the store of theological writings – most of them unpublished at his death – but had much more to write and think. He was reluctantly led to radical solutions for the future of his Church and the teaching of theology. He was not a martyr, but according to their lights, rightly condemned by the Nazis. Although his resistance to German Christians was theological, he was not condemned for that, but for subversive actions against the state. He had decided that it was right to pray and work for the defeat of his country, that civilisation might survive.

When Eberhard Bethge, the friend to whom he wrote most of his letters from prison, began to collect his papers after the war and publish them in volumes of *Collected Writings*, it fell to me to edit and in some cases translate them into English. As I worked through these writings from his earliest period to the end, a man of great stature emerged, very human, but a brilliant thinker whose mind was tuned to the problems of his day and country. Over a period of fifteen years I edited volume after volume and became convinced that there was a consistency about his thinking. Events shaped him, of course, and he reacted to the violent forces of his day, but there was a continuous thread running through from his student letters and articles to the *Letters and Papers from Prison* which caused such a stir in the sixties, when John Robinson extracted quotes from them to support his thesis in *Honest to God*. The radical statements he quoted were valid. Bonhoeffer was a radical theologian – but essentially biblical, as Luther was. In this book I hope to show the wholeness of the man, who lived and died a disciple of Jesus Christ, aware that he had often misunderstood, even done and said the wrong things, but sincere in his actions and thoughts, always rooted in the Word of God. From a child, his life ambition was to make a good and beautiful death and to show the world how a Christian can face death. Those who saw him at the end bear witness to his fulfilment of this wish.

ONE

A Child Fascinated by Death

Dietrich was born ten minutes before his twin sister, Sabine, and he never let her forget it! They were born in Breslau, the chief city of Silesia, then part of Germany, now Poland. He was one of a large family, eight children eventually, of whom the twins were sixth and seventh. Their birthday was 4 February 1906.

The family lived in a pleasant house, next to the Scheitniger Park where the father, Karl Bonhoeffer, was director of a mental hospital, as well as professor of psychiatry and neurology at the university. The house had its own large gardens in which the older children dug caves and played games which Dietrich entered into with gusto. They remembered him at the age of five, in the sultry summer of 1911, with his shock of flaxen hair framing his tanned face, hot from romping about and reluctant to obey the nursemaid's call to leave their games and come in!

Karl Bonhoeffer was happy with his large family. An entry in his diary at New Year, 1909, when he was on a visit to New York, shows his frame of mind: 'In spite of having eight children which surprises many people at the present time, we do not have the feeling that it is too many. The house is spacious, the children have developed normally, we parents are not too old, and we try not to spoil them, but give them a happy childhood.'[1]

The mother, Paula, also welcomed a large family and until Dietrich and Sabine were born took charge of the children's education herself. She was a fully qualified teacher, highly intelligent, an excellent hostess and a beautiful singer. One large room in the house was fitted out with desks as a classroom. Dietrich and Sabine, however, had their first schooling from a governess, Kathe Horn, with whom Dietrich kept contact certainly until he was in his twenties.

Karl Bonhoeffer was a busy man but he organised his life so as to give himself time with the children. And when he was with them he was totally with them, dancing round the table with the girls or devising games. He walked with them during the holidays and was always ready to hear their questions. He was not a dominant father. Paula was probably far more demanding than he was. But he demonstrated the standards he expected

21

them to live by. It was a stable household with mother and father supplementing each other's role.

Dietrich recognised in later life that his home had given him a sense of security. His youngest sister, Susanne, tells how on a walking tour with her during their student days, he said: 'I should like to live an unsheltered life for once. We cannot understand the others. We always have our parents to help us over every difficulty and, however far we are from home, that gives us such a shameless sense of security.'[2]

Breslau

In the early years of this century, Breslau had been a provincial Prussian town for 160 years, but it had a long history which had left its mark on traditions and buildings. Originally a town of Bohemia, it passed into Polish and Austrian hands, alternating with a period of Bohemian rule, until it was taken by Prussia eventually in 1742. When Dietrich was a boy it retained many of its old medieval buildings and was rich in baroque. As the capital of Lower Silesia it had a cultural heritage and good museums, art academy, theatres etc. It was the seat of a bishop and had several fine churches. During the nineteenth century, industry had grown rapidly – textiles, machinery, metallurgy and food – so that by 1900 it had a population of about 300,000 and was still growing. A large provincial town, lively and attractive. Dietrich was too young to take all this in, but his elder brothers were not and he must have absorbed some of their attachment to the town.

Karl Bonhoeffer had come to Breslau from Stuttgart in 1893 to be assistant to Carl Wernicke, the distinguished psychiatrist, and he had not liked the change. The tall houses and the factory chimneys compared most unfavourably with the gracious approaches to Stuttgart. But he dug himself in and almost became a Silesian. He specialised in the treatment of alcoholism and soon was recognised as the leading psychiatrist in Silesia, securing a special appointment to deal with the rehabilitation of psychologically disturbed prisoners. He married Paula von Hase on 5 March 1898 and in the same year received an independent appointment succeeding Carl Wernicke. He was much in demand from other universities, but for a time he found Breslau the best place in which to develop his researches.

The young Dietrich would know nothing of these important affairs, but he did know that a short distance away he could find his grandfather and his beloved Aunt Elisabeth, who ran the household after the death of his grandmother. And Dietrich remembered the holiday house they had at Wölfensgrund, which remained all his life an ideal place, even featuring in the one novel he wrote in prison at the end of his life.

The twins were particularly close and shared an early fascination with funerals! Opposite the house in Breslau was a Catholic cemetery, with the river flowing by. The twins loved to watch the river from their window and when a funeral cortége arrived with the black-draped horses drawing the hearse their excitement increased. They would never miss a funeral and indulged in long discussions about what it felt like to be dead.

The Move to Berlin

Dietrich was only six when his father was appointed to the most important chair of psychiatry in the country – to a professorship in Berlin. It was a long journey from Breslau to Berlin, not only in miles or kilometres. Journeying from a provincial town to the capital of the Prussian Empire was like moving to another world. Karl Bonhoeffer must have felt the advantage at once. The family originally moved into a house in Brückenallee, but later (1916) settled into a larger house at 14 Wangenheimstrasse in the Grunewald. It was an area where many of the academic staff of the university lived, teachers from widely differing faculties. He knew that his family would grow up there with cultural opportunities and intellectual stimulus. The holiday home in Wölfensgrund was now much too far away and, to the sorrow of the children, it had to be sold and another bought in the Harz mountains, near Friedrichsbrunn.

That move at Easter 1912 tore up many roots for the young Dietrich, but as the family was so self-contained the damage was limited. The whole family moved together and they brought their world with them. Far more disturbing than the move, although associated with it, was the beginning of school. At Breslau his school was at home with his mother or the governess, Käthe Horn. All the children had now to go to school in Berlin – the boys to the Friedrich Werder Gymnasium. The father would have liked the boys to have studied science but all chose the humanities. Dietrich was so far too young to choose! He began school in the autumn of 1913. The seven year old boy showed signs of nervousness and shyness. He was most unhappy. His father watched anxiously, with paternal care and a professional eye. The move had disturbed Dietrich more than he had expected, but he soon found satisfaction in the ease with which he could do the work. His father breathed a sigh of relief and commented, 'He does his work naturally and tidily. He likes fighting and does a great deal of it.' Dietrich was robust and developing a fine physique. He did not take to the elementary science taught at that age, but he did progress rapidly in music. The whole family was musical and often formed quartets in German fashion and Dietrich would never be left out. He soon proved outstanding and took the lead despite his age. Many sought his friendship at school, but he did not easily make friends. The large family was partly responsible. He had captive playmates at home in his brothers and sisters, bringing his school-fellows home sometimes, but only to join the family. It was a home where children played. His sisters said that Dietrich always played to win!

The Death Wish

The two little faces at the window in Breslau watching the funeral cortéges were pondering matters they could not fully grasp. Later, when Sabine and Dietrich were eight and sharing a room in the house in Berlin, they lay awake at night talking solemnly about death and eternal life. This would follow evening prayers and the singing of hymns with their mother. Sabine recalls that they would keep one another awake trying to imagine what eternal life must be like, how they would feel when they were dead. As they concentrated their young minds on the word 'eternity', excluding all other thoughts, they would think how long and gruesome it was. Dietrich liked thinking about death. He imagined himself on his death-bed, surrounded by all those who loved him, and secretly he would compose what he would say. He thought that death would not be grievous or alien. He would like to die young, a fine devout death! He wanted them all to understand that for a believer it was not hard to die. He wanted to show that it was a glorious thing. But, sometimes in the evening when he was over-tired, he would feel dizzy, and he began to think that he was going to die. Then he knew he was a fraud, because he cried out to God not to let it happen yet!

In later years, Dietrich talked and wrote about this period of his life, between the ages of eight and eleven when he both desired and feared death. Of course, it is never possible to be sure that later experiences have not been fed back into a remembered childhood, but he seems to have recalled these nights with Sabine in their shared room quite vividly. It was a kind of self-analysis for him. This comes out most clearly when he writes of his fear that he had an incurable disease. He wrote as though observing another person and perhaps he intended this to be fiction based upon memory:

> One day, he had a grotesque idea. He thought he was suffering from an incurable fear of death. No one could free him of this illness, because in reality it was no illness, but the most natural and obvious thing in the world – it was the most inevitable. He saw himself going from one person to another, pleading and appealing for help. Doctors shook their heads and could do nothing for him. His illness was that he saw reality for what it was. He could tolerate the thought of the inevitability of death for only a few moments.[3]

That was the texture of a dream and indicates that he was about to bury within himself something which could not be spoken. His favourite subject for discussion and for his imagination to dwell upon had suddenly acquired a bitter taste. He spoke no more about a fine, devout death.

Meanwhile, life in Berlin took a rapid change with the outbreak of war.

The First World War

Karl Bonhoeffer did not expect war! For the children it was exciting, but for the father and many of his acquaintances it was a gloomy and frightening prospect. The professional class of Germany had been mildly amused by the Kaiser, to whom they were all loyal, smiling at his strutting across the stage with the harmless trappings of uniform, armour and medals. His inflammatory speeches were regarded as no more than rhetoric.

Professor Bonhoeffer, with his international practice, was convinced that economic interests among the nations of Europe would prevent an armed conflict between European nations. A colonial war, perhaps, not a European one. But he was wrong. The nation seemed to go mad with enthusiasm as the Kaiser made more and more gestures, but when it came to it, the enthusiasm evaporated. Karl Bonhoeffer and his class tolerated bombast, but they sensed that real war would shatter their world.

On 4 August, a warm summer evening, he walked along the tree-lined avenue, Unter den Linden with three of his boys. The enthusiasm of the crowds in front of the palace, which had been so boisterous during the past few days, seemed now to yield to gloomy silence and he talks of it as 'extraordinarily oppressive'. The news had come that Britain had declared war on Germany. There was no gloomy silence among the children, of course. They picked up the early enthusiasm and prolonged it. Dietrich was the most enthusiastic of them all. In 1915, at the age of nine, while staying at the holiday home near Friedrichsbrunn, he wrote for maps and pins to plot the German advances and wanted newspaper cuttings so that he could be up-to-date! Back in Berlin, he reconnoitred the food markets and reported on what could be found. He knew when special rations could be obtained, the food prices, and where you could get the best bargains. He revealed hidden talents. One must admit that part of the reason for this burst of energy was his own huge appetite! Actually the family did not fare too badly at first, for Paula's brother, Uncle von Hase, was in a rural parish and it was always possible to find food there.

The First Casualties

By 1917, the war began to make more serious inroads on the family. News came of cousins killed in action or severely wounded and the older brothers who were still at school approached military age. Karl-Friedrich and Walter were then called up. Neither would allow the family to use its influence to get them commissions or safe jobs, although both Karl Bonhoeffer himself and the mother's branch of the family, the von Hases, had considerable influence. They both enrolled as infantrymen in the Fifth Regiment of Guards at Spandau, Berlin. After a short period of training they were sent to the front, Walter as an officer and Karl as an ordinary soldier. Walter left in the spring of 1918 at the age of just eighteen. Dietrich, on his own initiative, practised a song and sang it to him: 'Now as you leave we say: 'God speed you on your journey.' Walter was deeply moved by his twelve year old kid brother's act. Next morning he left, and as his mother ran beside the departing train she said, 'It's only space that separates us.'

These words impressed themselves on Dietrich's mind, perhaps because of the tragic events that followed. A fortnight later, Walter was killed on the Western Front. Paula was shattered and the whole family felt its defences had been broken. It took all Karl's loving care to restore his wife to being the inspiration of the family which she had always been – and eventually became once again. These war years had brought Dietrich face to face with the death that had long fascinated him.

The sense of security in the family had been breached by the first casualties, but it had also been divided by experience in a way that Dietrich was soon to recognise and explain. In 1918 when Walter was killed, the eldest brother, Karl-Friedrich, was nineteen and had experienced war. This put him in a different generation and, although Dietrich was to argue with him, he knew that the experience of war had set Karl-Friedrich apart and perhaps explained his cynicism. Klaus had not been old enough to go to war, but he too at seventeen seemed in another generation from twelve year old Dietrich. His two big sisters were moving into a strange world, Ursula at sixteen and Christine fifteen. He found himself grouped with the other two 'little ones' – his twin sister Sabine and the youngest child, Susanne, then only nine. Dietrich was the strongest and the only boy of the three little ones, and he quickly developed a protectiveness towards his sisters. This became most evident after Walter's death when Paula was more withdrawn. Both the younger sisters remember Dietrich's care. Sabine tells how, when gathering strawberries on a hot summer afternoon, Dietrich who had toiled with his usual enthusiasm for hours, carefully filled her half empty pot with his hard-won berries, so that she would not have less than he had. He was a tough little boy, well and strongly built, while training at the horizontal bars had hardened his muscles. He had only one serious illness in his childhood – in 1917 he had appendicitis and much enjoyed the experience of the nursing home.

But Friedrichsbrunn remained his joy and the younger children found that holiday home particularly therapeutic after Walter's death. There he discovered German literature, and there he played with the village children.

The house had a lovely view of the mountains and quite a large meadow, where everyone played together. It was mostly suited to the children, who often stayed there with the servants. The house had no electric light, but it did have a telephone and the children took turns telephoning Berlin to involve their parents in all they did and discovered.

The Decision

Friedrichsbrunn was for holidays, but Berlin meant school. Dietrich, for all his exuberance and love of games, was a thoughtful boy. He was capable in the midst of a lively conversation of suddenly withdrawing into solitude. Once in a Greek class, when he was in the first form, he was awakened from his dreaming by a question the master put. It must have corresponded to what he was thinking, because he did not stand up to reply, but spoke quietly as though he were still talking to himself. The master had asked, 'What will you eventually read at university?' Quietly, he replied, 'Theology!', and then he blushed. The master saw that he had embarrassed Dietrich and paused only to say, 'Well, you are in for some surprises.' The boy absorbed that brief moment into himself. It was a relief to get it out and he partly enjoyed the shock he had caused, but he was also a little ashamed. Now they all knew and he wondered if he had behaved as he should. Did he look serious enough? Was he firm or uncertain in his statement? He was becoming aware of his own vanity, but there was also the sense of awe before the immensity of the choice that he had made. He did not understand the master's remark, but he now realised the grandeur of his confession and his task. This incident is probably a piece of fictional writing, although based upon his experience.[4]

There had, of course, been many religious influences in his life before that incident in the Greek class. The Bonhoeffers were a Christian family, although not enthusiasts. The mother had involved herself earlier in Moravian piety; the father was a middle-of-the-road Lutheran. The family kept the festivals and attended church. Dietrich was confirmed, as were all the children. Sabine and Dietrich both took confirmation classes under Pastor Priebe, but separately as was the custom at the time. The twins were confirmed together on 15 March 1921, which seemed more natural to Dietrich than being segregated with the boys.

He had also been much moved at an Evangelical Rally of the Salvation Army when Bramwell Booth visited Berlin to preach. Dietrich was impressed by the joy he had seen on Booth's face and he watched those who had been carried away by the message, to affirm their allegiance to Jesus Christ. He almost went forward, but thought that at fourteen he was too young. He began to attend church regularly and his mother went with him. Her side of the family had been more closely associated with theology. Her father, a moderate and kindly man, was the son of the Church historian and court preacher, Karl von Hase. He was himself chaplain to Kaiser Wilhelm II.

Family Friends

There were two other families in the Grunewald district who soon discovered the Bonhoeffers and created with them a healthy society within the collapsing German Empire. They shared war and defeat, privation and disappointment, but never allowed despair to linger too long among them.

The first was the Delbrücks. Hans Delbrück was professor of history and a liberal. Klaus Bonhoeffer eventually married his daughter Emmi. The two families mingled in their games, entertainment and friendship. At the age of twelve, Dietrich began to join them. Emmi adored him, because he was like her beloved younger brother, Justus – strong, blond and blue-eyed. So much alike were they that Hans Delbrück frequently mistook Dietrich for his own son. It was soon discovered that Dietrich played the piano very well, Klaus, the cello, Sabine and Emmi the violin, while Ursula and Christine had good singing voices. They joined forces to make music together. At the piano Dietrich kept them all in order and in a sensitive way listened to the music they created. These two families produced young people who could enjoy each other. They went to concerts and parties, sometimes as a group, sometimes in pairs; they danced and talked and skated on the lake until it was dark. Klaus and Dietrich performed waltzes and figures on the ice with elegance. Soon another family joined them – the Dohnanyis, who also later married into the Bonhoeffer family.

Of course, they gossiped and quarrelled as any group of young people do, but they had style, a clear standard of taste and an intelligent interest in a wide range of subjects. It was hard to believe that a whole world was collapsing around them, but they were aware of the fact. Dietrich was really too young for such company, but he had to replace Walter. They probably all felt that these halcyon days in the shadow of defeat and deprivation were a gift which at the same time carried an immense obligation.

Dietrich was the most intense of that young group. Many commented on his rather stiff manner – old for his years. When he learnt to dance, the teacher was heard to say, 'Bonhoeffer, that's not a bow, it's a bend!' He walked with very straight knees and played his games with great intensity and seriousness. He had strong hands, but Emmi remembers that even at fifteen his firm grip never hurt.

He was troubled by what he saw of deprivation and despair in Berlin and could never condemn a suicide after that experience of witnessing a hopeless people with no prospect of relief. What he saw as the war dragged on, the blockade starving the civilian population, the news of defeat stunning a proud people and the terms of the Versailles Treaty giving them no hope of recovery, raised questions that rapidly became theological. He saw the hunger and the unemployment, although personally shielded from their worst effects. Was he spoilt? In a way the whole generation of prosperous middle-class Germans who managed to survive with their standards of living hardly impaired were all spoilt! But Bonhoeffer was even more vulnerable. He was the last to leave home, the only one of the Bonhoeffers who did not marry. Did Paula cling to him even more because she had lost Walter? He had a sheltered childhood and every advantage.

But I like to believe that Emmi (later Klaus' wife) understood him when she answered that question whether he was spoilt by saying: 'You can tell a person who comes from a home where the parents have taken their duties very seriously. In a nursery, the delphinium grows taller and its flowers are of deeper blue than those in the field.'[5]

TWO

The Humiliation of Defeat

The happy picture of those privileged young people in the Grunewald, with which the last chapter ended, needs some qualification. They were better off than many, but they too felt the shortage of food. Dietrich Bonhoeffer was able to say to an American audience several years later:

> The consequences of the blockade were frightful. I myself was in those days a schoolboy and I can assure you that I was not the only one who had to learn what hunger means. I wish you could have to eat, just for one day, what we had to endure for three or four years. I think you would then get a glimpse of the privations which Germany had to suffer.

Going into details of food during those war years, he added: 'Instead of a good meal there was largely sawdust in our bread and the fixed portion for every day was five or six slices of this bread.'[1]

He may have been generalising and forgetting the relief he had from Uncle Hase's rural parish, but he suffered. And the peace did not end it. The same 11 November which brought the end of the war, was the beginning of a new epoch of suffering as the corruption of public life and the humiliation of defeat by a merciless enemy was blended with the general poverty and the starvation. Again, the Bonhoeffers had the advantage of access to foreign currency through the father's clients . . . but they suffered too.

Germany Learns of Defeat

At the age of twelve Bonhoeffer's attitudes were changing, but it occurred neither to him nor to the rest of Germany that they would have to reckon with a defeat. He was discovering that war was nasty and his early enthusiasm for military victories was dampened, but it was assumed that Germany would eventually win. It was not until 1918 that news came of serious reverses in the advance of the German armies. Dietrich had given up sticking pins in the map by then! On the Western Front, a massive offensive was launched by the Germans and it promised some final success, but it failed – and when the civilian population heard news of the failure on 8 August 1918 the first real fears of national disaster were felt. Earlier in 1917 there had been rejoicing at the defection of Russia from the Allies, but what supplanted Czarist Russia did not please the bourgeois population of Imperial Germany. The revolution in Russia, although removing an enemy from the Eastern Front, had also threatened to destroy Germany from within. Just as Russia had collapsed through the disaffection of her troops, so the unheard of rumour was whispered which could hardly be believed in the Grunewald – there was disaffection among the German soldiers! The small communist party in Germany tried, but with little effect, to declare a Soviet-style regime. What troubled the Bonhoeffers far more was a statement by US President Wilson on 23 October, when the war was virtually won by the Allies, that if they had to treat with German militarism and the military autocrats of Germany, they must demand 'not negotiations for peace, but surrender'.

The Kaiser was eventually persuaded to abdicate and it was hoped that this would make negotiations for peace possible. Klaus Bonhoeffer was also called up and attached to the staff headquarters of the army, serving as an orderly at Spa. There he saw General Hindenburg leave the conference room after the decision to abdicate had been taken. He never forgot the sight of the man who had asked his Kaiser to resign – 'lifeless as a statue in expression and gesture'. The communists in Germany were on the verge of a take-over, but the socialists forestalled them and set up a republic. This, it was hoped, would avert a revolution. It was a very uneasy state of affairs, with much disorder and sporadic fighting between rival groups.

Life in Berlin

Despite the dangers of disorder in the streets of Berlin, Dietrich continued to walk to school. His young eyes were wide open as he watched detachments of troops marching in disorder, a thing almost unknown in Germany. He describes how soldiers mingled with civilians, who were carrying posters reading, 'Don't shoot!' The soldiers were not greeted as heroes, but failures. Civilians were pulling their guns out of their hands – 'pale, starved figures covered with sweat'. He saw no shooting, but the atmosphere was tense. Most people, however, simply tried to behave normally and hurried to their work. There they might find the communists in control. Dietrich's father tells how he arrived at his department in the hospital, to be met by the porter wearing a red cockade. The man intended to bar his way and was about to declare a communist take-over when Karl Bonhoeffer simply greeted him and passed on to his room. There was no further resistance. Germany was not ready for a revolution yet, but it seemed to be just below the surface.

There were two extreme wings – the communists and the right-wing nationalists. The nationalists were fashioning the myth that Germany had not been defeated, at least their soldiers had not, but stabbed in the back by cowardly civilians. The two extremes were responsible for a great deal of unrest in the streets, but not enough to prevent the Weimar Republic from being born. It was supported, without much enthusiasm, by the Bonhoeffers and their class as the least harmful form of government.

The Treaty of Versailles

The new government was now expected to negotiate a peace treaty. The militarist autocrats had been removed and it was hoped that the Allies would not insist upon an 'unconditional surrender'. The Armistice was agreed but that was no more than a ceasefire. The blow came in May 1919 when President Wilson's fourteen points were turned into a 'peace treaty'. That appeared to be reasonable until the French insisted upon draconian terms which were drafted into the Treaty of Versailles, and presented to Germany as an ultimatum to sign. The treaty was intended to crush Germany and make any recovery from the war impossible.

What troubled Dietrich most, however, were not the harsh terms but the acceptance of sole guilt for the war. Dietrich could repeat that offending clause years later. With a burning sense of injustice, Germany was compelled to sign a statement which no German believed to be true. It is doubtful whether the Allies believed it either, but France wanted her 'pound of flesh'. The clause read:

> The Allied and Associated Governments affirm that Germany accepts the responsibility of Germany and her Allies for causing all the loss and the damage to which the Allied and Associated Governments and their nations have been subjected as a consequence of the war imposed upon them by the aggression of Germany and her Allies.[2]

The offending article was No. 231 and the number became infamous. Dietrich was as angry as the rest. A victorious army can impose hard conditions when it wins and the defeated nation must accept, but to be forced to sign an acceptance of guilt which was unjust inflamed his anger for years. As late as 1930 in America he could say:

> . . . there was one wound which was more painful than all the privations and needs, that was the Article 231 of the Treaty of Versailles. I will tell you frankly, that this is the wound that is still open and bleeds in Germany . . . When the war broke out the German people did not consider very much the question of guilt. We thought it to be our duty to fight for our country . . .

The German soldiers fought in the war in the confident faith in the righteousness of their country . . . I personally see many faults in our policy before the war, I am not going to defend my country in every point . . . but other countries had committed the same or greater faults than Germany.[3]

Although the young thirteen year old Dietrich could not yet muster all the arguments, he felt indignation at the injustice, and later he took the trouble to examine the documents and convince himself that Germany was not solely responsible for the war. There is no doubt that he felt strongly about it and few discussions in 1919 and 1920 can have passed without reference to the injustice of the treaty.

Privations and Needs

The humiliation smarted, but the privations and needs which he rated lower than the unjust accusation of sole guilt must at the time have been more evident. Food was not only short, but without variety – no butter, no sugar, with turnips the staple food for all meals. There is little doubt that the flu epidemic of 1918 which carried away more than 100,000 victims in Germany was all the more fatal because of malnutrition and hunger. There was little or no heating, because Germany was compelled to export her coal to pay reparations for war damage. Dietrich tells of undernourished and poorly clad children he passed on the way to school and of one black spot he passed each day, where a group of people standing by the river gave eloquent evidence of another suicide.

The Last Days at School

Once he had decided to read theology, Dietrich began to look forward to his university years. He would go to Tübingen to satisfy the family tradition, but at first he remained at home and continued with his schooling, while he wrestled with the consequences of that decision to read theology. The schoolmaster had said that he had some surprises ahead. He wondered what they were as he delved into his conscious mind to test his motivation. In view of his parents' and teachers' ambition for him, he seemed to be choosing a humble path – a country pastor perhaps, honourable but modest. Yet he struggled with his own inner sense of pride and ambition. He was glad when his older brothers came back from the war, but they had changed, bringing new ideas into the home, ideas from a new world. Both had been deeply affected by their experience and they returned as part of that defeated army. They found a stable home awaiting them and a welcome, but they were searching for a more humane world. Karl-Friedrich was not averse to Marx and had developed a deep concern for the lot of the ordinary soldier. He had given his support to the workers' councils which were attempting a form of communism. Klaus was more concerned with the evils of a corrupt government and public officials and sought practical ways of securing social justice within the existing system. Both now continued their studies – the one in science, the other in law.

Klaus and Karl-Friedrich began to appreciate the searching questions posed by their young brother and the three were much together. The only thing that separated them was Dietrich's insistence upon reading theology, which they hardly considered an important subject given the serious state of Germany after losing a war. All three saw the sorry state of the Protestant Church in Germany – *provincial*, in the trivial sense of that word, out of touch with the real world, and feeble. How could this brilliant young brother waste his time in such an outdated organisation? Dietrich's spirited, if joking, reply was, 'If the Church is feeble, I shall reform it.' The positive contribution which Klaus made to his thinking was an interest in sociology and the discovery of Max Weber. He never came to terms with Karl-Friedrich's scientific scepticism and he was a little over-powered by his clever arguments. One quote from these heated discussions is Dietrich's protest: 'You may chop off my head, but I shall still believe that there is a God.'

The two older brothers went on to distinguished careers in their respective fields and were sorry that 'poor little Dietrich' had turned off into a blind alley. The best he could hope for was a professorship of theology, an irrelevant object in a museum, however much applauded; at worst, and he seemed to prefer this, an obscure country living as a village pastor.

In later years, Dietrich had more to do with the men who married his sisters than with his brothers.

Eberhard Bethge makes the point that Dietrich set out on his path to the Church from a worldly basis. Those who came from Church or theological families usually discovered the existence of the world later. Dietrich began with the world. He wanted to make sense of his parents' world, only later did the Church as such come into his field of vision.

At seventeen, in 1923, he went to Tübingen for two semesters. Sabine comments, 'Our childhood was now over, and our paths diverged.'

THREE

Theologian in the Making

By 1923, the shadow of Walter's death had lifted and Paula Bonhoeffer was her old lively self again. The family responded with her to the acceptance of a world in which Walter did not share as they had once hoped. Dietrich took his place with his brothers and found himself in older company than his years might suggest. He seemed almost to pass from the childhood world in which his sisters, particularly his twin sister, were his intimate companions to a fellowship with Klaus and Karl-Friedrich on equal terms. And this passage happened suddenly in 1923. The house at Wangenheimstrasse became a centre of social life and of earnest discussion, cultural, political and philosophical. Karl Bonhoeffer belonged to a semi-political group sympathetic to the young republic and anxious about its development. It met at the home of Professor Delbrück the historian, but the younger generation continued their discussions in less organised ways. Dietrich, even after he left for university, still found home to be the real centre of his life. It formed his theological development far more than the lectures and technical discussion of theology at the university.

The elder two brothers were making their way in their careers as Dietrich prepared for Tübingen. In that year, Karl-Friedrich became an assistant at the Institute of Physical Chemistry of the Kaiser Wilhelm Society. He collaborated in the researches which split the hydrogen atom and was later invited to Russia and to the USA. In 1930 he was appointed Professor of Physics in Frankfurt. After graduating, Klaus worked in the field of international law at the League of Nations.

Ursula was married in 1923 to Dr Rüdiger Schleicher, who worked in the Ministry in Berlin. In 1925, Christine was married to Hans von Dohnanyi, a lawyer, the son of the Hungarian composer. In later years, Dietrich was to be much involved with him. Christine was in fact studying biology at Tübingen when Dietrich went up. A year later still, in 1926, Sabine married Gerhard Leibholz, a constitutional lawyer of Jewish origin. A few years later, the youngest sister, Susanne, became engaged to the theologian Walter Dress. The children, with their partners and friends, made a lively company who met whenever they could at the Grunewald house in Wangenheimstrasse. Dietrich had his roots there and whenever possible he returned home with joyful anticipation.

Germany in 1923

Most Germans remembered that year as one of 'the great inflation'. The value of money fell ridiculously, until it almost became impossible as a means of conducting business. Pensions paid for by a lifetime of premiums yielded inadequate pocket money for even the smallest child of the family. Dietrich travelled on the cheaper local train from Berlin to Tübingen with a French franc in his pocket for financial security. Germany had not paid her reparations in full and France marched her troops onto the Ruhr. A national strike in protest ruined the fragile economy of a humiliated and exploited Germany. The president intervened and called from the obscurity of the German People's Party a man who nearly saved Germany: Gustav Stresemann. He became Chancellor and the republic lived again – for a time. His policy was reconciliation, mutual understanding and goodwill, as the essential ingredients to preserve Europe. The word that conveyed his policy to the more rational of the people was *Erfüllung*, i.e. fulfilment, and by it he meant to make Germany great again. He denounced blind confrontation and put an end to the strike. He dealt with the rampant inflation more or less successfully. He made no secret of his desire to see Germany great again, perhaps the leading country in Europe, but not by military means. His policies would take some years to achieve any lasting results, but there was hope. Later, tragically, irrational forces overcame him. These irrational forces had been there from the beginning. When he was still at school, Dietrich heard in his classroom the shots that killed Walter Rathenau and once he knew who had been shot he reacted with indignation. His schoolfellows were surprised at 'Bonhoeffer's passionate indignation, his deep and spontaneous anger, asking what would become of Germany if its best leaders were killed.' Even at sixteen Dietrich knew exactly where he stood.

Military Training

The shot that killed Walter Rathenau was not the last bullet fired in anger. Germany was torn apart between the communists and that extreme right-wing movement that wanted to make Germany great whatever the cost. The way of Stresemann seemed too slow. Armed bands roamed the streets and the two extremes of right and left did battle. The Bonhoeffers remained mostly left of centre, and were certainly liberals, supporting Stresemann and the Weimar Republic despite its weaknesses. However, the terms of the Treaty of Versailles made any republic in touch with the people of Germany quite unworkable. Germany was allowed an army of 100,000, an inadequate force to police the country or defend its borders. Any extreme group which could arm secretly would easily be able to take over the country, and the Soviet Union was only a few miles away across undefended territory. The terms had to be broken or circumvented. One way was to train the student population. The Allied Control Commission attempted to prevent this, but prevention was impossible and unjust.

Bonhoeffer was soon involved in this issue, together with the other students. He had joined a student association called 'The Hedgehog', to which his father had belonged as a young man. He was the only son to do so, and in later years he withdrew his membership publicly because of its support for the Nazi laws against the Jews. As a student, he found nothing objectionable in the 'association' and enjoyed the discussions that were held on social questions. Some of his fellow students went on a study trip to the Ruhr, among them Rüdiger Schleicher. During the second term at Tübingen, the winter term of 1923, Dietrich joined the other members of the 'Hedgehog', of which by now he was a 'fox', in military exercises with the Ulm Rifles. This was illegal training because the Allied Control Commission maintained that it broke the terms of the Versailles Treaty and were about to crack down on this student training. There had been unrest in many parts of the country between left- and right-wing groups and Dietrich, together with most students, saw the necessity of being prepared to maintain law and order in the face of a possible military coup. His brother, Karl-Friedrich, had in fact refused to join the 'Hedgehog' because he understood in 1919 that its members were expected to help in the suppression of risings in Stuttgart and Munich. Dietrich saw things differently four years later. He had not really had time to consider the training carefully, because the original date had been brought forward unexpectedly when the proposed crack-down by the Control Commission became known. Instead of 1924, the training was to take place in November 1923 and at short notice. Dietrich decided to go, but wrote to his family asking for permission. Were it granted he would stay; if they refused he would withdraw at a day's notice.

The afternoon training at Tübingen was cancelled because of 'spies' and next day the Tübingen contingent left for Ulm. The family anxiously agreed to his staying and he did two weeks' military training during the second half of November. He rather enjoyed it, glad that he could stand up to the rigours of camp life and strict training. He was no pacifist and was prepared to defend his country. However, he did not enjoy privation and wrote of his pleasure on return at being able to sit down at table with knife and fork again and to have his own room and a comfortable bed! Illegal it might be but this student training was approved even by General Reinhardt, the commander of the Stuttgart military district. The only thing that troubled the young seventeen year old Dietrich was that so many of the students were reactionary, hoping for a right-wing revolution under Ludendorff which would overthrow the Weimar Republic.

Theological Studies

His most influential teacher at Tübingen was Adolf Schlatter, and despite later disagreements in relation to the National Socialism of 1933 and the attempts at theological resistance which Bonhoeffer supported, Dietrich never failed to regard his biblical work highly. To the end, Schlatter was, apart from Luther, the theologian most fully represented in his library. He already knew enough Hebrew to allow him to go to Volz's lectures on the Psalms and Rudolph's on the Prophets. He was gripped by the 'passion of the prophets'. He went to Heitmüller's lectures on Romans and there was recommended to read Karl Barth's *Epistle to the Romans*. He found Heitmüller himself rather dry, but he took down his notes carefully, learning how to dissect an ancient text. The lectures of Karl Müller were on medieval ecclesiastical history. He already had in mind a trip to Rome and absorbed these lectures in preparation for it. It was during the second term that he really opened up. He registered for dogmatics under Karl Heim. Bonhoeffer's principal interest here was not Heim's introduction of science into his thinking, for which he is most often remembered, but his treatment of Schleiermacher. He did not like Heim; Schlatter remained the major influence from the Tübingen period.

But, to be honest, one must admit that Bonhoeffer found little in Tübingen that he could not have found anywhere. His mind was at work and the study at university simply meant giving rather more time to his reading and concentrating it upon theology. Between the two terms during a holiday at Friedrichsbrunn, he read Schleiermacher, in preparation for Heim's lectures. It was a copy taken from the library of his great grandfather, Karl August von Hase.

Towards the end of the second term he had an accident while skating, after which he remained unconscious for a long time. His parents were worried and hurried to Tübingen to see him. The visit fell around the time of Dietrich's birthday and he said that he would like to leave Tübingen at the end of the winter term and continue his studies in Rome. His father thought that he should wait, but he got his way and, together with his brother Klaus, he left for Italy on 4 April 1924.

Rome and North Africa

The two brothers reacted quite differently to Rome. They were both German Protestants and therefore the real appeal of Rome lay in its classical antiquity. They knew little of the Rome of the Pope. Klaus was content to keep it that way. He loved the classical monuments, the colours and the light, the adventure of being where so many great people of the past had been. Dietrich fell under the spell of Catholic Rome and could hardly tear himself away from St Peter's. All his life he retained this love for Rome, 'The piece of earth that I love so much', as he wrote to Bethge in one of his prison letters many years later. He urged him again to look carefully at Michelangelo's *Pietà* and try to feel its spiritual power.

He was lucky to meet a cultured priest in Bologna who was also going to Rome and became Dietrich's guide, particularly during Holy Week, which they were able to follow together. The liturgical richness and the devotion of the people to their Church deeply impressed him and he began to feel his own 'Protestantism' was provincial, nationalistic and narrow-minded.

He kept a diary while in Rome and, as a guide to his inner development towards Catholicism, it is invaluable. What is evident is that he met a different kind of Catholicism from what he had known in Germany. The old German adage – Catholicism is in minority, a lamb; in equality, a fox; in majority, a lion – may be a useful formula in assessing the relation of German Catholics to their Protestant alternative in provinces of Catholic dominance (e.g. Bavaria), Protestant dominance (e.g. Hanover), or a balanced mix, as in the Rhineland or Westphalia. In Rome he met another Catholicism which did not have to relate to Protestantism – it could and did ignore it. None of his criticisms of the structure of theology of the Roman Catholic Church changed, but he met the full impact of a powerful liturgy at its strongest in Holy Week, as well as the simple devotion of the people. He saw that it was more than a religion of fear and 'must'. One discovery he made which stayed with him all his life was the deeply spiritual nature of *confession*, which he had not understood until then.

Earlier in the week he had been to his first mass in St Peter's, on Palm Sunday, and was impressed by the international character of the seminarists, monks, priests: 'the universality of the Church'. In the evening he had attended vespers at Trinità dei Monti and never forgot the beauty of it. 'I gained some real understanding of Catholicism,' he wrote. But the next day, he discovered *confession* amidst the glorious mosaics and Roman splendour of Santa Maria Maggiore:

> It is gratifying here to see so many serious faces, to which all the things that are said against Catholicism do not apply. Children as well as adults confess with a real ardour which it is very moving to see. Confession does not necessarily lead to scrupulous living: often, however, that may occur and always will with the more serious people ... To primitive people it is the only way of talking to God, while to the religiously more far-seeing it is the realisation of the idea of the Church fulfilling itself in confession and absolution.[1]

While Dietrich Bonhoeffer was deeply impressed by the worship which he attended up to the last with a magnificent *Te Deum* in St Peter's, his criticism of Catholicism remained. After church, in a discussion with the priest who had been his mentor, all his intellectual objections came out. He describes the result of the discussion as 'a big withdrawal of sympathy on my part', and then he adds, 'There is a great difference between confession and the dogma of confession.'

His studies were not the most important thing about the Roman visit, but he did attend lectures and had little trouble with the language. There was no course on dogmatics, which disappointed him; ecclesiastical history told him little new, except for its different point of view. He was far more interested in the catacombs and the Roman mosaics. He liked being in Rome and one comment shows how he might have spent his time if he had had the chance to return: 'It would be very interesting to study here for a longer time, for the pictures (i.e. mosaics, and wall paintings in the catacombs) are marvellous sources of understanding for dogmatics and ecclesiastical history.' It was a short term in Rome, but he learnt more there that influenced his subsequent thought than the two semesters at Tübingen had taught him. He and Klaus made a short visit to North Africa, no doubt to see the classical remains, but also in a spirit of adventure. He returned to Berlin in June 1924 just in time to register at Berlin University, for the period June 1924 to July 1927. His real theological studies now began.

Berlin

Dietrich was in his nineteenth year and the whole academic richness of the great university of Berlin lay before him. The emphasis was 'liberal' in theology and one of the dominant masters was Adolf von Harnack, the Church historian, of whom Bonhoeffer once complained, 'he never seemed to get beyond the First Epistle of Clement (ca. 98 AD)'. He wanted to hear Harnack on the Reformation, and he did study Luther with Karl Holl. But his main studies were in systematic theology with Reinhold Seeberg.

He greatly admired the teaching of Karl Holl, except he complained that Holl made everything seem much gloomier than it need be, and more difficult. He recognised Harnack as the key figure and developed an affectionate attachment to him, recalling the walks in the Grunewald and the seminars long after he left Berlin. But Bonhoeffer did not easily recognise masters – Karl Barth was his first. Most of his work at Berlin was with Reinhold Seeberg for whom he prepared his thesis on the Church, *Sanctorum Communio*.[2] He was critical of Seeberg from the beginning, although he attended his seminars throughout the Berlin period. He read Weber, Troeltsch and Husserl for his thesis and much else beside. Then he discovered Karl Barth, reading first the collection of his lectures published as *Das Wort Gottes und die Theologie*[3] *(Theology and the Word of God)*. This transformed him and he became an advocate for this book and the 'dialectical theology' of Barth.

In the winter term 1924–25, a controversy between Barth and Harnack was brought to the attention of the Berlin students who rapidly took sides. Barth had contended for the 'wholly other' character of God, whose new input into the life of man was discernible, but not explicable. Harnack defended scientific theology. The discovery of the dialectical theology of Karl Barth gave some direction to Bonhoeffer's studies which, apart from his thesis, were tending to roam a little too wide. It also gave a strength to his arguments for the faith and his proclamation in preaching.

Preaching

The family probably expected Dietrich to become an academic theologian and pursue a university career like his grandfather, Hans von Hase. But from the beginning his interests were geared towards parish work. And he always loved preaching. His first sermon was given in place of Pfarrer Koller in the Stahnsdorfer Church in Berlin on 18 October 1925. His mother went with him to hear her son preach his first public sermon; it was the 18th Sunday after Trinity and the text was Luke 17:7 – 10. The text, which suited his Barthian tendencies, ends with, 'We are unworthy servants; we have only done what was our duty.' The granddaughter of the famous church historian Karl August von Hase must have been a little shocked by her son's attack upon the piety, religiosity and spirituality with which she was acquainted. A new world of thought opened to her as she heard him saying in his first sermon, with all the conviction of a nineteen year old theologian:

> Christianity means decision, change, denial, yes even hostility to the past, to the men of old. Christ smashes the men of the past into total ruin. He smites and cuts through with his sword to the innermost nerve. And that is where the wound hurts most, where the apparently most noble feelings meet with a satisfied morality.[4]

Bonhoeffer knew why and against whom he was preaching. The world he was attacking had been his since childhood. It was secure, in contrast to that of many others. It was a world in which it was not the custom to speak of God as the judge of all men, including their culture and their intellect, cutting the high spiritual pretensions of men down to size. There was nothing spiteful in his attack, he simply wanted to show that it was a painful thing to put the highest of human endeavour under the judgement of the Most High God. This was a theme he developed in later sermons, but the note was already clear in this carefully prepared sermon, written out word for word. As his mother listened, she must have known that her son was attacking the very citadel of conventional Christianity. The same kind of conflict occurred in his academic work. When he produced essays on church history for Harnack or on Luther for Karl Holl, he was praised and encouraged to specialise; but when the Barthian influence came into his essays on dogmatics for Seeberg, there was trouble. Yet he chose the trouble and eventually pleased even Seeberg with his final essays and his doctoral thesis which he started quite early.

The conflict between preaching and theology, partially resolved for him in Barth's collection of essays, continued. His father took a very great interest in Dietrich's choice and there is a telling letter from him which shows how the importance of what Dietrich had decided, was eventually recognised:

> When I heard that you intended to enter the pastorate as a boy, I thought that this was not the way that you should go, confining yourself to a corner of life. I thought at the time that such a removed and unreal experience as a pastor, as I knew it from my uncle, was too small; it was a pity that you should do that. Now seeing the Church in a crisis that I never thought would be possible, I see that what you have chosen was very right.[5]

Licentiate of Theology

This is the equivalent of a doctorate and included: supervised study, in Bonhoeffer's case by Reinhold Seeberg; a thesis, which eventually became the first book he published (at his own expense), *Sanctorum Communio*; and a public defence of a series of propositions associated with the substance of the thesis.

His later relations with Seeberg were clouded, but in these early years Dietrich had the greatest respect for him and once he left Berlin he continued to correspond with him. Bonhoeffer owed a great deal to his seminars. The thesis, *Sanctorum Communio*, was about the structure and theological basis of the Church. It made use of Max Weber in determining the influence of sociological pressures in the structure of the Church, and of both Seeberg and Karl Barth in working out the significance of theology in understanding the Church. Seeberg liked the thesis; Karl Barth praised the book highly as a 'theological miracle'!

The propositions offered for public discussion were debated on the Friday morning of 18 December 1927. The debate was rehearsed in Seeberg's seminar the day before, when Dietrich Bonhoeffer first met young Franz Hildebrandt and a long friendship started. Bonhoeffer succeeded and graduated as a licentiate of the University of Berlin.

Assistant Pastor in Barcelona

After the academic training, practical work and at least one year as an assistant pastor were required. During his work on his thesis Bonhoeffer had had some practical work. We have already mentioned the sermon preached in the Stahnsdorfer Church. Even earlier, he had done work in the Sunday School to show his involvement in church work and had been very busy with a group of young men in the Wangenheimstrasse on Thursdays. But now he was to take up a full-time engagement with a parish.

He was appointed assistant minister to a German-speaking congregation in Barcelona. This brought him into contact with a world he had never known. Spain was strange to him, although he soon found it fascinating; but the real change was the nature of the congregation – a type of German he did not know. They were business men, most of whom were out of touch with the turbulent events in Germany. They regarded all change as unfortunate and were still living in the world of yesterday. They were nice people and, on his visits, Bonhoeffer enjoyed their welcome and pleasant conversation, but in his diary he complains in the first few weeks that he 'had not had a single conversation in the Berlin-Grunewald style'. There was no intellectual stimulus from his congregation. Yet, judging by the lectures he gave at mid-week services, he tried to raise their sights. They probably liked this eager young man whose lectures were a bit above their heads! His preaching was different and on Sundays they were more than once uncomfortably disturbed.

His stimulus came from the continuing work on his thesis for publication and his correspondence with Reinhold Seeberg. That correspondence shows that he had found another interest in the children's games of Spain. In them he detected vestiges of old theological disputes between Christian and Muslim. We have a parallel to this in our own nursery rhymes, many of which have reference to old disputes in our history. 'Mary, Mary, quite contrary, how does your garden grow', for example, contains a clear reference to the unpopular Mary Tudor who attempted to plant Roman Catholicism again in Reformation England. And her 'cockle shells all in a row' are, of course, her priests. Bonhoeffer found similar references dating back to the time of the Moors in Spain, when Christians and Muslims debated issues that found their way on to the streets and survived in children's games.

Another new interest was bull-fighting. This enthusiasm shocked both his family and his friends. Dietrich would have nothing to do with a boxing match, which he regarded as brutal, yet he could regard the elegance and brute force of a bull-fight with emotional satisfaction. This passion seems to have started at Easter 1928 when his brother Klaus visited him. After the Easter sermon they went to a bull-fight and Dietrich confessed that he felt none of the horror that people told him he ought to feel. He admired the elegance and the skilful release of emotions and was sucked into the emotional atmosphere. Afterwards he tried to explain the fascination and the purpose of the bull-fight.

He had been disappointed in the Catholicism of Spain for it in no way resembled the experience he had had in Rome. Nevertheless he saw that the people led highly moral lives. He saw the bull-fight as the release of passions which otherwise would have led to immorality.

Spain puzzled him and he never really understood it. He was, of course, there during a very unusual period of calm in the Spanish story. The monarchy seemed well established, although it would be overthrown three years later. The intellectuals he talked with were all anti-clerical. He travelled quite a lot in Spain, particularly when his brother came to see him, and the senior minister allowed him to take time off to visit Madrid, Toledo, Cordoba, Seville and Granada. It was not surprising that like many before and since he developed a keen interest in El Greco.

He read *Don Quixote* – in the original Spanish – but later bought himself a German translation. The figure of the romantic knight entranced him and he later saw his relevance for Nazi Germany. Many similar seeds were planted during this first Church assignment. Another was his grandmother's suggestion that he go to India, although that idea had perhaps taken root during his Tübingen days, at a time when the figure of Gandhi appealed to many young men in Europe.

The Parish Work

Bonhoeffer was not in Spain on a cultural tour; he was there to learn the craft of parish work and he did. His enthusiasm was mainly for preaching, but he did all the other things a young assistant minister has to do. The German congregation was isolated from Spanish culture and it must have seemed to Bonhoeffer that he was living in two worlds – the culture of Spain when he was on leave, and the duties of Germany in his parish work.

His senior minister was Pfarrer Olbricht, a kindly and courteous man who was forever trying to curb the enthusiasm of his young assistant, who wanted to start all kinds of activities during the weekends, when the congregation seemed to have free time. But Olbricht very wisely kept his organisations under control. He knew that one day this eager young man would leave and he would be left with more than he could cope with. He was not well and was glad of Bonhoeffer's eager desire to preach. In fact he did far more preaching than the directions for the training of young assistant ministers recommended. In 1928, he had to write and deliver nineteen sermons. He was meticulous in his preparation. Writing to his parents in November 1928 he gives us a glimpse of this incessant activity:

'Writing sermons still takes up a great deal of my time. I work on them the whole week, devoting some time to them every day.'

The Barcelona Sermons

Bonhoeffer was not always too careful in his exegesis. He was quickly captivated by his theme and went on to make what a German academic might consider rather wild statements. He was enthusiastic. He tried to stir these stable German burghers into a commitment to Jesus Christ. What impressed them was that the Gospel was a matter of urgency to this young man. As his favourite quote from St Augustine implied, he wanted to make their hearts, 'restless until they rested in' the God he loved.

Those Barcelona sermons are worth looking at, even though he later saw the cracks in his youthful theology. It was in Barcelona that he first felt the joy and compulsion to preach the Gospel. It was there, too, that his particular interest in the Advent season was awakened.

We do not have the text of all the sermons Dietrich preached in Barcelona, but among the twelve that have survived is the sermon on Advent Sunday 1928. This sermon would normally have been preached by the senior minister, but for some reason he did not return from his travel and Bonhoeffer wrote with evident excitement to his parents: 'On the first Sunday in Advent I shall be able to preach again, because Olbricht will not be returning until the following week and I am very pleased about that.'

On 2December, 1928, the young assistant announced his text; 'Behold, I stand at the door and knock' (Rev. 3:20) and his opening words were:

> To celebrate Advent means to learn how to wait. Waiting is an art which our impatient age has forgotten. It wants to pick the ripe fruit as soon as the shoot appears. But the greedy eyes are all too often cheated when they see the apparently luscious fruits, but find them unripe within. Then rude hands throw away what has brought them such disappointment. One who does not know the holy discipline of waiting, which means deprivation in hope, will never experience the blessing of fulfilment.[6]

He was speaking to a people who had not known the deprivations of war those in Germany had known. They were in Spain, where they could earn money. Some were, of course, poor and not successful. But in every community of expatriates they worked for profit and looked forward to the time when they could return to a homeland much as they had left it. Again, like most expatriate communities, they were impatient at the slowness of progress 'back to normal' at home. In many of Bonhoeffer's sermons there is a reminder that those who endured the war and defeat had experienced something unknown to this protected community. He was not hostile, but he reminded them of values they might have lost in their prosperity.

Advent is the prelude to Christmas and he could never fail to feel the sheer joy that had so often been his in the Grunewald home:

> God comes. The Lord Jesus comes. Christmas comes. Rejoice, let all Christendom rejoice! We hear the Christmas bells ringing again for the first time today. We hear already in the distance the angels' song of, 'Glory to God and peace on earth'. It will not be long. Learn to wait and learn how to wait aright. Make the time of waiting into a blessed time, a time of preparation.
>
> When the Advent comes and we sing and hear again the old Christmas carols, then gently there steals upon us a special feeling. The hardest heart is softened. Then we trace something which we had known as children, when we were separated from our mother. It is a kind of homesickness, with no hardness or bitterness in it. And it is a longing for a home beyond the clouds, for our eternal Father's home.[7]

He had a rich memory of home and could draw upon it to awaken a longing in the hearts of his listeners, but he very soon pointed out the limitations and even fantasy of wanting again that impossible dream of the past. He had to show this expatriate congregation that the old Germany has gone forever. In contrast, he portrayed the eternal homeland of the 'Father's house'.

There is much rhetoric in this sermon, as well as realism. The signs of the times that knock upon the door of a doomed culture and demand entry are contrasted with the presence of Christ, standing patiently at the door and seeking our willing acceptance of him. The longing for the past to return is contrasted with the joyous acceptance of the nature of Christ – 'Behold! I will make all things new'. It is for this renewal that we wait. Advent is a time of waiting in that creative sense, anticipation of renewal. And he concludes this early sermon with a paean of praise:

> Our whole life is Advent – that is waiting until the end. Waiting for the time when there will be a new heaven and a new earth, when all men will be brothers and will rejoice in the angels' song, 'Peace on earth and goodwill to men'. Learn how to wait! For he has promised that he will come: 'Behold, I stand at the door and knock'. And we call to him, 'Yes, come soon, Lord Jesus'. Amen.[8]

The Choice of Academic Work

When the presbytery formally invited him to stay in Barcelona, Bonhoeffer had two questions before him. Was he to make his life work in a parish? And, if so, was this the kind of parish in which he would want to begin his pastorates? He seemed to think that he needed to get back into the reality of life in Berlin *if* he was to be a parish priest. But the *if* posed the larger question. Was his family right in assuming that his contribution to the Church should be in the academic field? A parish or a university chair?

He had worked on *Sanctorum Communio*, which the publishers did not regard as a saleable proposition. He was persuaded to cut it and then publish with substantial subsidy. Academically it was acceptable, although his tutor, Reinhold Seeberg, tried to persuade him to work on some more historical or biblical theme and to establish himself in that field. But Bonhoeffer was not to be dissuaded from a theme to which he had already devoted much time and in which he had invested much emotional energy. It was not historical or systematic, but a theological enquiry into the question of consciousness that he chose to work on. He had been inspired by one of Seeberg's own remarks in class and a quotation from Luther on Galatians. This was the beginning of what was to become his second published work, *Act and Being*[9] and was to qualify him as a lecturer when he returned to Berlin. On 17 February 1929 he was back home in the Grunewald family circle. He did not forget Spain and even found time in his busy life over the next few years to visit Barcelona again. Yet he had turned his back on that kind of pastorate and, indeed, on purely parish work. He had learnt much from his Spanish interlude, not least to appreciate the liturgy of the bull-fight!

A Lecturer in Berlin

Although conditions had improved in Germany during Bonhoeffer's absence, there were ominous signs of right-wing reaction. Stresemann had worked wonders by accepting the harsh Versailles Treaty and gradually winning concessions. The galloping inflation eased and the Rhineland was set free from foreign troops. But there were those who regarded this democratic government as weak. Stresemann himself was labelled a traitor for acceding to the conditions of the Versailles Treaty and many refused to see that he was doing the best he could with an impossible position. The first signs of armed rising occurred while Bonhoeffer was still in Spain. In the autumn of 1929, the largest ex-servicemen's organisation in Germany, under the leadership of the right-wing nationalist leader Franz Seldt, was formed into the *Stahlhelm* ('steel helmet').

Other nationalist groups were also formed, including a very small movement called the 'National Socialists'. Aided by a number of Church leaders they had united to draft a 'national petition for the establishing of a law against the enslavement of the German people'. It failed, but was discussed in parliament (Reichstag) and those who opposed it were publicly derided as traitors. In the midst of all this, Stresemann died on 3 October

1929, Wall Street crashed three weeks later and, in the economic blizzard that followed, the Weimar Republic wasted away under the leadership of Chancellor Brüning. Karl Bonhoeffer was a strong supporter of Brüning, but his world and its values were passing away. The great liberals who had been fashioned in the early years of the century and lived through the Great War were now dying one by one. Stresemann was dead and two close friends and neighbours of the Bonhoeffers died shortly afterwards: Hans Delbrück and Adolf von Harnack.

Dietrich grieved at the loss of close friends and was aware of the deep concern in his own household, but his main concern was his own career. He was still uncertain about his future. He determined to get the necessary academic qualifications, in case he decided in favour of university rather than parish, but he also kept in touch with parish work.

In order to qualify as a lecturer at the University of Berlin, he had to submit a thesis which showed his ability to handle the subjects on which he would lecture. This was to be *Act and Being*, but a great deal more research was needed on his original thesis which concerned 'conscience in theology'. Meanwhile, he was still very young for the post of lecturer, and it was difficult to see where he would fit in.

While working on *Act and Being* he made efforts to publish his earlier doctoral thesis, *Sanctorum Communio*, and offered himself as a voluntary assistant lecturer. He began lecturing in systematic theology in the summer term of 1929.

Bonhoeffer completed *Act and Being* in February 1930, which meant that he had two academic works to his credit. For a long time both were undervalued. In fact, taken together, the two works laid the foundations for those *Letters and Papers from Prison* which stirred the world more than twenty-five years later.

The thesis was accepted and Dietrich Bonhoeffer was qualified, at the age of twenty-four, to lecture at the University of Berlin. The habilitation ceremony took place on 18 July 1930 and he was invited to give his inaugural lecture on 31 July. His lecture was advertised as, *'The Question of Man in Contemporary Philosophy and Theology'*.

> Two things keep alive the discussion of the question, *What is Man?* First, his work, and then the experiences which show the limits of his nature, his intellect or his will. When he begins to marvel at his capabilities, at his work, and when he is ruthlessly shown his limitations by reality, the old biblical question emerges once again: 'What is man that thou art mindful of him, and the Son of Man that thou dost care for him? Yet thou hast made him little less than God' (Psalm 8), and the other, 'What is man that thou dost visit him every morning and test him every moment?' (Job 7:17). On the one hand, a century of inventors, who have built a new world on the ground of the old;

and, on the other hand, a lost war, must put before us the question of man in a new and more acute form. Two great possibilities arise: man seeks to understand himself from his *work* or from his *limitations*.[10]

The lecture kept close to its theme, developing what he called the concept of possibility. This reflected the limitations of man. He argued that this concept has no place in theology and therefore in theological anthropology. He went on to show the essential role played by the Church in this self-understanding of man.

This highly trained and promising lecturer was not yet allowed to take root in Berlin. One further stage was necessary to complete his preparation – the New World had yet to try his mettle. He accepted the Sloane Fellowship at Union Theological Seminary, New York, and was granted leave of absence for one year to complete his studies.

FOUR

The New World

A lmost everybody around Dietrich Bonhoeffer seemed to assume that he was bent on an academic career. His dean guided him carefully through the bureaucratic machinery to speed his qualifications. He could now lecture in Berlin, but he felt some academic experience overseas would help him to see his work in a wider setting. Many German scholars were going to America and, for theological students, Union Theological Seminary in New York was the obvious place. There, a German would meet international scholars and break out of his isolation. The war had cut German scholars off from the academic world and they were only slowly restoring their international contacts. Those who had his best interests at heart recommended study overseas – Britain or America. Someone suggested Union Theological Seminary and the wheels were set in motion to secure an invitation for Bonhoeffer.

At first he was not enthusiastic. He was eager to lecture, not to be a student again. He made enquiries about the American system of 'credits' which was, and is, confusing to Europeans. Instead of studying a 'subject' you could pick up bits of subjects and be credited with them as you attended lectures and wrote essays. The system seemed to offer rather more freedom than the German method of supervision by a tutor. Most German students in Germany chose a university because they wanted a particular tutor. Bonhoeffer would not have to do that in America. He would in fact be doing research and learning about American theology. When the invitation came, offering him a Sloane Scholarship, with all expenses paid, to be an overseas student at Union Theological Seminary, he accepted it.

He sailed on the *Columbus* to America, embarking on 5 September 1930. He had not given up the idea of going to India to meet Gandhi. On board, he was delighted to discover that he would share a cabin with Dr Lucas, who was principal of a college in Lahore, then part of British India. Dr Lucas quickened his desire to visit India and invited him to Lahore, where he would have an expert guide.

First Impressions of New York

It was the America of the Depression. Only a year earlier, the Wall Street crash had left the American economy in ruins. Unemployment was higher than that in Germany, there was real poverty and homelessness, fighting in the streets and a general air of disillusion. Most people blamed the war and such conditions bred anti-German feelings. What he heard from the first Americans he met seemed to show that they had followed recent events in Germany far more closely than he had. Americans were afraid that Germany was hankering after another war. They took the National Socialists much more seriously than Bonhoeffer did. He had been too concerned with his own affairs to have noticed the changes that had taken place in Germany over the past few months. Earlier, the Nazis were unimportant. A pastor in Bochum decorated his church with swastikas; another refused entry to Nazis in uniform. Nevertheless, the National Socialists were regarded by most of Bonhoeffer's circle as an extreme movement that would soon go away. The September elections to the Reichstag took place while he was crossing the Atlantic. He hardly noticed that they had spectacularly increased their strength from 12 to 107 seats. The National Socialists were no longer an insignificant party in the German parliament.

Bonhoeffer's scholarship was one of a number granted every year to students from foreign countries. He was the 'German' student for the year. Because his advanced theological studies had already been completed, he was free to pursue his own line without the restrictions of a degree course. He was also free to explore the life of America on the verge of the Roosevelt era – and he made full use of this freedom.

He studied philosophy of religion under Professor Eugene Lyman, who was theologically far removed from his own Barthian tendencies. This was a deliberate choice. Bonhoeffer knew how to listen and to learn. Outside the seminary, American life confused and fascinated him. In particular he threw himself into an attempt to understand 'the negro community' – it had not yet become correct to call it 'black' – which was about as far from his experience of community life as he could possibly have chosen. His guide was a gifted black student, Franklin Fisher.

Discovering the Black Churches

Franklin Fisher was a striking young man to whom Bonhoeffer listened attentively. Here was a 'negro' student who could take him right into this new world. Everyone who knew Franklin Fisher was impressed by his appearance and he had an easy, friendly manner. Despite American racism he seemed to be unaffected when he was among his fellow students and they treated him as an equal. Bonhoeffer developed a spontaneous friendship with him and the American segregation pained him just as it had his brother. Once, when a group of them had gone to a good restaurant and Fisher was refused the service that the others were offered, he ostentatiously left the restaurant, leading the whole party out into the street, demonstrating his displeasure! Racism was not in his character and he could not tolerate it.

The church nearest to Union Theological Seminary is Riverside Church, of Baptist foundation, but in his time all-white. It did not debar blacks as some churches did, but it attracted only white congregations with the exception of a few students. Bonhoeffer disliked it from the beginning. He contrasted its thin preaching with the full Gospel of the negro churches. 'They will remain,' he said, 'long after this temple of Baal has been destroyed.' Harsh words, but he was still a young man.

He set about the study of the black Churches with vigour. He had to understand their problems in the minutest detail, so he read books, asked questions of Franklin Fisher and made many visits to Harlem. He taught in a black Sunday School and helped in the youth clubs. He developed a remarkable identity with the people and was received as though he had never been an outsider. He was particularly attracted to the 'negro spiritual', always taking care to point out that it arose in slavery. He concludes a report to his own Church with words that show his devotion to this part of the American people, of whom he notes 'one in every ten is a negro':

> The most influential contribution made by the Negro to American Christianity lies in the 'Negro spirituals', in which the distress and delivery of the people of Israel ('Go down Moses . . .'), the misery and consolation of the human heart ('Nobody knows the trouble I've seen'), the love of the Redeemer and longing for the kingdom of heaven ('Swing low, sweet chariot . . .') find moving expression. Every white American knows, sings and loves these songs. It is barely understandable that great Negro singers can sing these songs before packed concert audiences of whites, to tumultuous applause, while at the same time these same men and women are still denied access to the white community through social discrimination. One may also say that nowhere is revival preaching still so vigorous and so widespread as among the Negros, that here the Gospel of Jesus Christ, the saviour of the sinner, is really preached and accepted with great welcome and visible emotion. The solution to the Negro problem is one of the decisive future tasks of the white Churches.[1]

Plans for Cuba

Bonhoeffer was restless for travel. Dreams of India began to fade when he realised how much the fare would be to return to Germany via India, but the USA offered many opportunities. He was in demand as a preacher and he travelled around speaking, preaching and attending conventions. He enjoyed the richness of American Church life even when he found it confusing. There were many Protestant Churches, and despite their vigour and their strong convictions he found their theological bases shallow. He concluded that what he was witnessing was 'Protestantism without Reformation', for these Churches of the Reformation had never experienced the traumatic upheaval of the European Reformation. He also enjoyed the music and culture of America. Yet his eye wandered to surrounding countries where he might again encounter the Spanish culture which he had known in Barcelona: Mexico and Cuba.

He had a contact in Cuba, for his old governess, Käthe Horn, was working at a school there. Through her, he managed to get a Christmas preaching engagement and then looked round for cheap fares. Erwin Sutz was the Swiss student at Union Theological Seminary and their common language meant that they soon developed a friendship which lasted for many years. He was the natural companion to accompany him to Cuba and very soon Bonhoeffer was organising him and the trip. During a busy period in Washington he heard about 'Southern clergy tickets', but as Erwin Sutz was in New York at the Seminary he asked him to enquire about the prices. Both students were managing on quite small budgets and the fee for preaching in Havana was not going to be very high. With meticulous care, Bonhoeffer worked out the itinerary and the costs. The trip helped to cement the friendship with Erwin Sutz.

They visited Käthe Horn, of course, and her school. Then he preached at the German-speaking church in Havana on the last Sunday in Advent (21 December 1930). He found himself addressing a German colony in a Spanish setting and it was like Barcelona all over again. But Cuba was not Spain and he soon recognised its deep dependence upon America. These Germans were far more aware of the great industrial giant of America than his Barcelona congregation had been of Spain. His text came from Deuteronomy 32:48 – 52. It was the command to Moses to go up the mountain where he might view, but not enter, the Promised Land – a text that always moved him. Now with Christmas only a few days away he could compare the nearness of the joy with the seriousness of the preparation. Christmas cannot be taken for granted; perhaps we are not worthy to enter its joy. He stayed the laughter and the celebrations of Christmas for a while and pointed his hearers to the lonely and tragic figure of Moses – commanded to ascend the mountain, look upon the Promised Land for which he had longed all his life, and then die on the mountain. 'The Lord talked to Moses that day ... and Moses died according to the Word of the Lord.'

Bonhoeffer feels the deep disappointment of Moses as his life-long hope of leading his people into the Promised Land is denied him. He is quick to root the text in the lives of those who are his congregation, for they too have known hopes unfulfilled. The children may be disappointed, but there are deeper hopes that trouble us comparable with Paul's 'thorn in the flesh': 'How many times have we wrestled with temptations, with what agony of soul have we prayed, and how hard it is to see such fulfilment denied to us.'

It is not a hopeless message, but it brings his hearers face to face with the seriousness of their situation. Only when that is vividly experienced and the links between disobedience, unholy sin and death, are clearly seen, can the Gospel be accepted.

> God then promised to draw near to earth, to draw near to us; he has promised to lead us on the way to Redemption, Salvation, Sanctification. We know of this promise and we have our wilderness wanderings like Moses. But, if Moses dies on the mountain, we must die too if God is to deal with us according to his law. We must know that first, then we know also as Christians, that we shall not die, but live in the promise. That promise will be ours!

Bonhoeffer insists that we have to go through that process. We cannot go into the Promised Land unprepared, so the Advent message becomes a shattering call for repentance. It is this which is necessary before we can enjoy Christmas.

> Now, in three days we shall have Christmas again. The great change will take place, and God would have it so; out of the hoping, waiting, longing world, a world of promise will arise. There will be no more crying. Tears will cease to flow. No lonely sorrow will threaten us again, nor crush our spirit, because he is there who can help. He is there and will never leave me alone.

Although Bonhoeffer's sermon is not very different from his preaching in Barcelona, it was wider in interest, with a world view and a sense of world-wide suffering. The unemployment in America had troubled him, as had the deprived of that mighty land. So at the end of his Havana sermon we have a reference to more than Germany: 'People see such different things in their hearts as they approach the Christmas tree. And it is surely right that each of us, who have looked around the world a little, should celebrate this Christmas some of the wonderful things that have happened, perhaps especially this year.'

Earlier in the sermon he had said: 'God has seen the poor of the world and come to help them.' Now, in the joyous anticipation of Christmas in three days' time, he asks his congregation to see the poor of the world too:

There before our eyes stand a long line of unemployed, the millions of children in hunger and distress throughout the world, the hungry of China, the oppressed in India and in our own unhappy land. And while we all see this need, there is only confused counsel. Yet, despite it all, Christmas comes. Whether we want it or not, whether we ask for it or not, we must listen again to the angels' song. Christ the Saviour is here. The world he comes to save is our lost world.[2]

Longing for News of Germany

Bonhoeffer was homesick. He had never found Christmas more difficult to enjoy and he missed both the intellectual stimulus of his fellow-students and his family, as well as the joy of holidays in Friedrichsbrunn. He was also seeing Germany differently. While he complained of the theological grotesqueness of America and the fearful illusion of 'World Protestantism' as an ecumenical idea, he began to hear of changes back in Germany that made him fearful. His academic interests had prevented him from seeing that, despite the enormous steps taken in German theology, this had not led to any more relevant preaching. Some of the best minds in Germany were turning towards the attractions of National Socialism. His friends wrote to him about this attraction. The nation which had known the humiliation of defeat and was angry about the injustice of the Versailles Treaty was tempted to support a growing demand for national self-assertion, which National Socialism seemed to represent. Some people could see that this was a betrayal of the Gospel, but not everyone. Unlike Bolshevism, this party was not atheist, it supported the Churches. Its popular demonstrations were skilfully managed and created a stir among the younger people, which surprised many observers. It seemed a totally different Germany. He read of a new state of excitement. As he criticised American theology and felt the nerve of the 'negro' congregations pulsating, he tried to think how he could preach in this new Germany. From what he heard, the prevailing ideas were the struggle for freedom, the renewal of the idea of a Prussian state (with a Kaiser again), purity of race, the fight against the Jews, death to the Marxists, the Third Reich of German freedom and righteousness. How could you preach the Gospel to a people stirred by pride and hate?

One letter in particular made him sit up and take notice. It was from a much respected friend in Berlin, to whom he had written about the defects of American theology. Helmutt Rüssler did not mince his words in reply:

Your whole being is 'unpolitically' inclined and because you are not in the midst of the economic struggle for existence and the political inferno you are more easily able to explore from your high watchtower, 'what is the length and height and depth of Christ'. That does not mean that I underestimate your criticisms (of American theology). They are perhaps more comprehensive, but perhaps not so concrete as those of us front-line troops in the mud.[3]

What was happening in Germany was far worse than Bonhoeffer realised. The 'unimportant' National Socialism had become a popular movement and there was much in it that attracted the masses. It inspired young people with a purified, glowing national feeling. It was a new form of paganism, but it went about in Christian clothing. He was not fully informed, although he understood that the situation was desperate, that the threat to the Church was critical and that he should be back home taking his part in fighting against such corruptions of the Gospel.

Sabine

The whole Bonhoeffer family had been against the Nazis from the first, but a sense of revulsion came with the Nazi attitude to the Jews. Dietrich felt this all the more intensely because in 1924 his beloved twin sister, Sabine, became engaged to Gerhard Leibholz, whose father was a Jew. Gerhard, like all the children, had been baptised as a Protestant, although his father could not take that step. He was a very distinguished citizen, the owner of textile factories in Lichtenberg, near Berlin, a city councillor and then an alderman of Berlin, Wilmersdorf. He lived in the Kurfürstendamm, until he moved to a large house in Grunewald. When Gerhard first joined the Bonhoeffer circle of friends he was much liked, especially by Sabine's parents. Despite this they were not happy about the engagement, for Sabine was only eighteen. Paula already saw some difficulties in his Jewish background and warned Sabine that Gerhard would never be able to advance in his chosen profession of law as far as he deserved. That, she said, would be very painful for a wife to watch. Even in 1924 it was a disadvantage to be of Jewish descent in Germany. The couple had to wait, because Karl Bonhoeffer did not allow his children to marry until they were twenty years old. Gerhard passed his second law examination on 31 March 1926 and they married on 6 April.

They lived in Berlin at first and Marianne was born there on 30 June 1927. Meanwhile Gerhard made good progress, became a judge of the district, then a *Referent* in the Institute for Foreign Public Law and International Law. In 1928 he passed his lecturer's examination and in 1929 obtained his first professorship at the University of Greifswald. It was there that Dietrich sent his first letters from America to Sabine. They show very clearly his delight in her children (a second daughter, Christiane, was born in December 1930) and his growing respect for Gerhard. Soon the letters were to 'Dear Sabine, dear Gert'. They kept him informed of the growth of the Nazis and their behaviour towards the Jews, and were more sensitive than most to the political storm that was blowing up.

Nearly four and a half million unemployed destabilised the country and the NSDAP (National Socialist German Workers' Party) had made their enormous gains to hold more than a hundred seats in the Reichstag in September 1930. Quite early on, Sabine reports the appearance of SA uniforms – 'a man raking up the leaves who was dressed in a uniform which was unfamiliar and wearing jackboots'. The 'Horst-Wessel Song' was sung to them for the first time and they were shocked. Sabine also tells of a nasty incident in the marketplace of Stralsund:

> My father-in-law had visited us at Greifswald and had gone on an excursion with us and his chauffeur in his big 'Horch' car. He hardly ever had time for this and we had all looked forward to the trip to Stralsund. In the marketplace, the SA pressed insolently against the windows and took up a pretty threatening attitude of which my father-in-law was the object. Very quickly I took our four year old Marianne, who at that time was flaxen-haired and blue-eyed, from my lap and put her on my grandfather's knee. This saved the situation and we were able to drive on undisturbed.[4]

Writing to Sabine about that time from New York on the occasion of their shared birthday, Dietrich finds it hard to believe that either of them is twenty-five. He sadly regrets that he does not have her achievements behind him at this advanced age: 'If I had been married for five years, and had two children and a house of my own like you, then I would feel that I was fully justified in being twenty-five.'

In that same letter he shows that he has not yet fully grasped the full horror of what was happening in Germany.

Gerhard Leibholz and the Family at Göttingen

In May 1931, Gerhard Leibholz was offered an appointment in Göttingen as Professor of Constitutional Law. It gave him no pleasure for he was already aware that his days were numbered. A university lecturer and constitutional lawyer, however distinguished, who was of Jewish descent had no future in a Germany where the Nazis were gaining ground every day. Was there any point in making a new beginning? Nevertheless, he accepted, and the family moved to Göttingen in the October. Gerhard had foreseen the coming of the Nazis to power as early as 1930.

At first he was not disturbed. In 1932, the Union of National Socialist Students demanded the right to march in to the Opening Ceremony of the University term with swastika banners. Dr Ludwig, the Head of the

University at that time, forbade it.

Dietrich had returned to Germany and was already very busy in Berlin. Sabine sent him a cutting from a newspaper which indicated the popular image of the Nazis at that time:

> Tens of thousands from all political camps, from all professions and classes, lined the streets and felt themselves at one in spirit with the brown soldiers of the Third Reich who were greeted with tempestuous cries of 'Heil'. Anyone who saw the members of the SA and the SS, some three thousand strong, and the Hitler Youth marching by, caught up in the impetus of an inspiring movement and yet united in iron discipline, and in addition the many who marched with them in the rhythm of the Prussian marches must have felt that this was a great moment in history.[5]

The Leibholzs recognised the dangers and were already thinking of ways of escape. It did not take Dietrich long to recognise the truth of the situation. Gerhard Leibholz bought a car!

Bonhoeffer's Fastidious Choice of Friends

He took a long time to decide whether he would commit himself in friendship to anyone, but once the decision was made, he knew how to be totally open and generous with his friends. During his period at Union Theological Seminary he made four friends, two of these were his fellow students from Europe, although his more advanced theological education placed him somewhere between the professors and the students. The new European friends were Erwin Sutz from Switzerland and Jean Lasserre from France. They had similar scholarships to his and they were inevitably thrown together as Europeans.

With Erwin Sutz he could speak German and he shared a common German culture. Jean Lasserre was different. Bonhoeffer had probably never known a Frenchman in any close way and his strong opposition to the Versailles Treaty and the exorbitant demands of France in particular did not make it easy for him to choose Jean Lasserre as a friend. He was awkward with him at first, but the turning point in their friendship seemed to come when they went together to the cinema and watched the film *All Quiet on the Western Front*. Jean Lasserre describes the episode:

> In the early spring of 1931 most of us went to the movies in New York to see the film, *All Quiet on the Western Front*. The theatre was full. The audience was American, and since the film had been made from the point of view of the German soldiers, the audience immediately sympathised with them. When they killed French soldiers on the screen, the crowd laughed and

applauded. On the other hand, when the German soldiers were wounded or killed, there was a great silence and sense of deep emotion. This was rather a difficult experience for both of us because we were seated next to each other, he a German and I a Frenchman. It was all the more paradoxical because during the war the Americans had fought on the side of France against the Germans. For us, this was a profound experience. First of all from a fraternal point of view, it touched me to see how he could not do enough to console me, to be kindly to me after that movie when we had gone out.[6]

Burton Nelson, who provided me with the text of that description, said that when he was interviewing Jean Lasserre as late as 1977, the deep emotion was still there. '... he was overcome with emotion, and took two or three moments to reflect on it in tearful silence.' Lasserre continued by saying that he felt Bonhoeffer was also deeply affected by that experience 'because of me'.

Apart from the two European friends and Franklin Fisher, the black guide to the 'negro' community in Harlem, he had one other close friend, an American Paul Lehmann, who like the others remained in contact as long as it was possible. Paul and his wife Marion provided an American home for Bonhoeffer where he could relax. It was there that he celebrated his twenty-fifth birthday. Paul was working on a thesis at Union and was more or less on Bonhoeffer's theological level. He could understand the nuances of European theology and his grounding in systematic theology allowed him to argue and also sympathise with the aversion Bonhoeffer felt to some of the statements made by both professors and students. He was in the Reformed tradition – Evangelical and Reformed – later he became a Presbyterian. There was excellent scope for argument with Bonhoeffer's strong Lutheranism.

Of the four friends, Paul Lehmann was most able to stand back and assess Bonhoeffer. He understood the paradoxes which made up the discipline of his intellectual and spiritual life. Although a German, with his blond hair and heel-clicking, Bonhoeffer was often characteristically un-German, with his openness to every new experience, his humour, his total lack of condescension.

Each of these four friends played his part in the formation of Bonhoeffer and he contributed to their development. They did many things together during that academic year in the USA, as we shall see, but the lasting importance of their friendship was of even greater impact. In the years ahead, which would include years of war, he had links across the divide. Jean Lasserre would be the first to find the war dividing; Franklin Fisher and Paul Lehmann, a black and a white American, would give him access to the USA a little longer and Erwin Sutz was available in a neutral country. This was not planned, but was useful.

All four lived to look back on that year as students together and each in his own way expressed the memory of Bonhoeffer's personality. I think it was a very short comment by Paul Lehmann that rang most true for me: 'One did not notice the solitude which prepared him for fellowship, the discipline which sustained his abandon, the quiet piety which nourished the acumen of his lively mind.'[7]

That comment includes many of the paradoxes which made it so difficult to sum up this brilliant young man.

The Visit to Mexico

Despite the size of the USA Bonhoeffer became restless for travel again and nostalgic for some form of Spanish culture. After Cuba, Mexico. It seemed so obvious. Travel costs money and he soon saw that the only way to get where you want to go rather than where people wanted to take you was – to drive a car. Since he could not drive, he determined to learn. Perhaps over-anxious or, as some said, because he refused to bribe, he failed his driving test at least three or four times. Eventually he passed and to make doubly sure that he could drive he asked three of his friends – Jean Lasserre, Paul Lehmann and Erwin Sutz – to accompany him on the first lap of his cross-country marathon to Mexico City. By the time they reached Chicago, Bonhoeffer felt sure of himself and the highways were less threatened by his driving! The four set off on the long journey to Mexico in a venerable old car, but it held together and did not break down.

It was a wonderful adventure and deepened their friendship as they shared everything: hours of driving, looking for hotel rooms in remote places, sometimes camping, cooking their own food. They learnt more about one another in that summer of 1931 than they had in the whole academic year. Jean Lasserre has a vivid picture of one night of disturbance and no doubt there were many others:

> Once, at night, we had pitched our tent in a quiet grove of trees, without suspecting that we were taking over the dormitory of a herd of pigs. We had a hard time driving them away and discouraging these angry and noisy animals from reclaiming their bedrooms. After finally settling the matter we were worn out with fatigue and Dietrich fell quickly asleep. I was not so sure and I slept badly. At dawn I awoke with a start, because of a regular but ferocious snoring quite near to me. Thinking Dietrich quite ill, I threw myself towards him, only to find that he was sleeping peacefully as a child. The snoring which had terrified me was that of a huge pig who had stretched out against the whole side of the tent . . . Dietrich was undisturbed, apparently quite unflappable, whatever happened. He had an extraordinarily even temperament, capable of ignoring anger, anxiety and discouragement. He seemed-unable to despise anyone.[8]

What Jean Lasserre remembered most about the Mexican visit was the platform he and Dietrich shared with a Quaker called Herberto. It was a peace meeting and the audience of several hundred were impressed by the German and the Frenchman, both speaking earnestly about the Christian's responsibility to work for peace. It served to reinforce Herberto's witness for peace in Mexico. Bonhoeffer spoke forcefully and, according to Jean Lasserre, the convinced pacifist, made a statement which was even stronger than his own.

Union Theological Seminary

Bonhoeffer was a Sloane Fellow at this hundred year old seminary, Presbyterian in foundation, but ecumenical in every way. Bonhoeffer taught, heard lectures, participated in seminars and learned American theology. He avoided too much controversy and restrained his critical powers! There he became the champion of Karl Barth, whose theology had come very slowly to America. In Germany Barth's *Commentary on 'Romans'* had caused a stir when it was published in 1919, and his subsequent writings in the years that followed the war had divided many of the universities in Germany. He had attacked the liberal theology of his day, asserted the wholly other nature of God, called upon Christians to sit under the Word of God and developed a biblical theology which was called either the theology of crisis or a dialectical theology. John Baillie had seen its importance and welcomed a student who could interpret it. He therefore asked Bonhoeffer to speak to his seminar on Barth. He was nonetheless surprised to hear this young theologian beginning with total confidence: 'I confess that I do not see any other possible way for you to get into real contact with Barth's thinking than by forgetting, at least for this one hour, everything you learnt before.'[9]

John Baillie was aware that something important was going on in German theology which neither Britain nor America were taking seriously enough. He consulted Bonhoeffer about this and saw to it that an article by him was published in the *Journal of Religion*. Bonhoeffer's article was called 'Concerning the Christian idea of God'.

Another of the lecturers whom he got to know well was Reinhold Niebuhr. Baillie and Niebuhr found Bonhoeffer's writing somewhat peppered with paradoxes, such as 'the hiddenness of revelation', but put this down to German complexity and recognised in him a theologian of some weight. They both kept in touch with him after he left America.

Bonhoeffer's Assessment of America

The young German theologian made an impression on Union Theological Seminary and on many whom he met and who heard him lecture or preach in many parts of the USA. But what was his assessment of America?

He was obviously impressed by the freedom students had and the seminar system, which allowed a student to come into personal relationship with his tutor. The great teachers of America were more accessible than those of Germany. He found that American theology lacked the systematic treatment that Germany gave that discipline, but he greatly approved of what he called 'The Social Gospel'. He had many opportunities of criticising American academic theology for its shallowness, but its application in practical Christianity appealed to him. He saw that the Churches were much more involved in social and political issues than in Germany. In fact, he detected a theoretical contradiction in the American insistence upon the separation of Church and state, while permitting a very strong and continuous interference by the Church in political matters:

> Nowhere has the principle of the separation of Church and state become a matter of such general, almost dogmatic significance as in American Christianity, and nowhere, on the other hand, is the participation of the Churches in the political, social, economic and cultural events of public life so active and so influential as in this country where there is no state Church.[10]

He was also quite worried about the American attitude to Church unity. For him, unity was a matter of theological discussion, but his American colleagues seemed to think of it as a matter of 'give and take', good will and a little organisation. This did nothing to improve his assessment of American theology. But apart from all this, and his admiration for the 'negro' Churches, he had a deep concern for Protestantism in America. He met Lutheran Churches which felt none of the dynamic of the Reformation and he began to realise that the key to Protestantism in America was not the Reformation. American Churches cannot be understood without knowing of the beginnings of Congregationalists in New England, of the Baptists in Rhode Island, and of the 'Great Awakening' led by Jonathan Edwards. He admired the vitality of American practical Christianity, but was quite uncertain about what it had to teach Germany.

He was anxious to be back. He had enjoyed America and learnt to look at his own country with different eyes; but when he came to say what he thought he had learnt from America that would be useful in Germany, what he calls 'for our condition', he had to admit that it was very little.

Of course, he was not the best guide to what he had learnt. The years would tell, and there is no doubt that without knowing it Bonhoeffer had absorbed much which would later find its outlet in his theology and his dealing with the Church of his day in Germany. This influence would be largely without credits. America had introduced him to a new kind of churchmanship. He had started to know 'another part of the earth'.

FIVE

The Ecumenical Movement

Dietrich Bonhoeffer returned to Berlin in the summer of 1931 to lecture on theology at the university and to take an active part in Church life. He was committed equally to both tasks, but a third strand was soon to become evident in the pattern of his life: the ecumenical movement.

This movement had taken various forms since the Edinburgh Conference of 1910 when the Churches recognised that the mission of the Church to the world was hindered by its divisions. Long before 1910 there had been many organisations for practical cooperation, such as the YMCA and the Bible Societies, but what began to emerge with strong American support, can be divided into two parts – the Faith and Order Movement, concerned with theological discussion leading to unions of Churches, and the Life and Work Movement, concerned with practical help for Churches in distress.

There was another ecumenical movement established in the USA which attracted his attention. It was the World Alliance for Promoting International Friendship through the Churches, whose origins and aims were openly pacifist. It received moral and financial support from the Church Peace Union. It was a great deal easier to raise money for practical Christianity with peace as its aim, than for theological discussion leading to a hoped-for unity. The programme of the World Alliance was favourably received by Church leaders and an inaugural meeting was planned for Constance, Germany, for 2 – 4 August 1914. The conference was hurried through so that British delegates could reach the frontier before war broke out and enough was done to keep the organisation intact during the war years. After the war it assumed responsibility for victims and its message of peace was popular. The Life and Work Movement eventually cooperated with it to organise a conference at which Bonhoeffer played a significant part, on the island of Fanö, Denmark, in 1934. But that lay in the future.

The World Alliance for Promoting International Friendship through the Churches

Meetings of the World Alliance were held in Cambridge, on 1 – 5 September, 1931, and Bonhoeffer was invited. The German interest in the ecumenical movement had been very largely theological and that usually meant that their representatives were academics; unlike Britain, whose representatives were bishops and Church officials. Bonhoeffer did not direct his attention to Faith and Order, as one might have expected him to, but to the more practical issues of Life and Work. This may well have been the American influence upon him and led to his association with the Council for Practical Christianity (the German name for Life and Work). Bonhoeffer went to Cambridge in September 1931 and was elected youth co-secretary for Germany and Central Europe. Reporting on the Cambridge meetings, he pointed out that the Disarmament Conference then being held in Geneva dictated the issues discussed by the Churches in Cambridge. They did not, of course, hold the same political discussions as the nations at Geneva. However, they were primarily concerned with the question of the willingness of the nations at present arming, to stand by the word they had given in the articles of the League of Nations Charter. They also realised that if the nations broke their word, all efforts towards a moral ordering of international relations would collapse. On the brink of what appeared to be a return to complete moral chaos in international life, the Churches took a firm stand and appealed for truth and faithfulness in observing and discharging the pledges the nations had given. Bonhoeffer noted that this question of the honour of the nations now arming was seen as the paramount question by the English and the Americans. The conference was able to send out a unanimous message to the Churches of the world, stating that war as a means of settling international disputes was contrary to the spirit ('Mind and method') of Christ and the Church. It went on to demand:

a) A substantial reduction of armaments;
b) A reasonable and just relationship between the nations under arms;
c) Security for all nations under attack.

Bonhoeffer was not uncritical, but he saw the importance of the Churches of the world giving the utmost prominence to this message. The International Youth Conference, which was affiliated to the World Alliance, was unable to send out a resolution. They felt that high sounding words were taking the place of a serious attempt to rebuild new relationships and clearly Bonhoeffer shared this view. In his report of the Cambridge meetings he looked at two American resolutions which had been made on the sole guilt of Germany in the First World War. He detected a change in the American attitude. This was important for him, because he could not accept that Germany alone was responsible for the war. Looking at the YMCA resolution which the Twentieth International Conference had drafted about that time in Cleveland, he welcomed the denial that Germany bore the sole guilt for the war, and he compared it with the resolution of the Federal Council of Churches as recently as November 1930. These two resolutions showed a new humanity in American Christian thought. He echoed, however, what many Americans themselves were saying about the Federal Council resolution: 'Ten years too late!' His own comment was in the form of a question: 'When will the time come that Christianity says the right word at the right time?'[1]

The University Lecturer

During the autumn of 1931 Bonhoeffer was busy lecturing at the university. He enjoyed lecturing and related well to his students, but less well to his colleagues. There are many possible reasons for this. He was young and inclined to be rather sure of himself. He had a habit of finding a quotation from Luther that others had not noticed to clinch his arguments, while his dissatisfaction with theology as it was being taught estranged him from some of the older staff. His critical attitude to men who had been teaching theology when he was still at school could have been interpreted as arrogance. When he tried to put forward things that he had learnt in America his proposals were not readily accepted. The pressure on the university staff from inflation, political unrest and the propaganda of National Socialism made many feel ill at ease with the wide ranging thought of this young internationalist!

He himself thought that the reason for his estrangement was his support of Karl Barth. There were leading liberal theologians in Berlin – Bonhoeffer himself had studied under Adolf von Harnack and greatly respected him – but Barth had delivered a withering attack on liberalism. He recognised that his theology was beginning to become suspect in the eyes of his colleagues. 'They seem to have the feeling that they have been nourishing a viper in their bosom,' he wrote to a friend at Christmas.

There was no doubt about his continuing support for Karl Barth and it never occurred to him to change it. He had scarcely returned from his studies in America before he went to Bonn where Karl Barth lectured. That was 10 July, which left him only a few days to make the necessary plans and contacts to arrange his lecturing for the autumn term before meeting his mentor. He had not met Barth before, but his reading had assured him of his adherence to Barth's school of thought. He stayed only two weeks in Bonn, attending Barth's seminar as soon as he arrived. The story is told that

Barth heard, or had reported to him, a remark by Bonhoeffer which greatly pleased him. Bonhoeffer, ever ready with his quotes from Luther, recalled his comment that 'sometimes the curses of the godless sound better in the ears of the Almighty than the hallelujahs of the pious'. Karl Barth invited the young man to dinner and a lasting friendship was formed. They did not agree on every point. Bonhoeffer argued and disputed, but he was deeply impressed. The man was far better than his books, he was open, ready to listen to objections. Bonhoeffer commented that he showed such concentration and careful attention to the critical points made, 'whether they be put arrogantly or modestly, dogmatically or uncertainly'. That comment says something about Bonhoeffer, who could put his points in all four ways. But Barth was a very sharp disputant and he would not have treated this young man so seriously had he not recognised something unusual in him.

There is no doubt that his lectures would be greatly influenced by Barth's teaching. Delivered with the enthusiasm of youth, they could easily have displeased his anti-Barthian colleagues. He had discussed the themes of his autumn lectures with Karl Barth in Bonn and this discussion influenced in particular his lectures on ethics. Barth seems to have pleaded for a little compromise. Beside the one great light in the night, Barth said, there were also many little lamps, so-called 'relative ethical criteria'.[2] Bonhoeffer was not convinced. Barth had also said that Bonhoeffer was making grace into a principle and killing everything else with it. They differed, but the lectures on ethics are heavily dependent on Barth. This was the beginning of a long theological discourse on a subject which never left Bonhoeffer as long as he lived.

At this time, he saw the need to deal with the ethical decisions of the day. The unprecedented state of public life in Germany should have made that evident to everybody, yet some were still able to bury themselves in their academic research without reference to the grim outlook for the nation. Bonhoeffer was torn between his desire to continue his academic work, reading, studying, thinking, lecturing and discussing with his students, and joining 'the front line troops in the mud'. As he wrote to Erwin Sutz, 'Seven million unemployed, that is fifteen or twenty million people hungry; I don't know how Germany or the individual will survive it. Economic experts tell me that we are being driven at a tremendous rate towards a goal which no one knows and no one can avoid.'[3]

He wondered if the Church would survive and was disillusioned with the efforts the Church leaders were making. The other series of lectures he gave that term was also on a theme which would remain with him all his life: 'What is the Form of the Church in the World?'

But lecturing was too remote. He wanted to get into the Churches and work.

The Local Church

He was ordained in November 1931 and took his commitment to the work of the ministry very seriously. When the autumn half of the university semester was over, he threw himself into parish work. One local church task pleased him immensely – a confirmation class in the poorest part of Berlin. He gives a very clear impression of that class and his concern for it in a letter to Erwin Sutz:

> Something which keeps me far busier at the moment is the confirmation class which I hold for fifty young people in North Berlin. It is about the most hectic part of Berlin, with the most difficult political and social conditions. At the beginning the young men behaved like mad things, so that for the first time I had real problems with discipline. But what helped most was telling them quite simple biblical stories with great emphasis, particularly eschatological passages. Now there is absolute quiet, the young men see to that themselves, so I need no longer fear the fate of my predecessor whom they quite literally worried to death! Recently I was out with some of them for two days; another group is coming tomorrow. We've all enjoyed this being together. As I am keeping them until confirmation, I have to visit the parents of all fifty of them and will be living in the neighbourhood for two months in order to get it done. I'm looking forward to this time immensely. That is real work. Their home conditions are generally indescribable: poverty, disorder, immorality. And yet the children are still open; I am often amazed how a young person does not completely come to grief under such conditions; and, of course, I am always asking myself, 'How would I react to such surroundings?' There must be a great – and I think also a moral – power of resistance in these young people.[4]

That letter shows the earnest young pastor who, despite his academic interests and the world view he was acquiring of the Church, was deeply concerned with the pastoral problems of a local church. He devoted a lot of time to those young men, who kept in touch with him for years – even those who later became enthusiastic Nazis. He was not satisfied with the kind of instruction the young men were receiving at that time and even attempted, with his friend Franz Hildebrandt, to write a new catechism which related to the questions young people were asking in the thirties.

Richard Rother, who was one of the young men in his class, gives a very clear picture of him at that time. He says how composed he was and how he made them familiar with the catechism in quite a new way, bringing it alive with the telling of his personal experiences. The boys were impressed by the fact that he rented a room in order to be near them, and even more by the discovery that he had instructed his landlady to let any boys into his room when he was not there. This was the kind of trust that they had never experienced before. When he took ten of them to the Harz Mountains to spend a fortnight with him, for most of them it was the only time they had been out of Berlin. He went to great lengths to let them know that God loved them by spending time and care showing them the meaning of love. Whenever they needed him he was there. They were confirmed on a Sunday in March 1932 and, despite the critical elections being held that day, his mind was entirely on the boys. This was Hitler's first bid to become Chancellor, when he challenged Hindenburg and lost.

The Confirmation Sermon

As assistant preacher at Zion Church where the boys were confirmed on 11 March 1932, Bonhoeffer preached the sermon. He asked them beforehand what he should speak to them about. They replied that they wanted to hear that life had some serious meaning. He thought about that for a long time. These boys, particularly in Berlin at the time, must constantly wonder what life is all about. They had no prospects and, although they had grown fond of him, their relationship would soon end. He would do his job and pass on to other boys. For this period of preparation he really had given a meaning to their lives, but now what? He saw that he must explain to them what was happening in this strange ceremony of confirmation. What lay on the other side? Like many others who had heard him preach, they knew that he was capable of making his listeners recognise their own worth. They also knew that he could tell a good Bible story and make it come alive for them. A senior minister, Fritz Figur, who was the pastor of a nearby church, said that while Bonhoeffer's theological papers could be obscure and erudite, he had a way of holding his congregation when preaching, by his choice of the unexpected text and his strong use of metaphors.

Bonhoeffer put all his skill and love into that sermon. His text was from Genesis 32:25 – 32, the experience of Jacob on the night before he met his brother Esau, whom he had wronged. Then the stray verse from the next chapter: Genesis 33:10: 'For truly to see your face is like seeing the face of God.'

Even to read this sermon now is to be gripped by his dramatic account and to feel oneself in the darkness of the night with Jacob, about to face the awful presence which stands between him and the Promised Land. He compares that moment to the confirmation, which is like a door through which the child passes to become an adult, the young man passes to leave home and set up on his own, beyond which lies the rejoicing of the family and the first communion. Bonhoeffer paints the land into which they are entering with attractive colours, and then reminds them that God stands between them and this new world, protecting it and keeping it pure from our soiled hands. Like Jacob they must wrestle until he bless them:

God is there and bestows upon us his grace and his blessing and therefore we are in the promised land.

And now when God's day breaks, he sees the face of his brother (Esau) not as the face of an enemy, but as though he saw the face of God. He sees in his brother, God himself and his love. And the brother receives him and he is at home, for he had found God and his brother.

Have you understood aright? He who has found God has also found his brother. The face of his brother is seen as the face of God. And he who does not find his brother, does not find God either. For God himself has become our brother in Christ, in order that we might see him behind every brother.

And now it shall be day again for you. That does not mean that from tomorrow morning all your problems will be over and it will be smooth and easy. But you will know that God who blesses you will never leave you. That is the sun which rose over Jacob and rises also over you: God's love and grace, as you see them in Christ, your brother and Lord, on the cross and in his resurrection. You will find God and your brother in the Christian Church, you will find your home there, you will find your promised land there.

Here we are the Lord's and a Christ to each other . . . Love rules because Christ rules . . . Why should we fear?[5]

Bonhoeffer's experiences with the confirmation class in the suburb of Wedding led him to seek pastorates in the East End of Berlin, but he was not acceptable. The Nazi influence was already making itself felt in the parishes. He did however set up a youth club at the end of 1932 in Charlottenburg (Berlin) which aimed at providing unemployed young men with some creative occupation and a sense of belonging to the community. Unhappily, the events of 1933 soon brought this to an end.

The International Youth Secretary

Ecumenical conferences could be attended only between semesters because Bonhoeffer had lecturing duties. These were of vital importance to him, both because he enjoyed lecturing and because it was in his lectures that he developed his theology. The summer semester was May to July. In this semester in 1932 he took up two of his most consistent themes: 'The Nature of the Church' and 'Christian Ethics'. His dissertation, *Sanctorum Communio* had handled the nature of the Church, but in an academic way. He now had to think through his theme clearly enough to communicate it to students. In Berlin there were plenty of students, but you had to hold them. If your lectures were dull or did not communicate, they responded by not attending. Bonhoeffer's lectures grew and his classroom was always full.

It is not hard to understand why he held his audience when we read the drafts of his lectures which have survived. The following on 'What is the Church?' will serve as an example:

> We can only say what 'is' the Church if we say at once what it is from the human side and what it is from the divine side . . . The Church is a bit of the world, a lost godless world, under the curse, a complacent, evil world. And the Church is the evil world to the highest degree because in it, the name of God is misused, because in it God is made a plaything, man's idol . . . But the Church is a bit of the qualified world, qualified by God's revealing, gracious Word, which, completely surrendered and handed over to the world, secures the world for God and does not give it up. The Church is the presence of God in the world.[6]

He does not fail to relate this kind of thinking to the real situation in the Germany of his day. Many of his students must have remembered the words of, his lecture about the 'political word of the Church', when they heard so many preachers asserting their confidence in the National Socialist Party and the divine role of Adolf Hitler.

> The first political word of the Church is the call to recognise the proper limit, the appeal to common sense. The Church calls this limit – or rather the passing beyond it – sin, the state calls it the possible; both with different stresses might call it 'finitude'. Politics is finitude – that is the first eminent political word of the Church, and this word frees the Church from party politics and in the political sphere proper frees it from allegiance to any party. Note carefully, the first word of the Church is not, 'Make politics Christian' – that would be again to mistake the limits – 'but recognise finitude'.[7]

Events were soon to allow him to test that view against a powerful and popular political movement in his own Germany, and his appointment as an international youth secretary allowed him to test it on a broader canvas.

Although he had been an observer at the Anglo-French Conference in April, he was to be more involved in another regional conference after the summer semester. He had a hand in organising the Franco-German regional conference in Westerburg, 12 – 14 July. The subject was 'The Unity of Franco-German Protestantism between Catholicism and Bolshevism'. The political background did not help this conference. The German delegation had walked out of the Geneva Disarmament Conference because of the intransigence of the French, and even at Westerburg the old tensions were evident. Nevertheless, it was worthwhile for French and German young people to confront each other in a Christian context. It was also an occasion when August de Haas (a Reformed pastor from Dresden) spoke quite clearly about what was to be expected from the Nazis. It could well have been the first time French young people were made aware of the gravity of the situation in Germany 1932. A study group was appointed to prepare a similar conference for 1933.

But Bonhoeffer's main work for the ecumenical movement during the months since he was appointed youth secretary had been in the preparation of another conference to be held in Gland, Switzerland, 25 – 31 August 1932. However, before then, only ten days after the Westerburg conference, Bonhoeffer unexpectedly had to speak in Czechoslovakia.

The Youth Peace Conference, Czechoslovakia

The young Czechoslovak Church, under its patriarch Prochazka, had called for a peace conference for youth to be held in Bad Schwarzenberg, now renamed Ciernohorské Küpele. Bonhoeffer had not intended to go, because he already had more than enough travel to cope with, but Superintendent Max Diestel, who had been partially responsible for his appointment in Barcelona, was unable to attend and asked him to take his place. Accident brought him there to make the most important contribution of his life so far.

His mind was not fully on the conference theme: 'Public Opinion and World Peace'. Of course, he sympathised with it, but the nature of the Church was far more important to him at that point and when he spoke on 'The Theological Basis of the Work of the World Alliance',[8] he went well beyond the theme of the conference. The delegates must have recognised that at once from his first sentence: 'There is still no theology of the ecumenical movement.'

He saw this defect as due to a failure to face up to the nature of the Church. In America he had felt that the ecumenical movement was understood differently, as a mere matter of organisation, while the Germans were more concerned with truth. His first statement was thus followed with some powerful and critical arguments:

> As often as the Church of Christ has reached a new understanding of its nature it has produced a new theology, appropriate to this self-understanding. A change in the Church's understanding of itself is proved genuine by the production of a theology.. . . If the ecumenical movement stems from a new self-understanding of the Church of Christ, it must and will produce a theology. If it does not succeed in this, that will be evidence that it is nothing but a new and up-to-date improvement in church organisation.

He saw the danger of ecumenical leaders failing to do theology, or leaving it to the specialised department of Faith and Order. Such neglect of theology left the Church a prey to changes in the political climate, defenceless against attack. This led him to attack the nationalistic tendencies of his own

Churches in Germany, naming Hirsch and Althaus, whose propaganda found a place in Lutheran church newspapers. He attacked the Anglo-Saxon talk of the Kingdom of God, with its premature resolutions about peace. Attempts to reach an agreement between the Churches in the World Alliance only had meaning, he said, if that agreement led to a great proclamation: 'Because there is no theology of the ecumenical movement, ecumenical thought has become powerless and meaningless, especially among German youth because of the upsurge of nationalism.'

He maintained that the situation was not very different in the other countries. There was no theological anchorage. He went on to outline some of the basic theological questions that had to be answered if the practical work of the World Alliance was to have a clear understanding of itself in the mirror of the Gospel. Otherwise it was skating on thin ice.

His first question then was: 'With what authority does the Church speak when it declares the claims of Christ for the whole world?'

If the answer is only the commandments of God, the Church has regressed into the synagogue; if it proclaims no commandment then it has lapsed into libertinism.

> The word of the Church to the world must encounter the world in all its present reality from the deepest knowledge of the world if it is to be authoritative. The Church must be able to say the Word of God, the word of authority, here and now, in the most concrete way possible, from knowledge of the situation. The Church may not therefore preach timeless principles, however true, but only commandments which are true today. God is always God to us today.

He sees that there are dangers here if the Church must know every detail of the situation before it can make a statement. The usual practice of the Church, he maintains, is to act upon this by evading any action and turning instead to general principles. The real choice does not lie there. The Church should look squarely at the situation and either keep a 'qualified and intentional silence of ignorance' or take the risk and put the commandment, definitely, exclusively and radically. Then the Church would dare to say 'Do not engage in *this* war!', uttering this commandment as the commandment of God in the clear recognition that this can be so. Then he added: 'In so doing the Church must recognise that it may be blaspheming the name of God, erring and sinning, but it can speak thus in faith in the promise of the forgiveness of sins which applies also to the Church.'

Thus he shows that the prophetic word of the Church, spoken as the word of God in the concrete situation, is grounded in the preaching of the forgiveness of sins. The arguments of this young man, not yet twenty-seven years of age, bewildered his hearers. He was saying that the Church must proclaim the divine commandment to the world. The World Alliance must so act. This commandment can only be given on the basis of the forgiveness of sins. 'But it must be given, as long as the world is not the Church.'

Then he asks how the Church can know the commandment of God to proclaim to the world and he has two answers. The first is, the biblical Law and the Sermon on the Mount. The second is that the church must find God's commandments in the orders of creation. The address was a long one and into it he poured his theological wrestling. He was at that time preparing lectures on the first three chapters of Genesis and much of this material which was published later as *Creation and Fall* enlightened his understanding of the orders of creation. Bonhoeffer was essentially a biblical theologian from the start.

A Critical Commitment to the Ecumenical Movement

Bonhoeffer was in the first instance committed to his own Church. He was a Lutheran for whom the Word of God had primary authority. He found in the writings of Martin Luther, which he knew thoroughly, an inspiration which enabled him to understand and interpret the Bible better. He also found comments on the Christian life which corresponded to his own strong sense of practical reality. Both Luther and Bonhoeffer prized common sense highly! He was brought up in the discipline of the Church of the Old Prussian Union and was firmly on the Lutheran side of that Church. The Church of the Old Prussian Union had been formed in 1817 under state pressure to bring under one administration Reformed and Lutheran Churches, but the Lutheran was always in the dominance. While Bonhoeffer later learnt to appreciate much in other Churches, from the Roman Catholic Church of Italy to the Baptists of New York, he saw everything from the point of view of his own Church. Thus when he accepted the invitation to go to the conference in Cambridge, and there agreed to become youth secretary for Central Europe, he did so to represent his Church in an international setting.

His first commitment to the ecumenical movement was, as we have seen, over the peace issue. Closely associated with this was the international aspect of the movement. He began to see that peace was possible only if the Churches of the world united in their efforts to avert war.

He put little faith in the various schemes for Church union. In Germany it was a different problem from that in America or in Britain. In Germany the Free Churches were small and the two major Confessions (Catholic and Evangelical) were geographically divided. The Evangelical Churches were further divided into Lutheran, Reformed and United, but again geographically. Each had its own territory. There had been many battles in the past and few Germans could forget the devastating effects of the Thirty

Years War. There were also examples of discrimination, which made it difficult for a Catholic to obtain employment in a Protestant area, and vice versa. But, on the whole, the system worked well. They were not competing Churches in the sense of the American Churches he had seen.

Further, he saw that many of the Church union discussions had been about organisational matters and few dealt seriously with theological difficulties. The trauma of the Reformation in Germany had put 'truth' as the main issue, not administration. It was for this reason that his lecture on the 'Theological Basis of the Ecumenical Movement' was so important. The ecumenical movement could be taken seriously only if it developed a theology of Church and world.

If all the Churches were to pool their theological resources to answer the question, 'What form should the Church of Christ take in the world?', a question which he later cast in the form, 'Who is Christ Jesus for us today?', then the venture would have had Bonhoeffer's full support. The tidying up of Methodists in England or Presbyterians in Scotland, the different Lutheran Churches in America did not rouse him to great enthusiasm. He did not seem to feel the 'scandal of division' except to the extent that it prevented the Church from discovering its role in the world. Thus, while he was to be found at a number of ecumenical conferences, he was nearly always trying to get the representatives of the Churches to speak and act clearly on a specific issue.

In his theological arguments for action he was radical, in the sense of getting to the root of things. He would not accept ready made answers. But his authority was biblical. The Word which the Church must speak to the world and act upon had to stem from that promise and fulfilment, which is in Christ.

His criticism of the ecumenical movement when it was trying to deal with the issues of the day was that its fine words were too often not matched with any action. And the words themselves were cleverly devised to take in a variety of points of view. He saw that much of the time the drafting of these documents was really playing games and not seriously addressing the real problems. And he believed that the hour was late for Europe and the world, too late for playing games.

A few days after he left the conference in Czechoslovakia, there were two elections in Geneva which would affect his adherence to the ecumenical movement, although he was not fully aware of that at the time. Karl Barth was elected to the theological committee of Life and Work, while the Bishop of Chichester (George Bell) was made President of the Ecumenical Council.

The Conference at Gland, Switzerland

There was no accident about Bonhoeffer's presence at this conference. He had been preparing for it for almost a year, since his appointment in

74

Cambridge as youth secretary. It was an International Youth Conference, 25 – 31 August 1932, a joint conference of the youth from the Ecumenical Council and the World Alliance. The organisers were the three youth secretaries, of whom Bonhoeffer was one, and Mr Steele from Life and Work. The theme was 'The Proclamation of Christianity in the Present Crisis'.

Bonhoeffer was very critical of the British because they seemed to relegate the Christian proclamation to the level of the economic and international crisis. The chairman of the conference was Dr Burroughs, the Bishop of Ripon, and clearly he thought Bonhoeffer rather tiresome. Reporting in the *Yorkshire Post*, he said that Bonhoeffer was pessimistic and could only quote, 'We know not what we should do, but our eyes are unto Thee.' This was not pessimism, as we can see from the text of his address.[9] He began by a reference to a German friend who had said to him that the Church is dead and the only thing to do was to give it a decent burial. He was critical of the conference, comparing its pomp with the funeral service of the Church and insisted that 'the Church lives in the midst of death' and that only the miracle of God can call it out of death into life.

The Anglo-Saxons may have thought that he was going off into the vagaries of German theology, but in fact his address was the most practical of the conference. He condemned pessimism as illusory, no better than optimism. He described what God could do with a Church that admitted that it was dying and looked to him alone for life. Optimism and pessimism both have the same root – they come from being concerned with our own cause, with the defence of a particular view of the world, with a predetermined theology or the honour of the Church. While defending these well-worn paths, he maintained, we do not hear where Christ is calling us. That call we have to hear from our brother, who comes sometimes with a strange message to us, even that the Church is dead and all our liturgies are funeral services: 'Brother encounters brother,' he said, 'in all openness and truthfulness and need.' When we listen to this strange brother, and one suspects that he meant himself at that point, 'only then will Christ encounter us at this conference.'

Bonhoeffer's address became almost a sermon as he compared the events in Europe and the call to the Church which he wanted the conference to hear, to the call Paul heard to go over into Macedonia and help. 'The second time the call comes to us. The second time, Europe calls, "Come over and help us!". Europe, the world, will a second time be won for Christ.'

The Clouds Gather

The National Socialist Party gained steadily in the elections. In September 1930, the spectacular gain had been a jump from 12 to 107 seats in the

Reichstag, now on 31 July 1932, they had 230 seats. Bonhoeffer was well aware of the danger – especially to the Church. When he returned from his summer of ecumenical conferences, it was in his sermons that he expressed this concern most clearly.

Three sermons illustrate this awareness and deep concern. These are: The university sermon in Trinity Church on the nearest Sunday to Reformation Day, 6 November;[10] notes of a sermon given 1 December;[11] sermon at the evening service in Trinity Church on 15 January.[12]

The first, appropriate to the celebration of the Reformation, was given the title 'God's protest against all Protestant pride', and the text was based on Revelation 2 verses 4, 5, 7. He began dramatically:

> It is becoming clear that we are in the eleventh hour of our life as a Protestant Church, that there is not much time left before the decision is made whether it is all over with this Church, or whether a new day is to dawn. We should also know that you do not comfort a dying man with fanfares or try to call him back to life. Fanfares belong in funeral processions, there where a cold silence is overcome by an even colder noise, there where wreaths and the dead march decorate the decay. Children frightened in the dark streets, whistling and stamping their feet firmly and making a noise to give them courage.

His notes of the sermon given on 1 December begin with a reference to the Westerburg youth conference. His text is Daniel 10, ending with verse 19: 'O man greatly beloved, fear not, peace be with you; be strong and of good courage. And when he spoke to me I was strengthened and said "Let my Lord speak, you have strengthened me".'

It was a Frenchman who read this text at the Westerburg Conference. They were earnestly seeking peace, and the words of Daniel seemed to change everything: 'And as he came to the words "courage", "peace be with you", then we were all transformed, our gloom dispelled and together we said, "Now, speak Lord for you have strengthened us".'

The third sermon on 15 January 1933, also talked of fear and its overcoming. His text was Matthew 8 verses 23 – 27, the stilling of the storm: 'Overcoming fear, that is what this text is about. The Bible, the Gospel, Christ, the Church, Faith, they are all one great war cry against fear in the life of man. Fear – that is somehow the original enemy himself. Fear dwells in the hearts of men.'

The title of this sermon is, 'The cry of victory over fear'. And those who heard it that evening in Trinity Church must have remembered the note of triumph as the awful and fearful events of 1933 unrolled.

On 30 January 1933, Hindenburg called Adolf Hitler to become Chancellor of Germany.

SIX

Nineteen Thirty-Three

When Hitler was appointed Chancellor of Germany on 30 January 1933, he came to power on a wave of popular support. He promised much – discipline to a nation that had almost disintegrated, dignity to a people whom the other countries of Europe despised and humiliated. Germans wanted to be proud of their country again and Hitler promised it a future and a destiny, after he had purged it of foreign elements. It was the young who were most enthusiastic. They wanted to restore the greatness their fathers had surrendered in defeat. They did not believe that Germany had really been beaten on the field of battle, rather stabbed in the back by cowardly civilians. There was a widespread belief that the victorious Allies intended to reduce Germany to a nonentity in Europe, and that their main instrument was the iniquitous and unjust Versailles Treaty.

The Churches too saw Hitler as a welcome change from the colourless Weimar Republic which seemed to have little time for Christian aspirations or any desire to restore the Church to its former place beside the throne. The Churches talked of recalling the people to their moral heritage and Hitler supported them.

When this new 'will to live' stirred in the hearts of the people, the heroic programme of National Socialism made an immediate appeal. Hitler seemed to be saying, 'Lift up your heads! It is good to be German.' The threat of Bolshevism was also very real and with it the fear of chaos and domination by the old enemy to the east. Poland and Russia seemed to threaten again, and the only bulwark against them was seen as National Socialism. Its propagandists talked of renewal in public life, the place of the Church as a People's Church and the need to build up political and Church life in harmony, as a guarantee of the moral fibre of the nation.

The Bonhoeffers

The academic circle to which the Bonhoeffers and their neighbours belonged could not possibly share that enthusiasm. They had already experienced something of the horrors of the Nazi treatment of the Jews and were seriously worried. After all, Sabine's husband and Dietrich's closest friend, Franz Hildebrandt, were of Jewish descent and daily they had evidence of the horrors yet to come. They supported the Weimar Republic with little enthusiasm and were as critical as the rest of the Versailles Treaty, but they did not find Hitler the solution to their problems, even if they did look for a fresh start.

Dietrich's father, writing as a psychiatrist, described the symptoms aptly:

> I disliked and mistrusted Hitler because of his demagogic propaganda methods, his telegram of condolence after the Potempa murder (a Silesian village where a communist, Pietrzuch, was kicked to death by five Nazis in front of his mother), his habit of driving about the country carrying a riding crop, his choice of colleagues – with whose qualities we in Berlin were better acquainted than people elsewhere.[1]

That sounds a little like a class comment on people not considered fit to govern. Truth to tell, those considered 'fit to govern' by his class had not done too well since the end of the war. Dietrich Bonhoeffer had more serious comments to make and he made them in a broadcast on 1 February 1933, two days after Hitler came to power. In 1933 he had been working with the Student Christian Movement and it was probably in connection with this that he was broadcasting. He spoke on 'The Younger Generation's changed View of the Concept of Führer'.[2] A remarkably relevant subject. In the course of showing the development of a 'leadership principle' in youth work he made no secret of his contempt for what he called 'the unnatural narcissism of youth made vain by old fools'. He gave a theological talk on the structures of authority and the dangers of a growing tendency to make idols of the 'leader' (Führer). The danger lay in the temptation of a leader to 'succumb to the wishes of those he leads, who will always seek to turn him into an idol. Such a leader soon believes himself to be infallible, making himself and his office an idol, thus mocking God.'

The broadcast was interrupted at this point. Perhaps censorship had already started on 1 February!

Church and State

The Protestant Church was particularly vulnerable to the appeal of the Nazis, for it had long been separated from the people. After the war the new German Constitution declared: 'There is no state Church.' The 'separation of Church and state' was one of the first acts of the new republic. With the fall of the monarchy the old tie of 'throne and altar' had gone. The Evangelical (Protestant) Church felt lost: it belonged neither to the head of the state nor to the people. The opportunity to create a great Church in

Germany dependent upon the support of the people was let slip. Germany's only experience of 'Free Churches' was of small pietistic groups with no political responsibilities. The theological question of the day was how the Church could assume any political responsibility now that the link with the state was gone. What is the Church? What responsibility does it have in the world? Dietrich Bonhoeffer had seen a Church separated from the state in the USA and used that experience as he made the nature of the Church one of his prime theological concerns. The Church leaders were in sharp disagreement and Martin Dibelius and Karl Barth took opposing views. The two poles in this strong disagreement were, on the one hand, those who wanted to purify the Church by exercising discipline until only the true Christians remained, and on the other hand, those who wanted to build a Church to which all belonged, a People's Church.

The appeal to forge a link between a strong government with the right ideas and a People's Church was almost irresistible. Many young pastors saw a great appeal in a government which claimed to resist evil, abolish vice, clean up literature and the arts, send young people out of the beer cellars into the countryside and camps and raise the general tone. The watchword 'purity', however hypocritical, made it appeal to some. When, after the war, I met pastors and former Church youth leaders who had joined the party in 1933 I had the greatest difficulty in understanding why such obviously good men were taken in by this propaganda. Many of them left when it became too extreme, or slipped quietly into obscurity.

If for a moment we step a year ahead into 1934 and listen to the kind of things being taught in schools we begin to see the horror that must have come over such people. As early as 1934, the following prose passage was being learnt in schools:

> As Jesus set men free from sin and hell, so Hitler rescued the German people from destruction. Both Jesus and Hitler were persecuted; but, while Jesus was crucified, Hitler was exalted to Chancellor. While the disciples of Jesus betrayed their master and left him in his distress, the sixteen friends of Hitler stood by him. The apostles completed the work of their Lord. We hope that Hitler will lead his work to completion. Jesus built for heaven; Hitler, for the German soil.[3]

Even earlier than this, a pamphlet circulated in Witten/Ruhr stated: 'Without Hitler there is no National Socialism; without National Socialism there is no Third Reich; without the Third Reich there is no German Christian Movement; without the German Christian Movement there is no German Evangelical Church.'

That is the full grown error. It did not begin like that, but was more seductive in its wooing of the Church. As one man put it: 'The Church wished to take full responsibility for the people and drew near, perhaps too near, to the state.'[4]

The Strength and Dangers of the German Situation

When Germany became a republic, there were not many Church leaders who eagerly seized the opportunity to break the old 'throne and altar' link. The compromise worked out in those years after the war continues to this day. It is an imitation of the old system of Church government, whereby Church and state work hand in hand for the good of the people. Each *Land* or province had its own Church. The association is closest at that level, because Germany is a federation of different *Land* governments. A special Church tax is collected by this *Land* government from all who claim membership of the Church (or rather all those who do not dissociate themselves from the Church) and this is available for the ministry and for the community services of the Church. The German minister is a paid official of the government and is expected to conform to its laws. Of course, the Church has its own courts and councils, its schools and hospitals, social services etc. It has control of all these and has considerable authority in the *Land* government. But its association within the government structures has meant that Church and state have departmentalised their activities and authorities. The Church is expected to be obedient in matters that properly concern the government.

The peculiar state – Church relationship, characteristic of European Lutheran Churches, has tended to make the minister a state official. The people have so regarded him and he has so regarded himself. Even more than in England, the word 'parish' (*Gemeinde*) has the double meaning of a political area and a Church. Those living within the 'parish' expect the services of the Church, for which they pay their taxes. A person may opt out of this tax, but by so doing he cuts himself off deliberately from the Church and is no longer the minister's concern. The deep pastoral concern of many a minister softens this relationship, but the situation encourages a certain coolness of spiritual temperature in the Church – except in times of revival or crisis.

The strength of the Church is that the minister has an authority in official matters. He cannot be ignored, although he can be dismissed if the government brings pressure to bear upon his superiors. A few years after Hitler's rise to power, Paul Schneider went to Buchenwald concentration camp because he refused to let the Rhineland government separate him from his parish. A bishop to whom I spoke after the war said that he had to be careful how he spoke in public, 'Because on every word I say hangs the livelihood of a thousand ministers.' Apart from this danger in times of crisis, the official character of the minister and his relation to the government has led to a great deal of formal Christianity. The minister performs his duties; the people accept his services. Membership of the Church tends to be on the level of political franchise. Against this cold, official religion has come the protest of pietistic groups, asserting, sometimes in an exaggerated form, the need for a personal religion. The result has been that the parish church is not a community, but a political entity, formed by the accident of where people live or work. There is often no local Church in the sense of a religious community, but simply a number of people who attend church, a larger number who belong but never attend, and a minority who develop an intense form of fellowship in groups separated from the Church in all but the sacraments. These pietistic groups are often strongly opposed to the minister as a symbol of formal religion.

The German Christians

Within this historical structure there grew up with the National Socialist Party a movement, favourable to it and used by it. They called themselves the 'German Christians' because they saw Germany's destiny fulfilled in them. The founder of the movement was Wilhelm Kube, a politician in the *Land* government of Prussia. Its national leader was a Berlin minister called Joachim Hossenfelder, who joined the Nazi Party in 1929 and was much attracted by its organisation: regions, districts and local groups. He copied this like a shadow organisation to the party, as he developed his German Christian Movement. Each political group was related to an equivalent religious group and leader. Its rallying cry was, 'The Renewal of the Church'. The first *Land* Church to accept this organisation was the Church of the Old Prussian Union and it was followed by others. The next step was to make this shadow organisation national and legal. He wanted the German Evangelical Church to be represented abroad officially only by German Christians. The pattern was to be a steady progress towards a united Protestant Church with a Reich bishop, a kind of spiritual equivalent to Adolf Hitler. He was able to influence an important Church election on 26 May 1932. For this he prepared a statement on German Christian beliefs.[5] Rosenberg, whose philosophy of the German people lay at the root of National Socialism, was his major source. It was his phrases which recurred repeatedly throughout Hossenfelder's statement: 'German believers', 'the strong faith of our people', 'heroic virtues', 'the danger of racial mixing, especially with the Jews'.

There were ten points and No. 7 was the most precise: 'Our race, people and nation are gifts from God to be kept pure.' Of course many who supported the German Christians wanted a national Church because they feared the effects of disunity. They were not attracted by Rosenberg's fantastic philosophy, nor by the excessive 'German' emphasis.

Much was written about the up-building and renewal of the Church. The special needs of 'our time' were described and the futility of petty squabbles in the Church condemned. The times were grave. A strong Church was needed to combat godless Marxism and rampant materialism. So much theological hairsplitting about the slightest differences between the twenty-nine provincial Churches, often debated with passion and prejudice, seemed irrelevant to the serious task of building up a strong, spiritually-centred Germany. Of course, Church and state must work hand in hand to achieve this. The German Christians made much of God's call to Adolf Hitler to achieve his will for Germany. How could the Church be disobedient to the heavenly vision? Here, for once, was a political party in power seeking the same objectives as the Church. Instead of twenty-nine provincial Churches there should be One Church in One State.

As 1933 opened, the German Christians were a mixed group and they had no consistent theology. Some who could see the need for unity were not so keen on the 'German' emphasis, while the admiration for Luther confused the issue and was used by the more radical elements. Some of the German Christians claimed to be completing Luther's work, making the ultimate German contribution, as he had made the initial. It was an easy step from saying that Luther marked the emergence of the German people into the Christian world, to saying that Germany was destined by God to play a leading role in Christian history and therefore needed a purely German Church, purged of all foreign elements.

It was in 1933 that the strain emerged between those whose emphasis was 'German' and those whose emphasis was 'Christian'. About a year after Hossenfelder's statement, a revised list of basic beliefs was drawn up. The 'Germanisation' was much milder, but this modified document took no root in the movement and within a few days of its appearance the radical wing moved into the ascendancy. Even Hossenfelder was not radical enough for them, although he was allowed to retain the leadership a little longer. Now the 'German' was more important than the 'Christian'. Hitler himself came out in favour of the German Christian movement. The Churches were beginning to understand what Hitler meant by his declaration, on 1 February 1933, that he would take Christianity, 'the basis of our whole morality', under his 'firm protection'.

The First Christian Opposition

The German Christians were not alone in wanting to see some changes that would lead to the renewal of the Church. National Socialism and the theological perversions of the German Christians had gained the initiative, but the German theologians generally could not accept their facile arguments. Few were ready to grasp the nettle, but instead were moving around it, uncommitted. After Hitler had assumed full authority the natural caution of the academic corresponded well with the interest of self-preservation.

The first organised expression of Protestant opposition came with the 'Young Reformation Movement'. Like the German Christians this movement was opposed to Marxism and it sought to renew the Church. It was a mixed bag, sometimes sounding just like the German Christians, but it brought together some who were later to become leaders in the resistance. Its chairman was Walther Künneth and his advisory committee included Martin Niemöller and Hanns Lilje. A manifesto was issued on 12 May 1933[6] and it was signed by those who later would find themselves on both sides of the struggle. In Berlin the manifesto was distributed with an appendix, much sharper and more critical in tone. Bonhoeffer signed the appendix, but not the manifesto! His support, however tentative, gave grave concern to Gertrud Staewen, who wrote to Karl Barth about what appeared to be a 'lapse on Bonhoeffer's part'. She obviously thought he was in danger of joining the German Christians.

In fact, the movement fell apart when it came to the election of a Reich bishop. This was an innovation for Germany – a kind of archbishop who presided over the bishops and superintendents. Hitler needed such a figure through whom he could control the Church or 'take Christianity under his firm protection'. He wanted Ludwig Müller elected Reich bishop. Some of the Young Reformation Movement wanted this too, but part, including Niemöller and Lilje, wanted Friedrich von Bodelschwingh, whose work at the epileptic colony in Bethel, near Bielefeld, put him above reproach. Bodelschwingh was elected in May and his high prestige made possible the acceptance of one Evangelical Church for Germany. Bodelschwingh was, in the realm of Church politics, the kind of moral guarantee that Hindenburg had been in the secular realm. But the Nazis did not leave him alone, for they had their own idea of the kind of man needed to direct the Church. Because his independence was threatened, Bodelschwingh resigned and, in a rigged election on 23 July 1933, Ludwig Mü.ller was elected.

During that rigged election the Young Reformation Movement first used the phrase 'Confessing Church' (*Bekennende Kirche*).[7] Their call included the words 'We work for a Confessing Church. It is not enough that our credal confessions remain unchanged. The Church must learn anew how to confess before men the crucified Lord.'

The Reichstag fire, which led to the arrest of thousands of communists, was the political signal for Hitler's reign of terror. This was the end of February 1933 and it was clear that the targets were communists and Jews. Bonhoeffer's brother-in-law, Gerhard Leibholz, was threatened and the family was alarmed at the turn events had taken. Bonhoeffer expressed deep concern when

Bernhard Rust was appointed Prussian Minister of Cultural Affairs and this concern was intensified by Rust's statement: 'First thing on Monday the Bolshevik cultural invasion will come to an end. I shall ask the Churches outright whether or not they intend to help us in our fight against Bolshevism.'

Germany's Last Free Election

It is generally accepted now that the Reichstag was burned by the Nazis to give them a pretext for arresting the communists and destroying their political organisation before the elections of 5 March. In this atmosphere the word 'free' is a euphemism. The Nazis did not have to rig the election. Bonhoeffer, in fact, voted for the Catholic Centre Party, an almost unheard of thing for a Protestant minister to do! He felt that it was the only party with international connections and he feared the isolation of Germany more than anything else. The Nazis polled forty-four per cent of the votes – not enough to give them an absolute majority, but they could always count upon the support of the German National Conservative Party.

Following the election, laws were passed to make it treachery to speak against the Nazis and these were rapidly turned into anti-Jewish propaganda. A boycott of Jewish firms on 1 April found Dietrich's grandmother, at ninety-one, walking ostentatiously through the SA cordon round a Jewish store. The first non-Aryan law to 'reconstruct' the Civil Service was soon passed on 7 April.[8]

But the most serious step taken in those troubled weeks was the passing of the Enabling Act on 24 March 1933,[9] which gave Hitler and his party powers above the Constitution. Hitler was, however, anxious to retain the support of the Churches. On the eve of this Act, his speech was an attempt to win that support: 'The National Government sees the two Christian Confessions (Catholic and Protestant) as the most important factors safeguarding our national heritage'.[10] He promised to secure for them the 'influence which is their due', for he saw 'in Christianity the unshakable foundations of our people's ethical and moral law'.

Hitler was courting the Churches, but he would grant them power and influence only in as far as it suited his purposes.

Church Elections

On 24 June 1933, von Bodelschwingh resigned because he would not be used. A few days later students associated with the 'Young Reformation Movement' issued the following manifesto: 'The present situation in the Church demands a consideration of the true faith, because the visible Church may only maintain its structure through faith in the forgiveness of sins.'[11]

In its first thesis it reaffirmed its faith in the historic confessions and then listed its comments:

> a. any person can become a member of the Church, without distinction of race and social position;
> b. any reduction of the Gospel to a bourgeois trust in God or a liberal moralism is repudiated;
> c. the offices of the Church are held as spiritual offices, and not political.

The second thesis stated categorically that they wished to be responsible only to the Church and not to any political party of the Church.

The third thesis stated the conviction that the peace of the Church can be restored only by a common understanding of the cross of Christ. The manifesto ended with a protest against any interference in the affairs of the Church, a rejection of Hossenfelder and his German Christians, an appeal for the withdrawal of state commissars and support for Friedrich von Bodelschwingh.

Franz Hildebrandt drafted an election pamphlet which was even more explicitly an attack on the German Christians as heretics. Bonhoeffer, however, preached:[12]

> Close by the precipice of the valley of death, the Church is founded, the Church which makes confession to Christ its life. The Church possesses eternal life just where death seeks to take hold of her; and he seeks to take hold of her precisely because she has possession of eternal life. The Confessing Church is the eternal Church because Christ protects her. Her eternity is not visible in this world. She remains despite the attack of the world. The waves pass right over her and sometimes she seems to be completely covered and lost. But the victory is hers, because Christ her Lord is by her side and he has overcome the world of death. Do not ask whether you can see the victory; believe in the victory and it is yours.

The sermon came at the end of a week of activity for Bonhoeffer. He and Gerhard Jacobi had been canvassing for the Young Reformers and fallen foul of the Gestapo. A compromise was reached, but both were threatened with arrest if they did not keep to the conditions.

After the Church elections, with the German Christians in control, there was a period of anti-climax. The more moderate German Christians tried to prevent a split in the Church and it looked as though the extreme element would not be given its head – not yet! The extremists were prepared to wait for the National Synod which was to be held in September. That would be their star performance.

Bonhoeffer's participation had been strong enough to threaten his security in Germany, but that threat was somewhat exaggerated among his ecumenical friends who thought in terms of rescuing him! Bonhoeffer assured them that he was not on his way to a concentration camp. But he did have ideas at that time of leaving Germany.

He did not leave, however, before he had taken part in an historic act. A National Synod would normally see it as no part of its task to decide upon a 'Confession of faith'. The historic Confessions were not altered – simply accepted and interpreted. But the serious situation in Germany seemed to call for new action. The German Christians were not only reorganising the Church, they were also changing its faith. Niemöller was among those who pressed for the writing of a new Confession. This was agreed upon and at Bethel (Bodelschwingh's 'city of hope') the first Confession of the Confessing Church was written. This was decided upon towards the end of July and the meetings at Bethel were held in August 1933.

Bonhoeffer was, at that time, also considering the proposal to go to London and take charge of two German-speaking communities: one in east London and one in Sydenham. He preached 'with a view' at the two churches and looked at the Sydenham vicarage. He left Berlin on 27 July and preached in Sydenham on Sunday 30. Theodore Heckel, who had responsibility for the overseas German congregations, recommended him strongly. Bonhoeffer was undecided. If he went to London he was out of the fray, perhaps preserved for a more important later battle; if he remained in Germany he would inevitably move into a position of leadership in what was soon to be called 'The Confessing Church'. The decision was made, partly as a result of disappointment at the meetings in Bethel. He was deeply impressed by what he saw there and retained an admiration for the work of Bodelschwingh, but he was disappointed by the discussions on the Confession. Throughout August he wrestled with his problems. He attended no ecumenical meetings.

Bonhoeffer and Hermann Sasse hoped to produce a worthy 'Confession' for the issues of the day and set to work on 15 August. The first draft of a Bethel Confession was outspoken in its condemnation of the German Christian Movement. Bonhoeffer was clear that the German Christians represented a threat to Christianity. The issue was between Germanism and Christianity, and the sooner that came out into the open the better. However, this first draft was not accepted, for many were reluctant to split the Church and wanted to tone down its statements. The first draft was presented on 25 August and, the next day, Bodelschwingh sent the draft to twenty experts for comment and eventual signature. Bonhoeffer was unhappy from the start. He disagreed with the list of experts and, when the comments came in, they all seemed to him to be watering down the strong statements of the Confession. He refused to collaborate in the final draft and at that point decided to go to London.

Relations with Karl Barth

Bonhoeffer was at this time deeply concerned with the Jewish question. The German Christians accepted the Nazi view that the Jews had polluted the structures of German society and they must therefore be excluded from all government offices. They accepted also that anyone of Jewish origin could hold no office in the Church, and that Jewish Christian congregations must be segregated. Bonhoeffer opposed this with great vigour. He even headed his paper with two quotations from Luther. It was generally assumed that Luther was anti-Semitic and his statements denigrating the Jews were freely circulated. But Bonhoeffer, whose knowledge of Luther was encyclopaedic quoted:[13]

> *Luther 1546*: We should still show them the Christian doctrine and ask them to accept the Lord whom they should by rights have honoured before we did . . . Where they repent, leave their usury, and accept Christ, we should gladly regard them as our brothers.
>
> *Luther 1523*: If the Apostles, who were also Jews, had dealt with us Gentiles as we Gentiles deal with the Jews, there would have been no Christians among the Gentiles. But seeing that they have acted in such a brotherly way towards us, we in turn should act in a brotherly way towards the Jews in case we might convert some. For we are not yet fully their equals, much less their superiors.

Bonhoeffer's careful statement, which was not just a diatribe against the German Christians, but a carefully argued theological paper, denounced the monstrous legislation which divided the Church into Jew and Gentile. His objection to the Aryan Clauses was based upon a clearly understood doctrine of the Church.

Karl Barth also declared himself on the Jewish question in the first of a series of booklets with the general title, *Theological Existence Today*. Bonhoeffer wrote to him on 9 September 1933:

> In your booklet you said that where a Church adopted the Aryan Clause it would cease to be a Christian Church. A considerable number of pastors here would agree with you. Now the expected has happened, and I am therefore asking you, on behalf of many friends, pastors and students, to let us know whether you feel that it is possible either to remain in a Church which has ceased to be a Christian Church or to continue to exercise a ministry which has become a privilege for Aryans.[14]

Bonhoeffer went on to express his own view and told Barth that they had drawn up a declaration asserting that the Evangelical Church of the Old Prussian Union had cut itself off from the Church of Christ. He even said that he was considering the possibility of a Free Church.

Karl Barth agreed and confirmed that there was a *status confessionis*, i.e. a situation which required a new Confession of Faith. He approved of the act of telling the Church authorities and those who supported them that they were no longer the Church of Christ. He was wary, however, of any Confession coming out of Bethel, which he regarded as the home of the 'middle-line'.

A Letter from London

For the second half of September, following almost immediately upon his correspondence with Barth, Bonhoeffer accepted his one ecumenical engagement of the summer and went to the World Alliance Conference in Sofia.

On his return he obtained leave of absence from Germany to serve the two German-speaking congregations in London which he had visited earlier. Although he was in correspondence with Karl Barth about the Aryan Clauses, he made no mention of his decision to go to London. Perhaps he feared the undue influence of the older man. Bonhoeffer knew that this was a decision he had to make on his own. He resisted the pressure to accept certain conditions that would have made him virtually a representative of the German Christians, or at least mute over the cause of the Confessing Church. He decided to go to London and it was not until he was established there that he wrote to Karl Barth:

London, 24th October 1933[15]

I am now writing a letter to you which I wanted to write six weeks ago and which perhaps at that time would have resulted in a completely different turn to my personal life. Why I did not write to you then is now almost incomprehensible to me. I only know that there were two contributory factors. I knew that you were busy with a thousand other things and in those hectic weeks the outward condition of one person seemed to me utterly insignificant and I simply could not think it important enough to bother you. Secondly, I believe that there was also a bit of anxiety about it; I knew that I would have to do what you told me and I wanted to remain free; so I simply withdrew myself. I know now that that was wrong, and that I must ask you to forgive me. For I have now made up my mind 'freely'.

He went to great lengths to explain to Barth why he had decided to leave. The choice was between being a pastor of a church or a lecturer and he was now quite sure that his vocation lay with a church. He would have taken a church in East Berlin, after his experiences with the boys in the confirmation class, but the Aryan Clauses made it impossible for him to compromise. If his best friend Hildebrandt could not serve the Church because he was a Jew, Bonhoeffer could not indulge his privilege as an Aryan. He told Barth that he had invited Hildebrandt to London. It was obvious from his long letter to Barth that he was making excuses at great length and very nervous about what Barth would say. He knew that he should have consulted him! But a great deal of this young man is revealed in the way he tries to be honest about his motives:

> If one is going to discover quite definite reasons for such decision after the event, one of the strongest I believe was that I simply did not any longer feel up to the questions and demands made upon me. I felt that I was incomprehensibly in radical opposition to all my friends, that views of the situation in Germany were taking me more and more into isolation, although I remained in the closest personal relationship with these men – and all that made me anxious and uncertain.

He adds that the disappointment about the Bethel Confession, when hardly anybody saw the importance of what he was saying, was another reason for getting away for a while. Then he told Barth that the decision to go or stay was taken out of his hands by the Church authorities. He would have been glad if they had prevented him. The whole letter shows the uncertainty of the man and his nervousness in dealing with Karl Barth. It was a difficult letter to write and in the end he explains this: 'So now this letter is written. They are only personal things, but the sort of things I would very much like you to know about. It would be good if I could hear a word from you again.'

He waited in great anxiety for the reply and Barth kept him waiting for four weeks. Then it came – as he had feared.

> Dear Colleague,   *Bonn, 20th November 1933*[16]
> You can deduce from the very way in which I address you that I do not think of regarding your departure for England as anything but a necessary personal interlude. Once you had this thing on your mind, you were quite right not to ask for my wise counsel first. I would have advised you against it absolutely, and probably by bringing up my heaviest guns. And now, as you are mentioning the matter to me *post eventum*, I cannot honestly tell you anything but 'Hurry back to your post in Berlin!'

What is all this about 'going away', the 'quietness of pastoral work' etc., at a moment when you are wanted in Germany? You, who know as well as I do that the opposition in Berlin and the opposition of the Church in Germany as a whole stands inwardly on such weak feet! That every honest man must have his hands full making it sharp and clear and firm! That now perhaps everything is going down the drain not because of the great power and deceit of the German Christians, but because of the pigheadedness and stupidity, of the desperate shallowness of, of all people, the anti-German Christians! Now, one can on no account play Elijah under the juniper tree or Jonah under the gourd, but must shoot from all barrels! What's the use of the praise you lavish on me – from the other side of the Channel!

Look, I have now been to Berlin twice in recent weeks and I think that I know quite well what is going on there. I have also honestly tried to snatch round the helm, and I have probably had some degree of success; but if things had turned out well, I should have had quite different success, and so I went from the place extremely depressed, particularly the second time. Why weren't you there to draw on the sail with me, the sail that I could hardly shift by myself? Why aren't you always there where so much could depend on there being a couple of game people on the watch at every occasion, great or small, and trying to save what there is to be saved? Why, why? Look, I gladly suppose, as I have already said, that this departure was personally necessary for you! But I must be allowed to add, 'What does even "personal necessity" mean at the present moment!' I think that I can see from your letter that you, like all of us – yes, like all of us! – are suffering under the quite common difficulty of taking 'certain steps' in the present chaos. But should it not dawn on you that that is no reason for withdrawing from this chaos, that we are rather required in and, with our uncertainty, even if we should stumble or go wrong ten times or a hundred times, to do our bit, whether we then help our cause or damage it? I just will not allow you to put such a private tragedy on the stage in view of what is at stake for the German Church today, as though there were not time afterwards, when if God wills we have got a little way out of this muddle again, for the study of the different complexes and inhibitions from which you suffer, as indeed others also must. No, to all the reasons or excuses which you might perhaps still be able to put in front of me, I will give only one answer: 'And the German Church?' 'And the German Churches?' – until you are back again in Berlin to attend faithfully and bravely to the machine-gun which you have left behind there. Don't you see that an age of completely undialectical theology has dawned, in which it just won't do to keep oneself in reserve with a 'Perhaps – but again, perhaps not!' – Don't you see that any biblical saying you like formally cries out to us that we, lost and damned sinners, should now simply believe, believe, believe? With your splendid theological armoury and your upright German figure, should you not perhaps be almost a little ashamed that a man like Heinrich Vogel, who,

90

wizened and worked up as he is, is just always there, waving his arms like a windmill and shouting 'Confession! Confession!', in his own way – in power or in weakness, that doesn't matter so much – actually giving his testimony? I cannot really give you the prospect of taking part in a triumph, when I ask you to return to Germany. Here everything is as wretched and as dismal as you can imagine, and as far as one engages in tactical or historical – theological thought even a little bit, one can realise every moment that – the sea rages and will have its victims – in spite of any efforts, the German Church is lost. One simply cannot become weary now. Still less can one go to England! What in all the world would you want to do there? Be glad that I do not have you here in person, for I would let go at you urgently in quite a different way, with the demand that you must now leave go of all these intellectual flourishes and special considerations, however interesting they may be, and think of only one thing, that you are a German, that the house of your Church is on fire, that you know enough to be able to help and that you must return to your post by the next ship. As things are, shall we say the ship after next? But I cannot tell you emphatically and urgently enough that you belong to Berlin and not to London.

The impact of that letter was devastating. Barth had tried to soften it a little by adding a word of affection: 'If I were not so attached to you I would not let fly at you in this way!' Bonhoeffer did not reply and he did not return to Berlin, although he was sorely tempted to do so. But he had met the Bishop of Chichester and saw how much could be done in London to keep the Churches of the world aware of what was happening in Germany. He also went to Bradford with Barth's letter in his pocket to rally the pastors of the German-speaking congregations in England against the German Christians. He convinced himself that he was in the right place at the right time, but he did not try to convince Karl Barth.

SEVEN

The London Pastorate

In one sense Bonhoeffer escaped to London, not because he feared for his safety, but because he was unsure of his own convictions and needed to go into the wilderness for a while. He had urged dramatic measures – a clear refusal to accept the Aryan Clauses, a separation from the official Church – which could have led to a Free Church, a Confession which condemned outright the German Christian heresies. Even Karl Barth advised waiting until worse things happened. Bonhoeffer was the 'odd man out' and he wondered if his dogmatism was leading him astray.

He recognised that at some point he would have to take his stand in resisting what was happening to the Church in Germany. His motives were not primarily political at that time, although he was firmly opposed to National Socialism. His prime concern was with the Church. He had already taken his stand on certain points – the leadership principle in youth work, the Aryan Clauses, the election of a Reich bishop, the need for a clear Confession etc. He had supported the Young Reformation Movement, the Pastor's Emergency League and the emerging Confessing Church. Had the time come for total resistance? He was not sure. A pastorate in London would distance him from the struggle sufficiently to think more clearly about it. He was nearly twenty-eight and a very acceptable candidate for the two small congregations in London. Bishop Heckel, who was responsible for the overseas congregations, would have liked him to be more pliable and made some attempts to impose conditions that would assure that he represented Germany favourably abroad. This was not unreasonable, for Germany had always regarded its ministers to German-speaking congregations abroad as kind of 'ambassadors'. But Bonhoeffer would accept no conditions.

In a letter he wrote just before leaving for London, he made it quite clear to Heckel that he was not going to 'toe the line' as a price for the leave of absence:

> I am not a German Christian and cannot honestly advance that cause abroad.
> I would, of course, primarily be pastor of the German community, but my

relationship with leading circles in the English Churches as a result of ecumenical work and my personal interest in the ecumenical task of the Church make it impossible for me not to take up some attitude to questions about the German Church and the German Christians, because I shall be approached with such questions.

I need not say that I will speak with complete loyalty to Germany. I would rather give up going to London than have any uncertainties about my position. I regard this as an essential act of loyalty to our Church. May I ask you to put this letter on record?[1]

Sydenham

Bonhoeffer began his duties in Sydenham on 17 October 1933. His first sermon was on the text, 'So we are ambassadors for Christ, God making his appeal through us. We beseech you on behalf of Christ, be reconciled to God' (2 Cor. 5:20). He began on a personal note, reminding the congregation that it is quite natural for them to regret the change of pastorate. Pastor Singer had been dear to them, had been with them in moments of sadness and joy, had ministered the things of God to them. They missed him. And they hardly knew this new man! Such a personal start enabled him to be quite personal in dealing with his text. They soon discovered that this young man could go to the heart of the matter and call them to repentance, which he did in no uncertain terms when he preached on 19 November – Germany's '*Busstag*' (Day of Repentance).

There is a good account of the manse in which he lived, given by Wolf-Dieter Zimmermann, a Berlin friend who came to stay with him for a few weeks at Christmas:

> The manse was situated on a hill in a southern suburb of London, Forest Hill. It was rather large, uninviting and cold. Only gas fires installed in the fireplaces heated the rooms, and of course they could not be kept going all the time. Cold, damp air penetrated through the windows. Thus we mostly lived only in one room and our morning baths were reduced to a minimum! A housekeeper looked after us (as Franz Hildebrandt was also staying with Bonhoeffer at the time, this meant three), on an hourly basis, but everything else had to be done by ourselves, including the fight against mice which had nested in the house. For some time we had nobody to help us at all, because the housekeeper had all of a sudden gone mad and had to be taken to a home . . .
>
> Usually we had a sumptuous breakfast about 11 a.m. One of us had to fetch *The Times* from which we learnt, during breakfast, of the latest developments in the German Church struggle. Then each of us went about his own task. At 2 p.m. we met again for a light snack. Then there were conversations, interspersed with music (Hildebrandt and Bonhoeffer both

played the piano to perfection, solo or duet). In the afternoon, we mostly separated again. Many evenings we spent together at home, only occasionally going out to see a film or a play or some other engagement. Evenings at home meant theological discussions, music, debates, story-telling, and following one upon another until 2 or 3 in the morning.[2]

Hildebrandt and Bonhoeffer were theologically opposed to each other and the meeting of their minds sparked off many a point for a sermon. They would jot down ideas in the midst of a boisterous evening and only agree when they sat down at the piano: 'This is perfect, this is clear, there are no misunderstandings in this.' Music remained one of Bonhoeffer's continuing delights and was often for him the only stable ground in a chaotic world.

There are many stories told of his time in Sydenham. One concerns an invitation to Christmas dinner at the home of Lawrence Whitburn. Bonhoeffer took a German friend along with him and faced a turkey for the first time. The Whitburns had bought an enormous turkey and cooked it, but neither they nor their guests knew how to carve it. Bonhoeffer did not hesitate. He took on the new task and soon organised the household to hold down the unfortunate bird while he went into the attack with the carving knife. They all ate well, but the sight of the dissected skeleton remained as evidence of his determination to prove what so many said of him – 'Bonhoeffer is capable of anything'.

Lawrence Whitburn recalls many of Bonhoeffer's adventures during those months in London. He tells of his humour, his love of playing tricks, his fondness for tennis, which he always wanted to win, and most of all about his music. This affected his conduct of Church services too, as Lawrence Whitburn recalls:

> Bad music was for him unbearable and thereby hangs a tale. As is often the case, our congregation (at Sydenham) at that time had the bad habit of gradually getting slower during the hymns, a fault which unfortunately was also shared by the organist. Bonhoeffer decided that the correct tempo when singing hymns must be maintained and asked me to help. So, the following Sunday we went into battle, with the result that during the first hymn, we were soon a whole verse in advance. It was useless, we had to give up the fight. Thereupon Bonhoeffer thought we ought to form a church choir – I should conduct and he would sing with us. It would not be quite truthful to say that the practices always ran smoothly![3]

The Twofold Task

There is no doubt that Bonhoeffer was a little confused about why he had come to London. This is clear in his attempted explanation to Karl Barth.

But gradually a twofold task emerged. He needed a local church. The university did not satisfy him and he saw quite clearly that students sympathetic to the Confessing Church would soon be excluded. Some new form of preparing for the ministry would have to be created in Germany. He wanted to have a hand in that and he needed parish experience. His confirmation class had shown him capable of pastoral work in a parish and he knew the importance of preaching, which he loved. All that was one side of his task. But he also saw that his ecumenical contacts would be important and that the outside world needed an interpreter of what was going on in Germany.

He was in London from October 1933 to April 1934. This twofold task is illustrated by two sets of material: on the one hand his sermons, and on the other his correspondence and meetings with the Bishop of Chichester.

The Sermons

As a preacher, Bonhoeffer continued to develop and respond to his environment.[4] His choice of texts remained striking and he was able to take a Bible study and bring it alive. He was never remote, leaving his listeners in the world of the Bible. His illustrations, which brought the biblical material alive, were drawn from daily experience. Those long discussions with his friends may have thrown up ideas that he felt able to jot down in – the heat of the argument, but his illustrations were worked out with the greatest thoroughness. As in Spain, he took care to use those which were familiar to his listeners, but never simply to hold their attention. His illustrations were graphic. A good example came in the Advent season leading up to his first Christmas in England. There had been a mining disaster in Wales and the newspapers had reported it in detail. One incident in the tragic drama caught his attention, as it must have that of many of his congregation. Some trapped miners had almost given up hope, when they heard the sound of knocking as their rescuers came towards them. It was still quite a long time before they were rescued and their fate hung in the balance, but they had heard the knocking and their spirits revived. They were eventually rescued. Bonhoeffer uses this as an illustration of Advent. His text on that Sunday in 1933 was: 'Now when these things begin to take place, look up and raise your heads, because your redemption is drawing nigh' (Luke 21:28).

At Sydenham, he had a regular congregation of between thirty and forty. The other church for which he was responsible was St Paul's in the east of London, a Reformed community dating back about 200 years. These two churches were not able to support a pastor each and despite the fact that they came from different traditions in Germany, they combined their resources. The two communities acted rather like Free Churches. St Paul's had about fifty in the congregation and while at Sydenham, the congregation included many from the embassy, St Paul's mostly attracted local tradesmen. His sermons must have been a little over their heads. His predecessor had preached comforting pietistic sermons that made little demand on the intellect, nor did they raise theological or political problems.

Bonhoeffer was loyal to his Fatherland and encouraged his people to give to the Winter Aid Programme set up by Goebbels, but he also called for help for German refugees now beginning to arrive in England. His pastoral work was considerable and much time was spent with the refugees, who probably needed him most. Bonhoeffer had to preach once a month in English and it was at the beginning of his first English sermon that he explained how he approached the special task of ministering to a German-speaking congregation abroad: 'When I came to a German overseas church, the question that concerned me most was: What brought all these people to this place? What different reasons and what significant purposes have brought them all here?'

He saw his task first of all as getting to know the people, their stories, their circumstances, if he was to preach to them. It was not therefore surprising to hear from many sources that he spent a lot of time with the refugees from Hitler's Germany. The fate of these refugees was of considerable concern to him. As a regular pastor, Bonhoeffer had to preach every Sunday. Even allowing for the occasional visiting preacher and holidays, he must have preached some seventy or eighty sermons, all of which he wrote out carefully. Unfortunately only sixteen have survived. It is from this sample that we have to generalise. The first impression is that he made only occasional references to the situation in Germany. He followed the Church's year and expounded the relevant Bible passages with skill, bringing the Bible alive and using few, but telling, illustrations. In the earlier sermons he had a strong bias towards the eschatological and sounds a great deal older than his years. It is strange to read of this young twenty-eight year old, full of life with a rich appreciation of all the good things life can offer, expressing his longing for 'the last days' and eagerly preaching of 'the last things'.

Thoughts on Suicide

The sermons became much more intense during the Advent period and some remnants of his earlier fascination with death are allowed to surface. Homesickness, of course, can be illustrated from the sermons and sometimes there is an indication of depression. There is no evidence that he was a manic depressive, but he does show times of great exhilaration and times of passing through a dark trough. In letters of the period and much later in his notes for his book, *Ethics* he records sensitive periods of hatred for his imperfections, and also what he calls 'headstrong resistance which earthly life in general opposes to its own fulfilment by God'. There is no doubt that both of these caused him grief. His Advent sermons, in particular, show that he could preach so passionately about the goal of life, that he must have doubted his own goal. These three things – failure to meet his own high standards, resistance to God's will for him, doubts about the goal of his life, are later listed as leading a person into great danger. He recognised that Luther had been through this and tried to take comfort from his master's successful survival! But he could still write, 'In such hours of trial no human or divine law can prevent the deed.' He is talking of suicide and, although he found many other reasons later not to judge a person for committing suicide, it was these three reasons which were uppermost at that time. He never condemned suicide as a moral fault, but as a failure of faith in God.

Although written years later, the following words from *Ethics* represent his own thoughts at times in that lonely London parsonage:

> Help can come only from the comfort of grace and from the power of brotherly prayer. It is not the right to life that can overcome this temptation to suicide, but only the grace which allows a man to continue to live in the knowledge of God's forgiveness. But who would venture to say that God's grace and mercy cannot embrace and sustain even a man's failure to resist this hardest of all temptations?[5]

That writing was yet to come. In his sermons we trace the melancholy. It is most evident on those few occasions when he makes a direct reference to Germany. The most memorable is the sermon he preached on Jeremiah, which reveals the sadness in the heart of this young man at a time of deep disturbance in Germany.

The Jeremiah Sermon

On 21 January 1934, the news from Germany had been bad. Ludwig Müller was further supported by Hitler and all professors of theology were ordered not to oppose him nor to be members of the Pastors' Emergency League. The congregation at Sydenham heard their young pastor announce his text:[6] 'O Lord, thou hast deceived me, and I was deceived; Thou art stronger than I, and Thou hast prevailed' (Jer. 20:7).

They had learnt to listen well to the opening words of this preacher's sermons and that morning they heard the empathy between their pastor and the reluctant prophet. The German word (like the Hebrew) can equally mean 'persuade' as 'deceive'. Bonhoeffer takes it to mean 'talked into it'. The sermon becomes Bonhoeffer's own confession of the way in which God talked him into involvement in the Church struggle. This was a decisive time for him and in his exposition of Jeremiah he shared his own struggle with his people. But how many understood? God had talked him into this struggle and there was no evading it, because 'Thou art stronger than I and Thou hast prevailed.' There is no triumph in that conclusion. It is the inevitability which predominates. We do not choose any more than Jeremiah chose. Bonhoeffer moves from the reluctant prophet to his own situation:

> Thousands of church members and pastors are today in our country in danger of oppression and persecution for their witness to the truth. They have not sought this way out of pride or stubbornness. They must choose it – because God is too strong in them. Because they can no longer withstand God. Because the lock has shut behind them. Because they can no longer retreat behind God's Word, God's Call, God's Command. How often they wished for peace and quiet and calm. How often they wished they did not have to threaten, to warn, to protest, in order to witness to the truth. But a compulsion was laid upon them: 'Woe unto us if we do not preach the Gospel' (1 Cor. 9:16) God, why are you so near to us?

There is in fact no getting away from God, any more than a child can get away from his or her mother. A time comes when we wish that we had never begun with God. The way is hard. Bonhoeffer was not eager for a fight with the authorities, he did not want to split the Church. He was a theologian and a preacher, asking the question: What or Who is Jesus Christ for us today? The answer he was getting to that persistent question was to lead him into the heart of the resistance. He would not take Christ there, but find him there. But it was not all gloom. At the very point when we feel that we cannot go on, when we break under the hand of God's command – and Bonhoeffer adds, 'such moments come to us all' – then God draws near and his comfort and strength and faithfulness support us. There is no doubt in the preacher's mind that the victory is with truth, and however strong the opposition to us, we shall share in that victory if we allow God to overrule us:

> If we are bound to his victory chariot, bound and hard pressed, we have part in his victory. He has overruled us. He is too strong for us. He will not leave us alone. Why should we worry about the bonds and the wounds? Why worry about sin and suffering and death? He holds us fast. He will never leave us. Lord, overrule us once again and be strong over us that we might believe, live and die in you. That we might see your victory.

It is not difficult to recognise in that crucial sermon the struggle which had been going on in Bonhoeffer's mind, his reluctance to throw himself into an opposition, to fight against his colleagues, to be the rebel. He did not know how far it would lead him, but in that sermon he declared his confidence in God to hold him – even if he was wrong.

Bonhoeffer and the Bishop of Chichester

The exchange of letters between Bonhoeffer and George Bell, the Bishop of Chichester, shows more clearly than the sermons his involvement in the ecumenical movement and his efforts to interpret the German Church struggle to the World Church.

In the first lively exchange of letters between the two, it is already evident that he is using his presence in London to explain the resistance in Germany to those who might know of it only through the channels of the official German Christians. This exchange began as early as November 1933. The bishop invited him to Chichester and he replied at once, accepting the invitation and adding:

> You certainly know of the recent events within the German Church and I think that there is a great likelihood for a separation of the minority from the *Reichskirche*, and in this case an action of ecumenic support would certainly be of immense value in this tense situation. There is no doubt that any sort of separation would become at once a strong political issue, and for this reason would probably be dealt with by the government in an exclusively political way. If the ecumenical Churches would keep silent during those days, I am afraid that all trust put into it by the minority would be destroyed. We must not leave alone those men who fight – humanly spoken – an almost hopeless struggle. I get news with every mail and also by telephone. If I may I will forward to you the recent information.[7]

The bishop had not been silent, but written to Germany. What Bonhoeffer calls the 'ecumenic' Churches have been active without his urging! An English translation of the bishop's letter to Müller was printed in full in the *Manchester Guardian*. He had learnt that other Church leaders had visited Müller and that there was a chance of a delegation from the ecumenical movement. Bonhoeffer visited Chichester on 21 November and stayed two days with the bishop. A few days later, after thanking the bishop for his hospitality, he wrote to inform him of rapidly changing events and the personal case of the arrested Pastor Wilde:

> May I draw your attention to the enclosed leaflets. Three pastors have been dismissed only because of their sincere confession to Christ as the only Lord of the Church. One of them, Pastor Wilde, is father of seven children. The

case is not decided yet definitely, but perhaps the moment has come when the ecumenical movement ought to provide for subsidies and financial support for those who will lose their positions for the only reason of their being confessors of their faith. Things are becoming very acute.[8]

A few weeks later the Bishop was asked to write an article on the crisis in the German Protestant Church in Germany by the editor of *The Round Table*. He did not have time to do it himself, but he recommended Bonhoeffer as a better choice. His recommendation of Bonhoeffer gives us a clear idea of what Bell thought of him at that time:

> . . . I should however like to suggest a man who would do the article with great ability and first-hand knowledge. He is Dr Dietrich Bonhoeffer, 23 Manor Mount, Forest Hill S.E.23. For the last three months he has been German pastor in London. I know him well and he was introduced to me by Professor Adolf Deissmann of Berlin, as 'one of our best young theologians'. He speaks English perfectly. He is under thirty. He spent a year in USA for theological purposes. He knows the personnel of the German church at Berlin extremely well and is a follower of Karl Barth. He is also in almost daily touch with the situation in Berlin. Further, he is one of the earliest members of the Pastors' Emergency League, now swollen to 6,000 members, and his name is actually the first of the twenty or so signatures to the famous manifesto which the pioneers of the Pastors' Emergency League presented to the Prussian Synod in September.[9]

As these two men grew closer together, Bonhoeffer used his influence to persuade the bishop to write to the National Bishop, Ludwig Müller, to publish the letter in *The Times* and to intervene as much as possible to bring about the collapse of the German Christians.

Franz Hildebrandt was with him at this time and both were shocked by the German Christian Demonstration in the Berlin Sports Palace on 13 November. News came to them of the scandalous speech by Dr Krause, the senior Nazi official in Berlin. He said that now that leading ecclesiastical positions had been taken over by 'men of the movement', there would be more dismissals and the Aryan Clauses would be enforced at once. He called for the 'liberation of the Church from the Old Testament with its Jewish money morality and from these stories of cattle dealers and pimps.' Even some of the German Christians were shocked by what they heard.

From their draughty manse in Sydenham Bonhoeffer and Hildebrandt followed the events in Germany through correspondence, lengthy telephone calls and the excellent reports in *The Times*. They were encouraged by the apparent collapse of the German Christians and Hitler's statement that he would not interfere in Church disputes. But it soon became clear that the Pastors' Emergency League was not united enough to take advantage of the favourable situation.

Niemöller, at the crucial moment, felt unable to meet with the German bishops who had elected Ludwig Müller and were ready to reconsider their position. The protests that came from Sydenham brought both Hildebrandt and Bonhoeffer into the public eye.

Bradford, 27 – 30 November 1933

The annual conference of German pastors in England which met in Bradford was disturbed by news of the Berlin Sports Palace demonstration of 13 November.[10] When they met on 27 November, they expressed their concern and eventually sent a letter of protest to the Reichsbischof, Ludwig Müller. It was signed by six German pastors and inspired by Bonhoeffer. His speech at that conference was unequivocal. The letter which was sent on the last day of the conference proper, 29 November, insisted upon the character of the Evangelical Church in Germany as the Church of the Reformation. It pointed out that any break from the theological norm of the traditional Evangelical Church would result in a break between the German churches in Britain and those in Germany, ending with a direct reference to the 13 November demonstration: 'Revolted and ashamed at the attacks on the substance of the Evangelical faith in Luther's year 1933, and on the occasion of the enthronement of the National Bishop ... we express our hope and expectation that the German Evangelical Church will always continue to remain the Church of the Reformation.'[11]

It was signed by three pastors from London, Schönberger, Rieger and Bonhoeffer; Hansen from Bradford; Böckheler from Hull; Schreiner from Liverpool. The next few weeks were critical for the Church struggle in Germany. The German Christians recovered and even gained power, with a government behind them and the National Bishop prepared to flex his muscles. Müller summoned the Church leaders to Berlin on 13 January 1934 to explain the measures that would be taken against those who did not conform. Naturally this struggle was watched carefully by the German pastors in England and Bonhoeffer was rapidly becoming their spokesman. On 15 January, he drafted a letter to the President of Germany and it was sent in the name of the pastors of the German-speaking congregations in England. Once again, the letter made much of the betrayal of the Reformation by the German Christians, particularly in this Luther Year. It also pointed out that the Church struggle and the behaviour of the National Bishop was damaging to German reputation in Britain. Copies were sent to all involved and the letter had a powerful effect.

Bishop Heckel's Visit and its Consequences

Bishop Heckel led a deputation to London on 8 February 1934. He met the pastors and insisted upon a declaration of loyalty. These pastors were all loyal Germans, but none were prepared to swear an oath of allegiance to the National Bishop. Heckel had an unhappy visit and he appears not to have been completely frank with them on many matters. One in particular was outlined in a letter Bonhoeffer wrote shortly after the meeting in London. It is also worth quoting for the description it gives of the atmosphere at the meeting with the delegation and Bonhoeffer's role. The letter is dated 18 March 1934:

> In the session with the German pastors in England on 8 February 1934, you yourself said in your detailed report on church developments in Germany during recent months that at one time Pastor Niemöller had been invited to accept office in the government department dealing with the clergy. When I intervened to remark that according to my own personal information such an offer had only been made in passing in a private conversation with Dr Oberheid, you retorted that Dr Oberheid had been officially authorised to make this offer. I then remarked once again that I had been told otherwise. I also know that even after the above-mentioned session with the German pastors the Lord Bishop of Chichester was informed by you of just this offer and of the reasons for his refusal. I can obtain the exact words used by enquiring of the Lord Bishop, if that is desirable. In view of the significance of the fact of such an invitation for the assessment and the course of the whole of Church politics in recent months, in the interests of the brethren here, I had to press for an explanation of the truth of the matter and put your account before Pastor Niemöller for his comments. His answer confirms my earlier information. You will understand that Niemöller attaches the utmost importance to complete clarification of this point and must dispel all rumour wherever he can. It is also very important here that the confusion in the account of this point should not remain any longer.[12]

The note of confidence in that letter, which also repeated what he had said before leaving, that he could not accept any conditions when coming to London, reflect two events in February and early March.

During Bishop Heckel's visit, the German embassy had arranged a reception for him. After all, he was now the head of the Foreign Affairs Office of the German Evangelical Church. This was on 9 February and some of Bonhoeffer's Church officers had been invited. There they had learnt from the plausible Heckel that the conflict in which their pastor was so much involved was not a 'Church struggle', but a regrettable 'Church dispute'. Bonhoeffer and Rieger had refused to attend the reception. He was taken to task for involving the German Churches abroad in internal German disputes. The discussion with his Church officers went on into the night and it was eventually agreed that Bonhoeffer should put the matter to the whole Church and explain what he was doing. He did this and the Church committee put the issue to the vote. The result was unanimous support for their pastor.

The other event was a visit to Berlin. He had been summoned there by the Church government and efforts were made to get him to drop his ecumenical work. Nothing could stop him and he refused to sign any declaration to that effect. But while in Berlin he had seen the leaders of the Emergency League – Niemöller and Jacobi, as well as some friends from the Rhineland. With them he started preparations for a Free National Synod of the Confessing Church to be held in Barmen, it was suggested, on 18 April 1934. Bonhoeffer was worried lest this delay would weaken the interest of the ecumenical movement and subsequently he wrote to the Bishop of Chichester.

Bonhoeffer saw the urgency of the situation and the need for the World Alliance in particular to condemn what was happening in Germany. He also saw that the key figure was the Bishop of Chichester. When he wrote to Henriod in Geneva where the ecumenical movement should have had its location and later did, he received uncertain answers and again the reference back to the Bishop of Chichester. Bonhoeffer received a reply from Henriod, dated 16 March, which gave the bureaucratic answer. So back to George Bell.

On 15 April, Bonhoeffer wrote to him[13] after receiving a very disturbing letter from Germany. Quoting that letter he includes the words: 'In the present moment there depends everything, absolutely everything, on the attitude of the Bishop of Chichester.'

The correspondence between Bonhoeffer and the bishop continued almost daily, feeding him with information about Germany, checking draft letters, commenting on articles and the 'Nazi' Seal which the German Church had adopted. Bonhoeffer's hopes rose and fell during 1934, which was obviously a critical year for the Church struggle.

The Barmen Conference and Declaration

At the end of May, the Confessing Church, which now became the accepted name of the resistance to the German Christians, held its first National Synod in Barmen: 29–31 May 1934. The Confessing Church, usually referred to as BK (*Bekennende Kirche*) grew out of the practical work of the Pastors' Emergency League and the theological objections to the German Christians. It retained this double character, assisting those who were victims of the 'powers that be' and attacking the statements of the official German Evangelical Church as heretical. The synod decided that a Confession must be written to assert the orthodox faith in relation to the German Christian heresies. Thanks to the attention given to it by Bonhoeffer and the Bishop of Chichester, it was published in full in an English translation in *The Times* a few days after the close of the conference.

It will be enough to quote two articles from this long document to show the intention and the direct reference to the German Christians:

> In view of the destructive errors of the German Christians and the present national Church government, we pledge ourselves to the following evengelical truths:
>
> 1. 'I am the way, the truth and the life and no man cometh unto the Father, but by me' (John 14:6).
>
> 'Verily, verily, I say unto you, he that entereth not by the door of the sheepfold, but climbeth up some other way, the same is a thief and a robber . . . I am the door: by me if any man enter he shall be saved' (John 10:1–9).
>
> Jesus Christ as he is testified to us in Holy Scripture, is the one Word of God, which we are to hear, which we are to trust and obey in life and in death.
>
> We repudiate the false teaching that the Church can and must recognise yet other happenings and powers, personalities and truths as divine revelation alongside this one Word of God, as a source of her preaching.
>
> 2. 'He is the source of your life in Christ Jesus, whom God made our wisdom, our righteousness and sanctification and redemption' (1 Cor. 1:30).
>
> Just as Christ Jesus is the pledge of the forgiveness of all our sins, just so – and with the same earnestness – is he also God's mighty claim on our whole life; in him we encounter a joyous liberation from the godless claims of this world to free and thankful service to his creatures.
>
> We repudiate the false teaching that there are areas of our life in which we belong not to Jesus Christ but another lord, areas in which we do not need justification and sanctification through him.[14]

That declaration was the character of the resistance. Rather than deny it, men lost their livelihood, accepted harsh imprisonment, were exiled and some resisted unto death.

The honour of keeping England informed about what was happening must be shared between Bonhoeffer, the Bishop of Chichester and *The Times*.

The Fanö Conference

Bonhoeffer was interested in the attitude, not only of the Church of England, but of the World Church. For this reason he made early reference to the ecumenical meetings planned to be held in August 1934 in Denmark, at Fanö. The first problem is which Church in Germany should be represented. The planners of the conference had not been notified that a second Church had been established in Germany and therefore continued to deal with the German Evangelical Church (German Christian). Bonhoeffer argued that that Church had been excommunicated and the Confessing Church was the only true Church in Germany. It had not chosen to become a Free Church, but regarded itself as the German Evangelical Church. In correspondence with Henriod and Schönfeld in Geneva, it was quite clear that no official notification had come to them that there were two Churches in Germany between which they had to choose. For that reason, they invited to Fanö only the official German Evangelical Church (German Christian). Representatives of the Confessing Church had to be there in other capacities. Bonhoeffer, for example, was on the committee as one of the youth secretaries.

This was also a period of great political upheaval in Germany. On 30 June, Hitler suppressed a large rebellious group in his own party – more than 200 people were shot with Rohm, one of his closest associates. On 2 August, Hindenburg died and the hoped for moderating influence upon Hitler was thus removed. On 19 August, a plebiscite was held to combine in the person of Adolf Hitler the two most powerful offices in the land – Führer and Reich Chancellor. Ludwig Müller's office, in gratitude to Hitler, proposed that all pastors should swear an oath of allegiance to him personally. At their ordination they had already sworn allegiance to the State, but Müller proposed something more specific: 'I swear before God that I will be true and obedient to the Führer of the German people and State, Adolf Hitler, and I pledge myself to every sacrifice and every service on behalf of the German people such as befit an Evangelical German . . .'[15]

Bonhoeffer disliked this service oath, but many in the Confessing Church wanted to be seen as the Church of the loyal German. For this reason while they opposed the German Christians, the majority did not oppose Hitler. Bonhoeffer did not belong to this majority, but he thought Niemöller did! Writing to Sutz, he says: 'Ingenuous visionaries like Niemöller still go on thinking they're the true National Socialists.'

Bishop Heckel was to lead the delegation to Fanö and it was a strangely mixed group. The issue of who would represent Germany was fought out at Fanö. Stephen Neill in his *History of the Ecumenical Movement* puts this quite clearly, saying: 'The biennial meeting of the Council at Fanö stands out perhaps as the most critical and decisive meeting in its history. Here the Council solemnly resolved to throw its weight on the side of the Confessing Church in Germany against the so-called "German Christians" and by implication against the Nazi regime.'[16]

Despite Bonhoeffer's protests, the Confessing Church had decided not to send a delegation to Fanö, although all agreed that Bonhoeffer should go in the dual capacity of conference speaker and representative of the views of the Confessing Church. The decision of the conference to support the Confessing Church is therefore due largely to Bonhoeffer's influence and his great supporter, Bishop Bell. This resolution was taken despite the statement of the official German delegation at the very beginning of the conference that they did not want the situation discussed at all!

Bonhoeffer spoke in English at the conference – still with a slightly American accent – and he called for peace:[17]

> How will peace come? Who will call us to peace so that the world will hear, will have to hear, so that all peoples may rejoice? The individual Christian cannot do it. When all around are silent, he can indeed raise his voice and bear witness, but the powers of this world stride over him without a word. The individual Church, too, can witness and suffer – oh, if it only would! – but it also is suffocated by the power of hate. Only the one great Ecumenical Council of the holy Church of Christ over all the world can speak out so that the world, though it gnash its teeth, will have to hear, so that the peoples will rejoice because the Church of Christ in the name of Christ has taken the weapons from the hands of their sons, forbidden war, proclaimed the peace of Christ against the raging world.
>
> Why do we fear the fury of the world powers? Why don't we take the power from them and give it back to Christ? We can still do it today. The Ecumenical Council is in session; it can send out to all believers this radical call to peace. The nations are waiting for it in the East and in the West. Must we be put to shame by non-Christian people in the East? Shall we desert the individuals who are risking their lives for this message? The hour is late. The world is choked with weapons, and dreadful is the distrust which looks out of all men's eyes. The trumpets of war may blow tomorrow. For what are we waiting? Do we want to become involved in this guilt as never before?
>
> We want to give the world a whole word, not a half word – a courageous word, a Christian word. We want to pray that this word may be given us today. Who knows if we shall see each other again another year?

The End of a Pastorate

Bonhoeffer was needed in Germany to lead a seminary for students of the Confessing Church. He preached his last sermon in London on 10 March 1935, but he still had some unfinished business. Bonhoeffer had long cherished a plan to go to India, where the art of inwardness and meditation, of silence and concentration had not been forgotten. He was also drawn towards Mahatma Gandhi, who seemed to value the Sermon on the Mount more than most Christians did. Bonhoeffer, in his sermons and study, had already started work on his next book, *The Cost of Discipleship*, which was to give detailed attention to the Sermon on the Mount. The Bishop of Chichester had introduced him to C. F. Andrews and later wrote to Gandhi seeking an invitation to India for Bonhoeffer. Writing to Gandhi, the bishop states that Bonhoeffer would like to spend two or three months in India early in 1935. He also refers to the plan for Bonhoeffer 'probably to have charge of the training of ordination candidates for the ministry in the future Confessing Church of Germany'. Clearly, Bonhoeffer had told him that he wanted to study community life and methods of training.

There was no time in the end for the visit to India, although the invitation came for Bonhoeffer to spend time with Gandhi and to bring a friend (Julius Rieger would have gone with him). When the plan fell through, the two of them went instead on a journey to the Midlands of England to study Anglican communities. They visited Mirfield, Kelham and the Cowley Fathers at the end of March 1935. These three communities had one thing in common, their remarkable achievement in the training of young Anglican priests. Each individual community, of course, had its own tradition. The oldest of the three was the 'Society of St John the Evangelist', known as the Cowley Fathers.

As Julius Rieger reports, 'In Oxford, Tobacco is anathema and smoking strictly prohibited; in Mirfield you may smoke; in Kelham, you have to.' It was in Kelham that they were received by the founder, Father Kelly, a chain-smoker and a very intelligent theologian. He had founded the Society in 1893 and his own contribution to theology earned him the reputation of being the English precursor of Karl Barth. Bonhoeffer eagerly read his lectures. This tour of the monasteries had its effect upon the way in which Bonhoeffer later disciplined his own students in the seminary. At first the regular hourly prayer seemed like a strait jacket, and yet it formed the students and made possible a religious community.

Another new idea to Bonhoeffer was 'the devotional life', a concept to which all three communities referred and which has no satisfactory translation in German. But Bonhoeffer saw that he would have to show German students that a scholarly study of the Bible was not enough. As his mind was beginning to form around the idea of devotional discipline he then realised that these Anglican communities also had a freedom which would be difficult to transplant into Germany. Something of this freedom came from the attitude to sport – the Anglican monks played tennis and football in their free time. And there was that secret strength that comes from being silent together, which he knew German Protestants with their love of disputation would find hard to learn.

A few weeks after this tour, he took up the responsibilities of a seminary of the Confessing Church in Zingst on the Baltic coast, later moving to Finkenwalde. But Bonhoeffer did not immediately lose contact with

London. Julius Rieger reports that he was in England at least four times during 1935 – April, May/June, August and October. It was a hard decision for Bonhoeffer to take – to return to Germany – but the call had come to train theological students for the Confessing Church. He was wise enough to make it possible to return to England if the task proved impossible. It was not an official appointment, no settled teaching, but a dangerous and uncertain venture. He did not know if he would have the freedom in Germany to do what he knew had to be done, but the task had to be attempted. On 26 April 1935 he met his first class of students at Zingst.

EIGHT

Students for the Confessing Church

During 1934, Bonhoeffer was in some turmoil about his future. He could not continue in the backwater of a London pastorate and yet he was of value there in maintaining communication between the ecumenical movement and the Confessing Church. But the overriding concern in his mind that year was the kind of theological training young German students were receiving in Nazi Germany. The news of Barth's dismissal from Bonn encouraged him to believe that he must return. He was losing faith in the universities and doubted their ability to prepare students for the struggle ahead. Indeed, he doubted their ability to teach the Christian faith, and the appropriate attitude of the Christian theologian to the problems of Germany in the thirties. The universities had lost their independence.

The Confessing Church realised this and began to make plans for the training of their own ordinands. The first to move was the Reformed Church of Elberfeld, whose theological seminary had been closed by the National Bishop. The closure was taken as an opportunity to open a Confessing Church seminary at Bielefeld. That was in March 1934. In June, Bonhoeffer was approached about similar work in the Church of the Old Prussian Union, but nothing definite was decided. He expressed his interest and the session which took place in Berlin on 4 July took note of this. Jacobi proposed Bonhoeffer as director of any seminary they might open and, after some hesitation about his suitability, it was agreed. Niemöller's summing up was definite enough: 'It is agreed that Bonhoeffer may take up the post of director of the Berlin-Brandenburg preachers' seminary on 1 January 1935.'[1] That was too early for Bonhoeffer and for the seminary.

Hildebrandt returned to Berlin in mid-September (1934) to say that Bonhoeffer needed to remain in London over the winter, but would be ready to take up the post in the spring. After preaching his final sermon on 10 March 1935, and making his rapid tour of Anglican monasteries, he spent the Easter vacation in Berlin. The first ordination students, who had been waiting for several weeks, began to arrive in Wilhelm Niesel's office in

Berlin. He thought they might temporarily use Burckhardt House, but on 25 April 1935, a new offer of accommodation materialised.

The Bible School at Zingst

They were offered the loan of the Rhineland Bible School at Zingst on the Baltic coast, but only until the beginning of the summer season. On 26 April, Bonhoeffer met his first class of students. They were men who had already received their academic theological training at the university. In this seminary they were to be prepared for the active pastoral ministry. All of them knew that as members of the Confessing Church they would be looked on with disfavour by the official Church (German Christian). The pastorates open to them would be limited and 'preference' in the Church was severely handicapped. They knew the price they would have to pay. One of their number was Eberhard Bethge. At that time he was fresh from university – he had studied in Königsberg, Berlin, Vienna and Halle. He had not met Bonhoeffer, but soon warmed to him. Later, he would become his closest friend, but at this time he was just one of the most senior students and he soon became Bonhoeffer's assistant.

The empty Bible School was simple, almost primitive, in its facilities. There was no heating and it was cold on the Baltic. At first the students lived in cabins among the sand dunes, but after a few months the seminary moved to Finkenwalde, still near the Baltic and near the town of Stettin. The premises were not luxurious, but they were better than at Zingst!

Finkenwalde

It was a tiny place, consisting of a few houses. The furniture was a medley of gifts from friends. The library, such as it was, contained no theological books. Bonhoeffer had to bring his own theological library for the use of the students, although some of them brought their own books. The students worked three to a room and in teams, but the rooms were simply furnished – a desk, a shelf and some chairs. They slept in one large room, all twenty-five of them, and were overcrowded. For recreation, they had a large untended garden, walks along the river and occasional excursions to the sea. Bonhoeffer kept some of the older students on after they had finished the course and attempted to form a community similar to the communities he had seen in England. These older men lived in a separate house attached to the seminary, called a Brethren House. The younger students envied them a little because each had his own room and washbasin.

Many of the students had come from quite 'solid' families, where they had all they wanted, and Finkenwalde was quite a revelation to them. Having overcome the first shock of physical privation they then had an even tougher one to face with the strict regime. In the morning there was half an hour of silent meditation on one biblical text in Luther's translation: the same text for a week! They were not allowed to consult the original text, a dictionary or any other book during this period. Two hours' rest after lunch. At night to bed in silence. From the beginning they revolted. There was too much 'must' for them. Bonhoeffer explained what help they would derive from this strict order, but they were not convinced. All they experienced was emptiness in themselves and in the texts, where knowledge and answers had been promised.

There were lectures and written work, but what the students remembered most was the discipline of living a monastic type of life. Every Saturday Bonhoeffer would speak to the students, as a pastor. He encouraged them to live as a community and share with one another what they felt about the events of the week. He very patiently took them through this experience of self-examination and gradually they came to see its value. Although Bonhoeffer was strict he was prepared to listen. When the students complained that despite all their meditation the texts still meant very little to them, he was prepared to alter the system. Instead of silence every day, once or twice a week they were allowed to meditate together and share insights with each other. So long as the object was achieved, he did not insist upon only one way of achieving it. The object was that the text should speak for itself. They had all been trained in exegesis and application of the text, here they learnt to listen to what God had to say to them in their situation through the text.

One of the students wrote about this difficult discipline: 'Half an hour of meditation: it is amazing what comes into your mind during that time. The mind moves around, memories arise, dreams awaken. Suddenly anger flares up. When we told Bonhoeffer of this, he said that was all right; things have to come into the open; but they must also be tamed in and through prayer. '2

Half an hour's meditation remained a burden for many of them, but it taught them that the biblical world is more than a subject that can be handled. It taught them how to prepare sermons and also how to listen to sermons. A text which has been meditated upon can no longer be merely dissected into different sources and layers. It can in fact be preached.

Bonhoeffer also taught them the value of open prayer; sceptical but curious, they went along with him quite early one Whitsunday morning. It was no second Pentecost, but out of their awkward silences and brief expressions of prayer, they learnt humility and knowledge which called to faithful service. Another practice which was strange to them and to which they were introduced was confession, not to a priest but to one another. Many of the revival movements in Europe have had this characteristic of mutual confession, but it is odd to the staid conformity of the German

Lutheran Church. Bonhoeffer stressed the urgency of confessing one to another before they received communion together, but he never made it a rule. Each was free to adopt this practice or not as he wished. He pointed out, however, that if they wished to be free, they would have to make a clean breast of any grudges they bore one another. A student describes the effect:

> So on this evening (before communion), we went to see one another and spoke of many grievances stored up in the last few weeks. It was a great surprise to realise how we had hurt the other person, without intention, by chance. Now we knew what it meant to consider other people. The atmosphere was pure again, we could go to Communion together without bearing a grudge against anyone among us.[3]

This did not become a routine, but was practised when needed. Bonhoeffer further suggested that they should each choose a brother to accompany their life in intercession. This was to give an outward sign that in the worst calamities they were never alone. Apart from this 'spiritual order' which the students continued to find a burden and often met with protests and jokes, mocking the imposed rules, which seemed to belong to the pietism and enthusiasm they rejected as good Lutherans, they had all the instructions of a preachers' seminary.

Bonhoeffer himself did the teaching – homilectics, catechetics, pastoralia, exegesis – and his lectures were given from very carefully prepared notes. His method of sermon instruction was peculiarly his own. He would set the students a very difficult text – often highly theoretical or remote – and require them to draft a sermon on it. These would be read out and then he would show by example how that remote text could be preached.

A rich community of life soon built up under Bonhoeffer's lively inspiration. He could be a hard taskmaster, but also a warm friend and he soon taught them to call him Brother Dietrich. They had practical work too – a 'Mission to the People' in Pomerania, house visiting and guided sermon preparation.

Out of this experience, Bonhoeffer produced two books: *Life Together*,[4] which describes the building up of a community life; *The Cost of Discipleship*,[5] which defines the meaning of costly grace, illustrated by a detailed study of the Sermon on the Mount. The students talked often of *The Cost of Discipleship*, much of which they heard in lectures, and looked forward eagerly to its publication.

Political Involvement

During 1935 the Confessing Church was most buoyant and almost confident of victory, but this was also the year which saw the most damaging legislation against it. Writing confidently to Niemöller,[6] Bonhoeffer said that Matthew 22:21 will have to have a substantially different interpretation from hitherto. 'Render unto Caesar the things that are Caesar's, but when, if ever, do they cease to be God's?' He was writing in connection with a circular letter that Niemöller had asked him to sign.[7] The letter was addressed to the officers of the Confessing Church. It pointed out that they had been wrong to keep striving and waiting for official recognition from the state: 'We have gone from one disappointment to another over the last months . . . We must now confess that it was our own lack of faith which caused us to put all our hope in men.'

Then the letter looked back to the two decisive synods of the past year: at Barmen, where the doctrine of the Confessing Church was spelt out and the Declaration; at Dahlem, where the structure of the Confessing Church was defined:

> We have brought this curse upon ourselves by denying what God committed to us in Barmen and Dahlem. Both synods called the church under the sole Lordship of the Lord Jesus Christ; Barmen that it should base its preaching and doctrine, Dahlem that it should base its form and order, solely on the one Word of the revelation of God. This should have kept us from any form of compromise.

The letter is a clarion call to abide by the earlier decisions and say 'No' to any form of compromise. God alone is to be their protection. This decision meant far more than appears at first. If the Confessing Church were to proceed on the basis of being *the* Evangelical Church in Germany, without official recognition, it committed its members to loss of livelihood, possible imprisonment and even death.

Bonhoeffer congratulated Niemöller on finding the right moment at which to take this stand and gladly agreed to sign the letter. He added, 'the whole seminar joins me in sending you their best wishes.'

Ecumenical Involvements

Bonhoeffer had reached the height of his involvement in the ecumenical movement during 1934, now his attention was entirely taken up by his preachers' seminary. He did not ignore either the Church struggle in his own country nor its implications for the ecumenical movement, but this had now to be done largely through his writings. Occasionally he was summoned away from his concentration upon his students, when the Confessing Church needed him, or when he was asked to intervene in a particular discussion. One such occasion occurred in May 1935, when a conference was arranged in Hanover to prepare for the World Conference to be held in Oxford in 1937. One visitor who was expected at Hanover was Joe Oldham, the secretary of the Edinburgh 1910 conference who was preparing for Oxford 1937! He was also trying to find out what was going on in Germany in order to report to Bishop Bell. He arrived at a time when matters were beginning to look very serious for the Church: Peter Brunner and two other pastors from Rhineland-Hessen had been interned in Dachau concentration camp for more than four weeks, and the Councils of Brethren had ordered weekly services of intercession on their behalf. On 11 May the Council's office in Dahlem was searched by the Gestapo for the first time.

It was against this background that Bonhoeffer made his position very clear at the meeting. He first pointed out that it was impossible for the Confessing Church to cooperate with the National Church (German Christian) in preparation for the Oxford Conference. Then he called upon Geneva, i.e. the research department of the ecumenical movement, to take a stand and refuse to recognise any other Church in Germany than the Confessing Church. He was angry with Geneva for trying to evade their responsibility to decide. The strongest point of his argument was that, on the basis of the Barmen and Dahlem Synods, it was impossible for Germany to prepare for Oxford unless its theology emanated from a real Church. The National Church was heretical. Schönfeld defended Geneva's neutralist position at a meeting six weeks later in Berlin – but not satisfactorily in Bonhoeffer's eyes.

Bonhoeffer wanted an ecumenical office in the Confessing Church, but he lost his battle. However, Präses Koch, organiser of the Barmen Synod and recognised leader of the Confessing Church in his part of Germany, twice sent Bonhoeffer to England during 1935. The reason in both cases was to warn Bishop Bell of what was going on. It was becoming clear that Bonhoeffer was the main German contact with Bishop Bell, who was now regarded as champion of the Confessing Church in England.

These constant absences from his seminary led Bonhoeffer to ask for an assistant director even before he left Zingst. Alternatively, he asked for a travelling secretary for the Church.

Niemöller's Manifesto

The circular letter which Bonhoeffer had so readily agreed to sign from Martin Niemöller soon became a manifesto for the Confessing Church, collecting forty-nine signatures from prominent people in different parts of Germany.[8] Bonhoeffer took this manifesto to Bishop Bell in August on his second visit to England of 1935. It convinced him that the Universal Christian Council could no longer ignore the serious charges made by a well-organised Confessing Church against the state's 'pacification measures'. It also convinced him that he must make an urgent visit to Germany. This he did in September, meeting Koch, Asmussen and Lilje. He also saw Rudolf Hess (Hitler's deputy) and Hans Kerrl (Minister for Church Affairs). He was too late to affect the Nuremberg Laws, which defined the inferior status of Jews, but Hess tried to convince him that the Jews would now be treated better because all was regularised by law. Kerrl tried to persuade the bishop that by his laws he was bringing back peace to the Church, and even suggested that he was optimistic about negotiations with the Confessing Church. Bell was not convinced. He tried to explain this view to the staff in Geneva, but failed to do so. The 'research department' in Geneva was really the staff preparing to administer the World Council of Churches when it was formed. It included Schönfeld and Henriod, both of whom found Bonhoeffer a bit extreme. They also felt that the Youth Section, which was largely in the hands of voluntary secretaries like Bonhoeffer, was carrying the whole ecumenical movement into an extreme position which made it impossible for Geneva to deal with the National Church in Germany. In order to call a halt to this they appointed a staff member to be youth secretary, who could supervise the work of the voluntary secretaries. He was an American – Edwin Espy. Trouble soon blew up because the decisions taken at Fanö had been put to one side. Schönfeld and Henriod both found it easier to deal with Gerstenmaier, who still wanted the Confessing Church to maintain some relationship with the National Church. One of the prominent figures in the Confessing Church to whom Kerrl had referred when talking to Bishop Bell was undoubtedly Gerstenmaier. Bonhoeffer rejected this and declared that he could not bring together a mixed delegation, which included both National Church and Confessing Church; but he was quite prepared to include the Free Churches in the delegation.

When Edwin Espy was planning a visit to Berlin, Schönfeld sent an effusive letter to the Church External Affairs Office:

> Perhaps you have already heard a lot of alarming things about the work of this ecumenical youth commission, and I might say that my feelings would be the same as yours, had not the position with regard to this work changed fundamentally now that we have found the right man for it. You may be certain that Mr Espy's work is in complete accord with the methods of the research department and with the problems and tasks we have set ourselves. I am telling you all this so that you will understand that a fundamental change is now under way. Myself, I have long thought it impossible that this part of the work should be determined exclusively – or almost exclusively – by a man like Bonhoeffer. But it is most desirable, particularly when this is about to be changed, that people should be available who will support Mr Espy in his work.[9]

With this letter and subsequent lively correspondence between Heckel's office and Geneva, Bonhoeffer lost the support of the ecumenical movement, except for Bishop Bell.

At Fanö, Bonhoeffer had won his battle to have the Confessing Church represented at ecumenical conferences, but he was pressing for more than that. After the synod at Dahlem, as Niemöller made clear in his 'Manifesto', it was impossible for the Confessing Church to send representatives if the National Church (German Christian) was represented.

Thus, at Chamby in 1935, where endorsement for the Fanö resolutions and plans for the Oxford conference of 1937 were considered, the Confessing Church was not represented. The moderate men in Geneva thought Bonhoeffer was asking too much. Bonhoeffer would not yield and refused every invitation to attend ecumenical gatherings in 1935. The last was a very attractive one – to be part of the Faith and Order Continuation Committee. It came from Canon Leonard Hodgson and Bonhoeffer would have loved to attend, but he refused unless he could have the guarantee that no member of the National Church would be there on equal terms. He seemed almost fanatic about this and to the organisers of ecumenical meetings he appeared tiresome. But it was an essential factor in his theology of the Church, and his acceptance of the Dahlem Synod compelled him to act in this way.

He was only twenty-nine and great career opportunities were passing him by. It was always Bishop Bell who spoke for the absent Confessing Church on these occasions and he was a good spokesman. Canon Hodgson persisted in his view that Faith and Order provided an excellent platform for the two disputing parties of Germany to argue their respective views. For Bonhoeffer, this was a matter not of disputing parties, but of the theology of the Church. Although he did not attend conferences, he put his views forcibly in writing.

The Confessing Church and the Ecumenical Movement[10]

This was the title of an article he wrote (for the seventh issue of *Evangelische Theologie*) during June and July. It was a most decisive article, asking searching questions of the ecumenical movement, posing the question whether it considered itself as a Church, and if it did not (and Bonhoeffer agreed that it should not) then arguing that it must undertake the task of defining the Church. Failure to do this called the Confessing Church in question. If the two were recognised side by side as Churches – the National Church and the Confessing Church – then the Church struggle had been lost. It was a powerfully argued paper.

In making statements of this kind, Bonhoeffer carried his students with him. Finkenwalde became a bastion of resistance and he carried these views beyond the boundaries of Germany. Bonhoeffer's reputation in the ecumenical movement meant that activities at Finkenwalde were watched with more than a curious eye by many churchmen outside Germany. And an interest in Finkenwalde meant an interest in the Confessing Church. Bonhoeffer cultivated this. His time in England had shown him how important it was for the world to know what Germany was about; his experience with the bureaucrats of Geneva had also shown him how easily the situation could be misunderstood. Early in 1936, he angled for an invitation which would take him and some of his students out of Germany. It came from the Swedish Ecumenical Centre, to visit Sweden and Denmark. Bonhoeffer picked his men and spent from 29 February to 10 March 1936 in Scandinavia. The party had very good opportunities in its visit to universities and churches, to build up support for Finkenwalde and for the Confessing Church. Bonhoeffer spoke frequently about the Church. Before leaving, he had prepared a paper on 'The Visible Church'[11] which probably represents what he said in many Danish and Swedish situations. In it he posed the question: 'Does the Church of the Word of God have a place in the world, and if so, what is the nature of this place?'

He began by pointing out two dangers: the other-worldly Church which lays no claim to relevance in the world; and the secular Church, derived from materialism associated with a magical attitude to the sacraments. Most of the paper, however, is taken up with a careful study of the New Testament. Before entering upon the study of certain passages chosen from the second chapter of the Acts of the Apostles, he outlines what he regards as the major themes of the New Testament when dealing with the Church:

1. The place of proclamation and confession;
2. The place of office, of officers and of gifts;
3. The place of Christian commandments (new life, discipleship);
4. The limits of the place of the Church,
   a. towards the sphere of the state,
   b. towards the natural law,
   c. towards the sphere of the Kingdom of God.

The presupposition is that the Church is the Church of the Word, and the question is that of the place occupied by this Church in all these relationships. Therefore it is a visible Church.

The lecture had four sections after this introduction, dealing in turn with the founding of the Church, the events of Acts 2, the new community described in Acts 2:42–47 and with very special attention given to the Apostles' teaching. This teaching is like no other teaching, particularly in its character of 'steadfastness'. This teaching is the work of God, the Holy Spirit is in this teaching. And it has one other characteristic. It does not

117

leave a believer as an individual. It creates fellowship. *Koinonia*, the special Christian kind of fellowship, is 'the waiting to drink of the wine of the eternal Lord's Supper that Christ will drink with us anew in his Father's kingdom. Fellowship stands between word and sacrament, between earthly feast and the eternal feast.'

There were twenty-four students who went on this Scandinavian tour, together with Wilhelm Rott (described as the Inspector of Studies) and Bonhoeffer. The invitation came from the Swedish Ecumenical Council and was given by the private secretary to Archbishop Erling Eidem. The Swedish hosts covered all the costs and the party visited Copenhagen, Lund, Uppsala, Sigtuna and Stockholm. It was a good tour. Not only did it provide the men with a wealth of valuable stimuli for the work of their own Church, it also gave their Swedish hosts a real glimpse of the problems of the German Church and renewed and strengthened the hands of friendship between the Churches of both countries. Bonhoeffer gave a glowing account of the warm hospitality. Three of the men had actually stayed at the home of the archbishop while in Uppsala and he assured them, 'that the Swedish Church remembered in constant prayer the struggling and suffering sister Churches in Germany, and would continue to pray for them.'

Bishop Heckel, responsible for the foreign affairs of the Church, was worried about this trip. The German embassy in Stockholm was told to regard the visit with suspicion and the Archbishop of Sweden was asked personally about the character of the tour and whether by issuing this invitation the Church of Sweden was taking up a one-sided attitude to the Church politics in Germany.

Support for Finkenwalde

Shortly after returning from Scandinavia, Bonhoeffer began to realise that the seminary needed support. He started to appeal for funds and help of all kinds from the churches of the Confessing Church and it was not long before it was pouring in, both in money and kind. Bonhoeffer pressed home the need for regular support. Here is an example of his appeals in the early summer of 1936:

> You heard last month of the threat to the existence of our house and at the same time of our work. We are now appealing to the friends of our house and asking them for a regular contribution towards our work. A number of people have already taken it upon themselves to help us each month with a gift; some of you have already heard our appeal, so that we can really only say, thank you. But you will understand our view that proper thanking demands proper asking, so that the old givers do not become weary and new givers are brought

in. We now have a great request to make of you, though I am sure that it will seem very small to those of you who know the value and the task of Finkenwalde: could each one of you show yourselves ready to help us monthly with a fixed gift? I am thinking in terms of 1 or 2 RM, though of course more will not be refused. It would mean a great deal to us if we received 50 or 60 RM a month.

As well as this request, which is the most important thing for us, some suggestions. Have you told your Confessing congregations about Finkenwalde? Could your congregation or even individual members of it join the circle of friends with a regular gift? And your Women's Guild - I am thinking particularly of those of you in the country – will certainly be glad to collect all kinds of produce for Finkenwalde. Recently the Women's Guild at Stemnitz sent us two hundred and twenty-five eggs as a thanks offering for their tenth anniversary, and another Women's Guild sent us sausages, bacon, eggs, butter and flour. When we asked them not to forget us in the future and to take our seminary into their sphere of help, the president wrote back to us, 'It is really wonderful that our women now have some definite work which they can do with all their hearts.'

And now we appeal to you, put yourselves in the forefront. We are sure that hands which pray for Finkenwalde will also be opened to give. Help us enlarge our circle of friends.[12]

The Olympic Games

These were held in Berlin in 1936. Hitler had need of foreign currency for the building up of his armed forces and wanted a shop window which would show the world how well Germany was doing. He had encouraged everyone who had any influence to press for Berlin and proved successful. This also provided the Confessing Church with an opportunity to play their part and let the world know the true situation behind the propaganda. August 1936 was a great opportunity. Daily addresses were given by leaders of the Confessing Church in a central church in Berlin and Bonhoeffer was one of those chosen to speak. He was invited in July and at first thought he should refuse. He was obviously going to be used for propaganda purposes and this fear was intensified when he was asked to provide a photograph, which he refused to send. He did however agree to lecture on the Wednesday of the Olympiad at 5 p.m. His chosen subject was 'The Inner Life of the German Evangelical Church since the Reformation', which he had to deal with in half an hour! He chose to speak largely about the hymns of the church, from Luther, Gerhardt, Zinzendorf and Gellert. Other speakers from the Confessing Church were to be Jacobi, Dilbelius and Niemöller. It was these other speakers who persuaded Bonhoeffer to accept the invitation. He began to prepare with thoroughness, reading all the hymns. When he was working through Zinzendorf, he wrote to Eberhard Bethge, 'What rottenness there is beneath all this piety. I tell you that I found things there that I am almost embarrassed to repeat to you. And all this in hymns too! Yes, that's man! pious man!'

He felt the air to be much cleaner when he was dealing with the Bible – 'We need the fresh air of the Word to keep us clean.' The lecture was eventually given in St Paul's Church. The day after, he wrote in a letter, dated 6 August 1936: 'Yesterday evening was very good. The church filled to overflowing, people sitting on the altar steps and standing all around. I wished I could have preached instead of giving a lecture! Some 1,500 or 2,000 people came and an overflow service was needed.'

That enthusiastic reaction was confirmed by the official report, although with no pleasure. *Die Christliche Welt* reported:

> While the lectures given in the church of the Holy Trinity were academically satisfying, they were hardly well attended; those in St Paul's were the opposite of this. Night after night the enormous church was not only filled to overflowing, but parallel meetings had also to be held in another large church to cope with the mass of visitors. Dr Bonhoeffer struck the same note as Dr Jacobi had done and illustrated his exposition with a number of hymns. According to him, the decline began as early as Paul Gerhardt; pietism and the Enlightenment and the nineteenth century sink lower and lower. Only in the present and especially in the hymns of Heinrich Vogel (!) do we begin to rise again to the heights of the Reformation. The speaker tried to prove his thesis by means of selected hymns and was even successful because of the complete arbitrariness of his selection. He did not shrink from quoting the first half of a verse, when the second, left unquoted, made the quite opposite point. When we consider that here we have a pupil of Harnack, we can only deplore this treatment of history. The third speaker, Dr Iwand of Königsberg, followed much the same line.
>
> To sum up: in Holy Trinity, valuable theology developed in a scholarly way, but a very small audience; in St Paul's, narrow and very suspect theology, but great religious enthusiasm and vast congregations, listening with the deepest devotion. This state of affairs must cause great alarm among those concerned with the future of the Evangelical Church.[13]

Scattered throughout Bonhoeffer's letters written during the Olympic Games there are remarks that tell of a gathering storm. The Confessing Church was in no doubt that something drastic was about to happen as soon as the temporary freedom of the Olympiad was over. The urgency of the situation led Bonhoeffer to change his mind about attending an ecumenical meeting at which the National Church was also represented. He realised now that the invitation to attend the preparatory meeting of the

Universal Council for Life and Work was probably the last he would be permitted to accept. That meeting was planned for 1936 in Chamby, Switzerland, and would prepare for the World Conference on Church, Community and State, to be held in 1937 in Oxford. Again writing to Bethge, he warns him that they may have to stay an extra ten days in Switzerland after the conference. He intended to have some peace to draft a letter which he hoped he could persuade the Council to send to Hitler. Bonhoeffer and Bethge went to Chamby and stayed on. Their mission accomplished, they spent a short holiday in Italy. The memory of that holiday remained with Bonhoeffer through the difficult and dark days ahead and he later refers to it in his letters from prison to Bethge. He did not use the occasion to see Karl Barth, but wrote to him at length.

Finkenwalde's First and Last Full Year

While the storms which were to break in 1937 were still gathering, amidst many controversies, Bonhoeffer managed to direct his preachers' seminary through 1936. He wrote a report on 21 December[14] with the slogan, 'He has done all things well' (Mark 7:37). He points out that such a text does not mean that *we* have done all things well. He urged his students to remember their failures and he did himself. 'You are no Christian . . . if you cannot say even of your guilt, "He has done all things well" . . .'

This report is addressed to former students (now in parishes) and friends. He takes the opportunity to assess also, the year for the Confessing Church and Finkenwalde's place in it:

> Over the past year God the Lord has deigned to give our Confessing Church great questions, great tasks and great sufferings. Since the intervention of the state Church committees in the life of our Church the Confessing Church has suffered great shocks. There have been hard decisions for you, dear brethren in the parishes. You have had to lead the struggle and in so doing have gone through much questioning, doubt and temptation. Our service here in the house was able to consist chiefly in continuing our work quietly and straightforwardly.

He reports upon the faithful keeping of the half hour of meditation which former students will remember, and the daily intercessions for all who have in any way been part of the community. He then tells them of their studies, in particular Bible study: 'No day of our life in office may go by without our having read the Bible in it. The very controversies of the last month have once again clearly shown to our shame how unversed in Holy Scripture we still are.'

He describes the quiet domestic scene of the seminary making music together and living as a learning community. He tells of the visit to Sweden and the missions conducted in the parishes. Reunions of old students are described with love, and he reports that almost all the brethren from the first and second term now have been ordained. He is saddened by three of the brethren who have cut themselves off from the Confessing Church, by joining the committees of the National Church: 'This has been a great grief to us. Our words here have not been enough. And in their life and their office we commend them to the grace of God in prayer.'

The Last Reunion

In April 1937, a reunion was held at Finkenwalde of those students who had started two years before in the first course Bonhoeffer had held after his return from London. It was a momentous meeting with his pioneers and lasted from 12–17 April. He and they were aware of the dramatic climate in which they met. Bonhoeffer responded to the occasion with one of his most moving sermons – preached on 14 March and circulated: The Judas Sermon.[15] His text was from Matthew 26:45b–50. It opened in a typical way – 'Jesus had kept one thing from his disciples right up to the Last Supper.' He had told them of his approaching death, the Son of Man had to be delivered into the hands of sinners. But only in their last hours together could he say to them, 'The Son of Man is delivered into the hands of sinners – by treachery. One of you will betray me.' The enemies have no power over him, it takes a friend to betray him. Two quotes from the sermon will show its power and its appropriateness to this fateful year of 1937:

> While he was still speaking, Judas came, one of the twelve, and with him a great crowd with swords and clubs. Now we see only the two persons concerned. The disciples and the mob fall back – both do their work badly. Only two do their work as it had to be done.
>
> Jesus and Judas. Who is Judas? That is the question. It is one of the oldest and most troublesome questions in Christianity. First of all let us keep to what the evangelist himself tells us about it: Judas one of the twelve. Can we feel something of the horror with which the evangelist wrote this tiny clause? Judas, one of the twelve – what more was there to say here? And does not this really say everything? The whole of the dark mystery of Judas and at the same time the deepest shock at his deed? Judas, one of the twelve. That means, it was impossible for this to happen; it was absolutely impossible – and yet it happened. No, there is nothing more to explain or to understand here. It is completely and utterly inexplicable, incomprehensible, it is an unfathomable riddle – and yet it was done. Judas, one of the twelve. That does not just mean that he was one who was with Jesus day and night, who had followed Jesus, who had sacrificed something, who had given up all to be with Jesus, a

brother, a friend, a confidant of Peter, of John, of the Lord himself. It means something far more incomprehensible: Jesus himself called and chose Judas! That is the real mystery. For Jesus knew who would betray him from the beginning. In St John's Gospel Jesus says, 'Did I not choose you, the twelve, and one of you is a devil?'

Judas, one of the twelve, and now the reader must look not only at Judas, but rather in great bewilderment at the Lord who chose him. And those whom he chose, he loved. He shared his whole life with them, he shared with them the mystery of his person, and in the same way he sent them out to preach the Gospel. He gave them authority to drive out demons and to heal – and Judas was in their midst. Nowhere is there a hint that Jesus had secretly hated Judas. On the contrary, by his office of keeping charge of the disciples' purse, Judas seemed to have been ranked above the others.

And then towards the end:

'Friend, why are you here?' Do you hear how Jesus still loves Judas, how he still calls him his friend at this hour? Even now Jesus will not let Judas go. He lets himself be kissed by him. He does not push him away. No, Judas must kiss him. His communion with Jesus must reach its consummation. Why are you here? Jesus knows well why Judas is here, and yet, 'Why are you here?' And 'Judas would you betray the Son of Man with a kiss?' A last expression of a disciple's faithfulness, coupled with betrayal. A last sign of passionate love, joined with far more passionate hate. A last enjoyment of a subservient gesture, in consciousness of the superiority of the victory over Jesus which it brings. An action divided to its uttermost depths, this kiss of Judas. Not to be able to be abandoned by Christ, and yet to give him up. Judas would you betray the Son of Man with a kiss? Who is Judas? Should we not also think here of the name that he bore? 'Judas', does he not stand here for the people, divided to its uttermost depths, from which Jesus came, for the chosen people, that had received the promise of the Messiah and yet had rejected him? For the people of Judah, that loved the Messiah and yet could not love him in this way? 'Judas' – his name in German means 'thanks'. Was this kiss not the thanks offered by the divided people and yet at the same time the eternal renunciation? Who is Judas? Who is the traitor? Faced with this question, are we able to do anything but say with the disciples 'Lord, is it I? Is it I?'

The End of Finkenwalde

Until 1937, the Church struggle had been theological and the only politics with which the Confessing Church was involved were Church politics. The struggle had been with the German Christians. Finkenwalde was a theological seminary and its community was conscious of serving the Church. Most of the disputes that had bordered upon politics had really been about the nature of the Church, and consequently its relation with the state. Bonhoeffer found himself now reluctantly pushed into a political struggle.

About the time of the last reunion in April 1937 he prepared some notes for a paper on Peace for the Oxford Conference in July whose theme was to be *Church, Community and State*.[16] It was not simply a pacifist statement, for it raised the political question of what the ecumenical movement should do if war came. Beginning with the simple statement that the Gospel is the message of peace, he listed nine points and the last raised the most pertinent political issue:

> A war is always a severe trial for the Church. At the same time it is a call for the Church to prove its faith and obedience towards its Lord. For this very reason, if war comes, the ecumenical alliance of the Church of Christ must not collapse. It must bear its witness in the fellowship of faith, love and intercession. The bonds of the Holy Spirit are stronger than the bonds of the created world.

In the following month in a retreat arranged at Finkenwalde for the ministers of the Confessing Church, Bonhoeffer turned his attention towards Church discipline and the authority of the Church. It was as if he knew that the main attack was about to begin and wished to see the congregations of the Confessing Church ready for it, disciplined and knowing their power. He turned to the New Testament and drafted a paper which was really a number of theses on *The Power of the Keys and Church Discipline*.[17]

These theses had the clarity of Luther's Theses nailed to the church door in 1517. They addressed the Church about to face an external enemy and called for a clear and severe discipline to sustain them when the blow fell. The attack came on 9 June with a law forbidding collections for the Confessing Church. It also forbade teachers from the seminaries of the Confessing Church to teach in Berlin. On 14 June, the Gestapo raided the offices of the Confessing Church of the Old Prussian Union and arrested Wilhelm Niesel. On 23 June, the Gestapo burst into a meeting of the national council of the brethren in the Friedrich Werder Church in Berlin, arresting Beckmann, Böhm, Iwand, Lücking, Müller (of Heiligenstadt), Perels, von Rabenau and Rendtorff. A few days later, the Provincial Administration of the Emergency League was closed and sealed.

Bishop Bell wrote to *The Times* on 3 July: 'This is a critical hour. It is not only the fate of individual pastors, it is a case of the attitude of the German state to Christianity.[18]

Almost at once he sent the Dean of Chichester, Duncan-Jones, to Berlin to make representations to the Chancellor and the Minister of Justice.

During the following month, students from Finkenwalde were persecuted – interrogations, house searches, confiscations and arrests. It seemed as though to have been a student at Finkenwalde under Bonhoeffer was itself a crime. The seminary carried on its work, expecting the blow to fall every day. Bonhoeffer finished the manuscript of his book, *The Cost of Discipleship*, as planned, spent a few relaxing days with the students on the Baltic and the last term came to an end on 8 September 1937.

NINE

The Fateful Years

On 1 July 1937, Martin Niemöller was arrested, and although at the time it looked like one more irritation from which the Church leader would be released, the imprisonment lasted until the end of the war in Europe, 1945. Niemöller had been arrested before in 1935, when together with five hundred other pastors he spent three days in prison. In the autumn of 1936, he expected to be arrested and calmly waited, but it was a false alarm. In the spring of 1937, he was told that the public prosecutor had forty charges against him, still he remained untouched. Then it came.

It was the first day of the school holidays. His two oldest boys had already left on their bicycles; Mrs Niemöller had just returned from seeing off the girls on an early train for the Baltic; Niemöller himself, after a late night at a church conference, was not yet dressed, but playing with his youngest son, Martin. The Gestapo arrived at 8.30 a.m. and asked him to come for interrogation. He dressed and went, thinking he would return a little later. These interrogations had happened before and they were always in the same place, the police headquarters in Alexander Platz. But this time he waited for hours. There was no interrogation. He was put in a prison, without charge, for the next eight years.

The Church never forgot him during that long imprisonment. In the little mission church of St Anne, attached to Niemöller's parish church, from the day after his arrest until the day after the end of the war, intercession services were held regularly – at first twice a week and then daily. These services were always well attended, especially by the women. Gradually other names were added and it became an intercession service for the martyrs of the Confessing Church. During the summer of 1937 the Gestapo tried to stop the services by mass arrests. The simple courage of the people outdid them. The more they arrested the more came, and at last they gave up.

On 24 July, Paul Schneider was banished from the Rhineland 'for endangering the public safety'. The statute of Hindenburg 1934, under which he had earlier been arrested and was now banished from his church and indeed the whole province, seemed to him falsely applied. Writing to the Chancellor himself he complains:

> The present announcement of my banishment is simply one more piece of evidence of the determined persecution of the Confessing Church, and thereby the Church of Jesus Christ in Germany. I must declare that the reasons for my arrest based upon the Hindenburg statute are both untrue and unjust. I deny the validity of the order. Like my arrest the banishment is also illegal. Hindenburg himself testifies against you when he says, 'Take care therefore that Christ is preached in Germany.' The Confessing Church does no more than that. I can neither recognise nor accept the banishment. I know that I have been called by God to my churches and cannot be separated from them by men. Not even the government can wrench me away from them, unless it has been clearly shown that I have done wrong. I must therefore reject this order to take up residence in some place outside the Rhineland. . . .[1]

Paul Schneider was the pastor of two parishes in the Hunsruck area of the Rhineland: Dickenschied and Womrath. He ignored the order and continued to minister to both. He was taken at first to Coblenz and later to Buchenwald, where he was beaten to death in 1939. There were many others like him, although he was the first to die. A little book, published in 1937 and circulated privately, told of these voices from prison. Most of the letters in that book were anonymous. After the war, the book was published and translated into English with the title *Dying we live*. All the letters tell of courage, of the acceptance of suffering as biblical, as redemptive and as part of God's purpose in the unfolding of something we do not yet see. They must have encouraged many to stand firm. But there were others, as the Church has always known, who wilted before the fires of persecution and betrayed their faith.

Dietrich Bonhoeffer was not tried in this way. In fact, he had often speculated on how he would behave if he were arrested. Later he would find out, but for the moment he was free to go off on holiday in Bavaria and make arrangements for the publication of his book *The Cost of Discipleship*. The book was dedicated to Martin Niemöller and the dedication continued, 'a book which he would have written much better'.

Almost as soon as the summer semester was over at Finkenwalde, the order from Himmler closed all irregular seminaries including Finkenwalde. The twenty-seven students were arrested, but not Bonhoeffer.

The Cost of Discipleship

The Cost of Discipleship contains the essence of Bonhoeffer's teaching at Finkenwalde. Read with *Life Together*, which describes the meaning of the

Christian community there, it gives a better idea of the value of this college of the Confessing Church than any amount of reminiscing by old students. These reminiscences are, of course, helpful to recapture the atmosphere and I have been privileged to enjoy long conversations with those of his students who survived. But it is these two books that can take us into the heart of Finkenwalde. They have, of course, a much wider interest than a description of life in the seminary. They outline what Bonhoeffer believed was the core of the Christian Faith. At the same time they come to grips with some of the weaknesses in the spirituality of the Church to which he belonged. In order to grasp this we need to read the two books side by side. The one deals with a Christian community and the spiritual responsibility we have one for another (*Life Together*), and the other challenges us to a more costly way of discipleship (*The Cost of Discipleship*).

In *Life Together*, Bonhoeffer defends his introduction of the practice of confession. He knows the dangers and spells them out clearly. No one should be the confessor for all, for he will turn it into a dull routine, he will be tempted to misuse the confessional for the exercise of spiritual domination. Instead he recommended that each student choose his own confessor, but that no one should hear confession who does not himself practise it. It is in describing the dangers of confession that he comes closest to one of the most profound essays he ever wrote[2] an essay which appears as an opening section in *The Cost of Discipleship*, but is best understood in the light of his attack on confession which becomes an example of cheap grace in *Life Together*. 'For the salvation of his soul let him guard against ever making a pious work of his confession. If he does so, it will become the final, most abominable, vicious and impure prostitution of the heart; the act becomes an idol, lustful babbling. Confession as a pious work is an invention of the devil.'

The essay in *The Cost of Discipleship* is called 'Costly Grace'. It opens with an attack upon 'cheap grace': 'Cheap grace means grace sold on the market like cheapjack's wares. The sacraments, the forgiveness of sins, and the consolations of religion are thrown away at cut prices. Grace is represented as the Church's inexhaustible treasury, from which she showers blessings with generous hands.'

While there is an echo there of Luther's attack upon the sale of Indulgences in his day, there is also a rejection of the Protestant pietism which seemed to practise religion as a virtue to be rewarded. Grace is not purchased this way, but is given freely at great cost and should be treated as precious. The essay is a defence of Luther against those who misuse him.

We Lutherans have gathered like eagles [or does he mean vultures?] round the carcase of cheap grace, and there we have drunk the pietism that has killed the life of following Christ. It is true, of course, that we have paid the doctrine of pure grace divine honours unparalleled in Christendom, in fact we have exalted that doctrine to the position of God himself. Everywhere Luther's formula has been repeated – by grace alone – but its truth perverted into self-deception.

This self-deception consisted of being satisfied with the proper statement of the doctrine of justification by faith. Then grace has to be handed out on the cheapest terms. 'We leave the following of Christ to legalists, Calvinists and enthusiasts,' he adds and then comes the most critical of his many critical remarks in that chapter: 'We justified the world and condemned as heretics those who followed Christ. The result was that a nation became Christian and Lutheran, but at the cost of true discipleship.'

After that opening section the book is about following Christ – in a costly way. It contains a detailed study of the Sermon on the Mount. In it he refuses to treat the 'commands' as idealistic; they are real and required of those who would follow Christ. He does not despise 'good works' as though they were in danger of leading us into heresy. The New Testament never makes that sharp distinction between good works and faith that Lutheran theologians favoured. Jesus expected his followers to do better than the Pharisees. Bonhoeffer is talking to himself as well as his students. Together they are trying to learn how to be faithful disciples in the peculiar situation of Germany under the tightening control of the Nazis.

Bonhoeffer was greatly affected by what he heard of the Mahatma Gandhi, who took the Sermon on the Mount as his guide for daily living. Few Christians took that section of Matthew's Gospel (Chapters 5–7) as seriously as he did. Bonhoeffer therefore felt bound to examine it and see whether he could live it. There were ideal conditions at Finkenwalde for such an attempt. They were a community of disciples, especially the older men in the 'house of brethren'. Confession allowed them to share with each other their failings of thought and deed. But it was not a monastic community, nor an escapist pietism, for the world impinged upon their devotions. They had to take up positions in relation to the German Christians, the Jews, the National Socialists, the international situation and Germany's search for *Lebensraum* (space to live and expand), the larger Germany to include all German-speaking peoples under one control, purified from alien elements, and many other issues of the day.

From the Beatitudes to the parable of the two houses, built on rock and sand respectively, he examined the nature of Christian ethics. How should a Christian live, how could the righteousness of a disciple of Jesus exceed that of the Pharisees? Just as Jesus had taken the Ten Commandments and shown that the literal way in which they are usually understood is not enough for a disciple, so Bonhoeffer took the accepted Christian standards of his day and showed how much more was demanded of a disciple. In this book we are back with his earliest sermon. A religious man is not necessarily a disciple. There are implications in accepting the call to be a disciple which separate a person from the crowd of nominal Christians, and this does not mean that the disciple is more religious. It probably means that he is more human. It is not in the light of his own good behaviour that a disciple asks if he has kept the commandments, but in the development of his relationship to other people. 'No one has the right to sing the Gregorian chants unless by the same voice he shouts for the Jews.' He saw that the creeds and confessions of his own Lutheran Church were honoured by the German Christians, but made to serve an alien philosophy. He argued for a personal relationship to Christ and to the other person which gave new meaning to the creeds and confessions. If at times he seemed to disregard the religious phrases, it was because they had been emptied of meaning by the new Pharisees.

Sometimes he sounds like Jeremiah standing outside the Temple on the Coronation Day (Jer. 7) and calling upon his fellow citizens to live lives worthy of the God they profess to worship. Bonhoeffer too would urge his fellow citizens not to trust in deceptive words, vainly repeating, 'The Temple of the Lord, the Temple of the Lord, the Temple of the Lord.'

When he describes the scene at the beginning of Matthew Chapter 5 before going on to expound the Sermon on the Mount in detail, it is not difficult to see how much he is trying to discover what a true disciple should do in the circumstances of Germany in the thirties. These verses give pause before reading or listening to the substance of the 'Sermon'. Bonhoeffer makes much of the deliberate pause: '*Seeing* the crowds, he *went up* on the mountain, and when he *sat down* his disciples *came to him*, and he *opened his mouth* and taught them . . .' (Matthew 5:1–2).

These phrases in italics are words designed to draw out the time and allow for consideration of the scene. The people see Jesus with his disciples. Those disciples were until recently part of the multitude, just like the rest. The people are faced with the disconcerting fact that these men have changed. These people are the lost sheep of the house of Israel, the elect people of God, the 'national church'.

Jesus sees his disciples. They have responded to the call which is for all Israel. Their very response makes evident that they are from the people. But, they have heard the voice of the Good Shepherd. This leads not to prosperity, as much of the Old Testament teaches that it should, it leads to poverty. These disciples have renounced everything, they have publicly left the crowd to live in want and privation.

It is the disciples that Jesus describes in the Beatitudes – blessed, because they have nothing, the poorest of the poor, the sorest afflicted, and the hungriest of the hungry. They have only Jesus, and with him they have nothing, nothing in the world, but everything with and through God. As you turn the pages of *The Cost of Discipleship*, it becomes evident that Bonhoeffer has seen quite clearly that the path of the Confessing Church will be one of persecution and not success. The events of 1937 were beginning to make this clearer. The German Christians had everything in their favour. The battle now had to be for the preservation of the purity of the Church, a remnant of which would survive and one day be ready to show the way out of the ruins to renewal. From 1937 onwards, Bonhoeffer's eyes were on the future, when the Nazi regime would be overthrown, the German Christians lose their powerful support and a shattered nation would need the help of true disciples of Jesus Christ. But he already sees that these disciples would be part of the crowd too, and would share its guilt.

The Commandments

In *The Cost of Discipleship*, Bonhoeffer deals with the disciples' attitude to the Ten Commandments, commenting in quite orthodox ways on the verses in which Jesus expounds the inner meaning of the commands. He came to fulfil the Law, not to abolish it. But there is one commandment which, above all, shows Bonhoeffer's development at this time.

The chapter on Thou shalt not kill, is called 'The Brother'. This does not limit the brother to the fellow Christian, but includes the Jew. The commandment which forbids murder entrusts our brother's welfare to us:

> The brother's life is a divine ordinance, and God alone has power over life and death. There is no place for the murderer among the people of God ... (For the disciple) the brother's life is a boundary which he dare not pass. Even anger is enough to overstep the mark, still more the casual angry word, and most of all the deliberate insult of our brother ('Thou fool').[3]

He writes that anger is always an attack on the brother's life and rejects the textual evidence for the qualification, 'without a cause' (Matt. 5:22), as does the RSV and the NIV. The disciples must be entirely innocent of anger. An idle word betrays our lack of respect for our neighbour, a deliberate insult disgraces him publicly and causes us to despise him.

Bonhoeffer has the Church very much in mind when he sees how the 'national church', the German Christians, despise their brothers, the Jews, whether they are Christian Jews or not:

> Let the fellowship of the Church examine itself today and ask whether at the hour of prayer and worship, any accusing voices intervene and make its prayers vain. Let the fellowship of Christ examine itself and see whether it has given any token of the love of Christ to *the victims of the world's contumely*

and contempt, any token of that love of Christ which seeks to preserve, support and protect life. Otherwise, however liturgically correct our services are, and however devout our prayer, however brave our testimony, they will profit us nothing, nay, rather, they must needs testify against us that we have as a Church ceased to follow our Lord. God will not be separated from our brother: he wants no honour for himself so long as our brother is dishonoured.[4]

The Cost of Discipleship established Bonhoeffer as a mature theologian, who could write in a popular way about the meaning of the New Testament for Christians in his day. Karl Barth had described his first book, *Sanctorum Communio*, as a theological miracle. His second book, *Act and Being*, received no such praise, partly because it was critical of the Barthian position. Both these books were academic and had a limited readership. *The Cost of Discipleship* was no less thorough in its exegesis, but it made a direct appeal to anyone who wanted to lead a Christian life and gave careful consideration to the teaching of the New Testament. In this book of 1937, he was not addressing himself to fellow academics, nor even to theological students, but to disciples of Jesus Christ. The title of the book in German was *Nachfolge* (Discipleship).

Even today, it raises serious questions about the integrity of the Church and calls in question many of its attitudes. The reader who takes it simply as New Testament commentary will find it enlightening and challenging. But there is more. The words of Jesus are brought to life in our time and we are not allowed to escape his searching questions about the quality of our Christian discipleship.

The Doors are Closed

Bonhoeffer had been allowed to complete his term at Finkenwalde in what might be called peace! He could attend neither Oxford nor Edinburgh for all the delegates of the Confessing Church for these two World Conferences had their passports withdrawn. As he read the English newspapers, he realised that the absence of the delegates from the Confessing Church, with their known interest in the ecumenical movement, spoke more eloquently to shrewd observers than a full delegation could possibly have done.

News of Finkenwalde's closure came on 28 September, in a telephone message from Stettin. The Gestapo had arrived after all the students had left and they found only Fritz Onnasch, the director of studies, and Frau Struwe, the housekeeper. Both were compelled to leave and seals were set upon the doors. The closure order was published in the newspapers next day, 'issued by the SS National Leader and Chief of the German Police'.

The order was, however, dated 29 August 1937. The closure of the other seminaries followed shortly afterwards.

Bonhoeffer travelled to Berlin to protest and ran into the celebrations for the arrival of Mussolini. The Confessing Church rallied its forces and fought the order, arguing, as Paul Schneider had done, that it was falsely applied – but all to no avail. When Bonhoeffer saw that he could accomplish nothing he turned his attention to the plight of his students ... but not before he had enjoyed the good things that Berlin offered at this festive time!

Wilhelm Rott had been released from prison and a party of them went to celebrate by attending a performance of *Don Giovanni* at the State Opera House. At the end of October, there was a festival of Church music. Eberhard Bethge joined Bonhoeffer in Berlin and was greatly appreciated by the family. Karl Bonhoeffer's comments at the end of the year: 'So far as we are concerned the (Gestapo's) intervention had its good side because we had Dietrich and his friend Bethge with us for a number of weeks.'

Bonhoeffer, despite the joys of home and music, was deeply concerned about his students. They usually wrote to him when in trouble and he answered them all, but now so many complaints and troubles came that he could see the danger of the collapse of the Confessing Church in Pomerania. In a circular letter to his students[5] who were serving the churches, he wrote: 'During the past few weeks, letters and personal comments have come to me which make it clear that our Church, and, in Pomerania particularly, our group of young theologians, has come to a time of sore trial.'

It is a strong letter. Bonhoeffer asks the recipients to read it personally even though the large number of letters he has received and the sameness of their complaints makes it necessary for him to send a circular letter, and try to analyse the malaise in the Confessing Church of Pomerania in general.

He begins with an appeal to their memory, eloquently recalling the epic period of their struggle, when they were students in Finkenwalde, or when the Barmen Synod spoke in such a way that they thrilled to its call to obey the Word of God, or when the Dahlem Synod clearly outlined the structures of their Church. He reminds them that they had the privilege of knowing the true Church of Jesus Christ. What has changed?

He then compares their miserable state with that of other provinces, where the Confessing Church is still strong and obedient and ready to suffer. Why is Pomerania different? Do they complain that the task has now become much harder? Do they think the congregations are not mature enough to understand their resistance and to participate with them? You can detect that many were saying that it was all right for Bonhoeffer, he didn't have to minister to an immature church.

'Are the congregations still too "immature"? As though a congregation could be too immature to hear God's Word and act in obedience to it and yet could be mature enough to act outside the Church! Who taught us to think so contemptuously of our congregations?' Bonhoeffer appealed to them to see that God was calling them, not in the nature of law, which they may well resent, but in the sense of Gospel, which brings them joy in obedience. He offers them the theological equivalent of 'blood, sweat and tears'. He appeals to the first chapter of Haggai, where the people who returned from the exile said, 'Wait! It is not yet time to build a temple.' Then came Haggai's word of the Lord: 'Is it a time for you yourselves to dwell in your panelled houses while this house lies in ruins?'

He deals with their questions one by one and answers them to his, if not their, satisfaction! Then with the peremptory conclusion of a commanding officer who has been very tolerant so far, he tells them to get on with the work.

A Sound Life

Albrecht Schönherr, one of the students at Finkenwalde, tried to assess the attraction that Bonhoeffer had for those young theologians.[6] He was in a good position to do this, because he had himself carried the battle into the theological faculty of the university and even set up a small community early in 1936 on the lines of Finkenwalde, by adapting an old student fraternity as a hostel. Bonhoeffer recognised the hard struggle Schönherr had in doing this, 'opposed by the entire faculty'. He was devoted to Bonhoeffer and trusted by him. What then did he think was Bonhoeffer's fascination?

'His appearance was imposing, but not elegant; his voice high, but not rich; his formulations were laborious, not brilliant.' He uses the words 'a sound life' to describe him, adding 'Never did I discover in him anything low, undisciplined or mean.'

Schönherr attempted to explain what he meant by 'a sound life'. He was not a one-sided intellectual. He outplayed all the students at games. He taught his students to see their value and lit up the pressure of their studies with music, which he played with them. His was a sound life also because he had a continuity with his past. He had learnt much from his father and he held his teachers in high regard, none more than Adolf von Harnack. 'A sound life', as Schönherr recalls, showed itself in the direct and vivid expressions that came when he was entirely concentrating upon something. It was only after profound concentration that he could deeply disturb the brethren with his statement that 'He who deliberately separates himself from the Confessing Church in Germany, separates himself from salvation.' The occasion of stating such a radical attitude was the attempt by the state to reconcile the Confessing Church with the National Church (German Christian). Albrecht Schönherr writes:

I shall not forget the moment when we heard the news, so fateful for the Confessing Church, especially in Pomerania, that the state had formed Church committees from both camps to bring about a pacification of the Church struggle. The postman had just delivered the newspaper. We were still standing on the stairs. Bonhoeffer thought it over for a few seconds, then he was quite clear about it: 'Church and un-church cannot come to terms.' From that moment there was no hesitation. One of the students who had submitted to the Church committees was sent away from us, in great distress, but also, after everything had been carefully explained, with great calmness.

Early in the Church struggle, one who later became quite prominent in the Confessing Church suggested that he might join the German Christians so as to break it from within. Bonhoeffer replied: 'If you board the wrong train it is no use running along the corridor in the opposite direction.'

In-Pastorate Training

Finkenwalde and all it stood for was not given up without a fight! Hans Iwand had tried to reopen his East Prussian seminary on the old lines in Dortmund, but students and teacher alike were arrested and expelled from the town. Some of the Confessing Church wanted to claim publicly the right to organise their own training, but wiser council prevailed and it was soon realised that the work itself was more important than the demonstration of rights. A kind of 'in-pastorate training' was developed, called by Bethge 'collective pastorates'. Each student was registered with an incumbent and was officially on his staff. Occasionally, a student might succeed him. It all depended upon having superintendents who were friendly towards the Confessing Church. These 'learning ministers' would be placed wherever possible near to each other and a centre found for instruction. Bonhoeffer's students lived in two vacant vicarages in rural Pomerania, much as they had lived in Finkenwalde. Of course, there were fewer of them and they were not so comfortably housed. These two 'collective pastorates' included seven or eight students each. None was registered as a member of a seminary, but each as a pastor in training with the name of the parish to which he was attached. This worked for about two and a half years. Other seminaries too worked in this disguised form.

Bonhoeffer's two 'collective pastorates' were in Köslin and Schlawe. Köslin was an obvious choice because the superintendent was the father of Fritz Onnasch, the director of studies from Finkenwalde. He installed his son as assistant minister and thus saved the Confessing Church one salary!

Köslin was a country town with a population of about 30,000. It was 100 miles from Stettin. Five confessing pastors in the town were able to accept up to ten students for 'in-training'. All of them lived together in the spacious vicarage of the superintendent. Schlawe was twenty-five miles to the east, a town of about 10,000 and it was here that Bonhoeffer and Bethge (now director of studies) were placed as assistant ministers. Eduard Block, the superintendent, always kept a bed for Bonhoeffer. The students, however, had to move further east to the tiny parish of Gross-Schlönwitz. They needed transport and when the pastor in charge of the parish married he needed his vicarage, so the students moved to nearby Sigurdshof.

A good picture of the collective pastorate at Schlönwitz comes in a letter from a student[7] who, after saying how reluctantly he went to this remote place, adds:

> It all turned out differently from the way I feared. Instead of the stuffy atmosphere of theological cant, I found a world that embraced a great deal of what I love and need: straightforward theological work in a friendly community, where no unpleasant notice was taken of one's limitations, but where the work was made a pleasure; brotherhood under the Word, irrespective of the person, and with it all, open-mindedness and love for everything that still makes this fallen creation lovable – music, literature, sport and the beauty of the earth – a grand way of life.

He added with a touch of humour that characterised Finkenwalde and the collective pastorates: 'Does it dull the objectivity of your theological view, when I write that it was the peripheral things which increased my delight in what is central?'

Ruth von Kleist-Retzow

One person who greatly regretted the move from Finkenwalde to a place so much further from Stettin was a member of the Pomeranian aristocracy, Ruth von Kleist-Retzow, a widow who had retired to one of her estates at Klein-Kössin near Kieckow.

She was a remarkable woman, always sympathetic to movements that brought new life to the Church. Even when she was very old she still read every new book written by Karl Barth. Bonhoeffer, when he entered the Stettin area, brought a new spiritual stimulus to her life and it was in her house that he started his fund-raising when Finkenwalde was in financial trouble. She was thrilled by the progress of his book, *The Cost of Discipleship*, and overwhelmed him with questions. He often wished his students had been so enquiring! He spent many of his holidays at Klein-Kössin and it was there that many of his students went when they were in need of rest.

Maria von Wedemeyer

Frau von Kleist-Retzow brought her grandchildren to Finkenwalde, among them an attractive and very natural little girl called Maria – Maria von Wedemeyer. Her main interest at the seminary was probably playing with the students in the garden, but her grandmother was concerned with the education of all her grandchildren and persuaded Bonhoeffer to undertake their preparation for confirmation. The closing of Finkenwalde rather disturbed this plan, but Bonhoeffer held classes and several of the grandchildren came with their grandmother, who probably enjoyed them more than the children did. He prepared Maria's brother Max for confirmation, along with the future husband of her sister, Ruth Alice, Klaus von Bismarck. Apart from the confirmation classes, there were many social calls and Bonhoeffer entered the world of the land-owning aristocracy of Pomerania and East Prussia – Kleist-Retzow, von Wedemeyer, von Bismarck. It was not the academic circle of Grunewald in Berlin, but it fascinated him and introduced him to a new level of political and military life in Germany. Dietrich must have met Maria many times during those visits to Klein-Kössin, but he hardly noticed the adolescent girl. It was years later in 1942, when her father was killed on the Eastern Front and he gave his spiritual support to her mother, that he fell in love with Maria. It was a tragic engagement as it turned out, but both were very much in love. The family thought she was too young and the mother tried to impose a sanction of absence for a year, against which Bonhoeffer protested strongly. He was an impatient lover and found the old-fashioned disciplines of the German Junkers hard to bear. But all that lay ahead in 1942 and 1943. In this fateful year of 1937 she was a child of thirteen and as far as we know unnoticed.

A Christian Spirit and a Prussian Sense of Duty

Maria's father was a landowner in Pätzig, some sixty miles north-east of Berlin. He was a successful farmer and took his responsibilities in Church and state seriously. He was a founder member of the Berneuchen Brotherhood, which sought to reinvigorate the Evangelical Church of Prussia. He was deeply concerned about the rise of National Socialism and, as a former comrade in arms of Von Papen, he helped to form a new Cabinet. When Hitler came to power, he withdrew and felt the consequences. He wavered between his loyalty as a soldier and his close association with the conspiracy against Hitler – Fabian von Schlabrendorff was his cousin and visited him frequently at Pätzig. But Hans von Wedemeyer never joined the conspiracy. He fought as an officer in Russia and was killed in August 1942.

Frau von Kleist-Retzow did not join a conspiracy either, but she waged a battle of her own to keep her grandchildren in the best tradition of her Evangelical faith. She saw through all the outward splendour of the Third Reich and, perceiving the decay at its roots, quickly turned away from it. Her judgments were clear and she wished to preserve her family from the corrupting influence of the day. She soon found an ally in Dietrich Bonhoeffer. He would provide the religious instructions and she herself would teach the spirit of her race.

To this end she rented a flat in Pölitzer Strasse in Stettin, and made of it a kind of Kleist boarding school. She planned the education of this whole generation of her family: to have a Christian spirit and a Prussian sense of duty! She built up a timetable of lessons, helping with the homework, educating the grandchildren to the extent that all conversation at dinner was in French. Werner Koch compares her to a prophetess of old! Perhaps like Anna. This woman could write letters of comfort and inspiration to all who needed them. She loved the Confessing Church and when its seminary was in need she came to help. She encouraged the faint-hearted, offered rest and security to the frightened, and when stores were low at Finkenwalde she would send practical help: a cartload of potatoes, meat, vegetables, eggs, money. Many of her letters have survived and in them she speaks of the experience of the awakening congregations which was her great joy. She shared the sufferings of others, but she could not read defeat into suffering. In February 1937, she wrote in a letter to Werner Koch that, despite the strange times, she could see real signs of hope: '. . . poor suppressed Christianity is coming alive in calamity, as I have never experienced in my seventy years.'

At Easter, Bonhoeffer and Bethge came to Klein-Kössin, partly to rest and partly to finish off *The Cost of Discipleship*. She wrote after that visit that she could hardly express in words the joy it gave her. Then she asserted her confidence in a way that must have encouraged both of these men, as well as Werner Koch to whom the letter was addressed:

> We have often spoken of you and in our evening prayers included those who are in prison and concentration camps ... I am certain that God will hear our prayers. Only his time is not our time. And yet there is always a meaning in it. Perhaps something like this: 'They meant to deal wickedly with us, but God meant to deal kindly.' It strikes me just how much and how long the men of the Bible had to wait. There is something special about such waiting I think.

In January 1938, Bonhoeffer was attending a meeting in Berlin when it was raided by the Gestapo, who had hoped to find an illegal meeting of the seminary in progress. They issued orders banning those who lived in Berlin from leaving, and those who lived in the country from entering the capital. There was nothing personal against Bonhoeffer himself, for he was allowed to return and continue as the assistant minister of Schlawe. The ban on the entry into Berlin was very tiresome, however, since it was his main source of information. His father intervened and, because of his reputation, had the ban lifted, so that it applied only to work in Berlin. When his parents had to discuss this matter with him, the place to which they went was the home of Ruth von Kleist-Retzow, in Stettin.

Political Involvement

In February 1938, Hans von Dohnanyi, his brother-in-law, who had kept him remarkably well informed about the progress of events in Berlin, introduced him to the four leading figures of the German resistance. They were, Dr Karl Sack, the chief of the army's legal department; Colonel (later General) Hans Oster, head of the Central Department of the German Intelligence (the Abwehr); Admiral Canaris, head of the Abwehr; and General Beck, a senior commander of the German army. The Bonhoeffer family, as a whole, in 1938 were waiting for the 'beams to crack' (i.e. Hitler's downfall), but until this point, Dietrich had taken no political actions against the state and he had been careful to keep his protests within the legal framework. His battle was not against National Socialism as such, however much he hated it as a system, but against the German Christians. His was a theological battle. It is for this reason that he is sometimes accused of caring only for the 'baptised Jews'. This is not entirely true, but his main objections in the early years were to legislation which would make a distinction between Jewish and Gentile Christians. Now he was to involve himself politically. The influence was his brother-in-law.

Hans von Dohnanyi had no sympathy with National Socialism, but as personal information officer to three successive ministers of justice, beginning in 1929, he was taken over as a good legal civil servant. The minister of justice in the first government after Hitler took power was Franz Gürtner and he greatly respected Hans von Dohnanyi. He discouraged him in 1935 from leaving to take up a lectureship at Leipzig. This trust kept Dohnanyi very close to the centre and very well informed. Sooner or later, however, someone was sure to complain. A party clique in the ministry, whose spokesman was Martin Borman, eventually denounced him and Gürtner protected him from any serious consequences other than dismissal. He was appointed a judge in Leipzig in September 1938. He did not lose contact with Berlin and he continued the dangerous practice of keeping a diary of the evil doings of his masters. His 'chronicle of shame' he called it, and intended one day to use it for indictment. It was not discovered and he was therefore allowed to make frequent visits to Berlin to lecture and his contacts with the conspiracy were not monitored. There were hopes for a coup and two attempts at revolution in 1939, but the conspirators were foiled by Hitler's success at Munich, his annexation of the Sudetenland and then the occupation of Czechoslovakia. On each of these occasions, the conspirators assumed that Hitler would drag Germany into a hopeless war. The Western powers remained inactive.

This high-power resistance was not confined to a few people and one is constantly amazed at the inadequacy of its efforts. This is particularly the case because, in these years before the war, the majority of people in Germany were fearful of war. While the mass of the German people responded enthusiastically to that part of Hitler's programme that called for national recovery, revision of the Versailles Treaty and a greater Germany, there was not much support for his expansionist programme in the east. Although there was anti-semitism in Germany before Hitler, it was not his attacks upon the Jews that gave him support. The majority of German people were soon opposed to his cruel treatment and the mass deportation and later the extermination policy never had popular support.

Dohnanyi, therefore, was not introducing Bonhoeffer to a small, fanatical group running counter to popular views in Germany. Had that group been successful in overthrowing Hitler, it could have been a popular movement. But Bonhoeffer's reluctance to join them was also natural, for it was totally contrary to his upbringing, both in family and Church. His class was accustomed to protest, but not to conspiracy to overthrow the government; his Church found revolution anathema. Yet, within this group, he found men of his class and some like those whom he had learned to respect in Pomerania. The officer class and the landed aristocracy were by tradition loyal.

It was also a dangerous game. A substantial potential opposition to the National Socialists had been ruthlessly crushed at the outset by the brutal annihilation of communists, social democrats, and independent trades union dissidents. The conspirators knew that unless they succeeded, or if they were discovered before they had done so, there would be no mercy. Bonhoeffer hesitated to act against all that he had thought of as right. The turning point in his mind came with the beginning of the deportation of the Jews. That was no longer a Church matter and could not be handled by resolutions at Church synods. It required political action which he interpreted as obeying the Word of God spoken to his people in all times of oppression of a minority: 'Open your mouths for the dumb.'

The Persecution of the Jews

Karl Barth, writing in 1967, when he had read Eberhard Bethge's classic biography of Dietrich Bonhoeffer, recalled with shame that Bonhoeffer had spoken out more clearly and much earlier than any of them about the treatment of the Jews – as fellow human beings, not simply when they were also fellow Christians. At that time, Barth reminds his readers, the Evangelical Churches were more concerned with self-preservation than the awful injustice done to the Jews. It was this that started Bonhoeffer's disillusion with even the Confessing Church and turned him towards a political action which was alien to him.

After that awful night of devastation and persecution of the Jews which has gone down in history as 'Crystal Night', Bonhoeffer wrote in his Bible the date, 9.11.38, beside the verse in Psalm 74, 'they burned all the meeting places of God in the land'. It was a night of terror, of which every German must be ashamed. Not far from the border with the West, in East Berlin (in the former German Democratic Republic) there is a derelict synagogue, left unrepaired, as a memorial to that night. What happened should have raised the voice of protest from every Christian soul. So many times, Bonhoeffer urged, and often urged in vain, 'Open your mouths for the dumb.'

The Protestant Churches of Germany have reason to repent of their acceptance, and even support at times, of the Nazi treatment of the Jews. There had long been an anti-semitic element in the German Churches and it can be traced to Luther. Nevertheless, as we have seen, Bonhoeffer could find writings by Luther which were in strong contradiction to those the German Christians were circulating. The anti-semitism had penetrated even the royal family as the scandalous memoirs of Prince von Bülow revealed. All this allowed many to tolerate anti-semitic statements and occasional acts which would not be tolerated today. Thus as anti-Jewish propaganda and activities grew the Protestant Churches were ill-equipped to deal with them.

Even the Bonhoeffer family with its strong liberal tradition and the welcoming of a Jew into their family (Leibholz) did not all see the seriousness of what was happening in Germany at first. Karl-Friedrich found the negro problem in America of far greater concern, before which anti-semitism in Germany was insignificant, the Jewish problem merely a joke in comparison. Dietrich quickly realised that this was not so, and on his return to Germany in 1931 he spoke out clearly of the dangers.

It was in 1933 that the Churches had their chance to speak out against the treatment of the Jews. Very few did and Bonhoeffer pressed for the Church to recognise its role as the social conscience of the state. He was one of the very few who gave careful attention to the consequences for the Church of the Aryan Laws of 7 April 1933. He spoke and wrote about the Jewish Question and by August of that year he was quite sure that he could not remain with a Church which excluded Jews. The events of that year led him to a systematic study of the role of the Church when faced with an unjust state.[8]

First, the Church must put the question to the state whether it can answer for its action as legitimate political action.

Second, it must care for the victims of injustice.

Third, if the Church found that the state was unscrupulously meting out too much or too little law and order, it could not be content with (to use the simile of a mad driver) 'binding up the victim of the wheel, but must put a spoke in the wheel'.

When he was involved in the drafting of the Bethel Confession he tried to incorporate an article on the Jewish Question. The dropping of this article was one reason why he was dissatisfied with the Confession. If that article had remained and found its way later into the Barmen Declaration, we should not have to listen today to legitimate criticism from the Jewish community that Barmen was silent about Jews.

The Brown Synod of August 1933 had said, to the continuing disgrace of the Protestant Churches of Germany: 'We understand and appreciate the measures taken by the state and recognise that the Evangelical Church also has cause for vigilance in the preservation of the German race . . .'[9]

Präses Koch objected and was shouted down.

A month later, Bonhoeffer wrote of these Aryan Laws when applied to the Church: 'The acceptance of such a scandal would be damaging to the congregation . . . Those who remain unaffected by these laws and are therefore privileged, will wish to align themselves with their underprivileged brethren rather than make use of their privileges within the Church.'[10]

After this crisis there should have been no question of cooperation between the Confessing Church and the National Church. For Bonhoeffer, there was no question, but as time dragged on and little seemed to be achieved, the sacrifices were less easy to bear. Bonhoeffer moved away from the compromised Confessing Church and increasingly found his time taken up with the conspiracy. Much of his work with Admiral Canaris was concerned with the rescue of Jews. He never wavered. It was the duty of every Christian to protect the underprivileged and such was the horror of Hitler's 'final solution' that he was prepared to be devious, to use force and to conspire against his own country. When I called the third volume of his collected letters and papers, *True Patriotism,* it was a comment, albeit paradoxical, on the nature of this man who loved his country so much that he conspired against it and prayed for its defeat.

TEN

Turning Point

When Bonhoeffer was first introduced to the conspirators, those senior militarymen did not think of themselves as engaged in a 'conspiracy'. For them, it was not so much the overthrowing of a government as the arrest of a maniac who was destroying their fatherland. They were patriots. Although they had long considered Hitler certifiably insane, they needed a scientific analysis of his actions by a competent psychiatrist. Hans von Dohnanyi thought inevitably of Karl Bonhoeffer and the route to him lay through Dietrich. It was for this reason that Bonhoeffer was important to what we have called the 'conspiracy'.

Hitler's Munich meeting with Chamberlain, Daladier and Mussolini seemed to provide the ideal moment for a *putsch*. General von Witzleben, a party to the 'conspiracy', was in command of the Berlin garrisons. It was assumed in Germany that Hitler wanted war and that the Munich meeting would not influence him in any way. Of course, the other nations – with the possible exception of Mussolini's Italy – would not agree to his demands for the German occupation of the Sudetenland, but he would none the less march into Czechoslovakia and popular opinion would be against him. In such a mood, the patriots would arrest Hitler, arraign him, find him insane and depose him.

The appeasement of the Allies allowed Hitler to take the Sudetenland without war and there was later no resistance from the West when he marched into Czechoslovakia. His popularity as the saviour of his people rose. The mood was wrong for any kind of *putsch*.

The Jewish Problem

No one in his right mind thought Munich had solved anything; it had only strengthened Hitler's position. War was inevitable sooner or later. The German people were beginning to believe in Hitler's almost divine powers. He now took over command of his armed forces, and although none of the conspirators had revealed his hand, the more senior posts were filled with reliable supporters. The exceptions were Admiral Canaris and General Hans Oster, at the Centre of German Intelligence (Abwehr). The National

Socialists felt able to tighten the restrictions on the Jews and to contemplate their annihilation. Until 1938, the Bonhoeffers had thought that they might contain Gerhard Leibholz within the family. Gradually, it became obvious that they would have to emigrate: Gerhard, Sabine and the children. On 9 September, 1938, Dietrich accompanied them to Basel for a 'visit' to Switzerland. It was clear that this meant that they would not return to Germany. Legislation proceeded apace to identify Jews and more easily exclude them from all professional work. Those of Jewish origin, even when that meant one grandfather, had to have a 'J' stamped upon their passports. While the Leibholz family was in Switzerland all passports belonging to Jews which lacked this 'J' were rendered invalid. That made it virtually impossible for them to return, so they went to England. At first sight that does not seem a very sensible choice for a German-speaking lawyer, but Dietrich had written to Bell, the Bishop of Chichester, recently appointed to the House of Lords, and he used his influence to get Gerhard placed at Oxford. There they remained.

Thus Dietrich was much concerned about the Jewish Question in his own family circle and for the next few months personal matters occupied his mind. The flight of Sabine affected him deeply. He believed that twins had a special affinity and the departure of Sabine, with whom he had shared so much when they were together as children, and even later when they were apart, affected him greatly. It became evident that this separation was for a long period, and he felt depressed, but like a manic depressive he had periods of great hope and exhilaration. As their common birthday drew near (4 February) he wrote of 'everything changing' and made frantic efforts to visit Sabine in England. When he spoke out for the Jews, or battled to keep them from further humiliation, he was like a knight errant fighting for Sabine. But there was another personal problem, affecting his own freedom.

Military Service

Germany was mobilising for war and Dietrich Bonhoeffer was eligible for military service. Placards appeared in Berlin informing all who were born in 1906 or 1907 that they must register at once. This was not yet a call-up but that would soon follow. Bonhoeffer faced the choice that many young men had to face, but with him there were certain unusual complications. This was January 1939 and since the arrest of Martin Niemöller and the closure of the Finkenwalde (illegal) Seminary, the pressure was on. Anything that Dietrich Bonhoeffer did could bring new dangers to the brethren. He had to choose between three alternatives.

He could register and then simply await call-up, taking his part like anyone else in the military exercises preparatory to the inevitable war; or he could register as a conscientious objector and appear before the tribunal which would most certainly send him to prison. The best solution, however, seemed to be a postponement until he was too old for military service. He even joked about the idea of having so many overseas invitations that he could just stay away from Germany until it was too late. In that mood he wrote to his brother, Karl-Friedrich in Leipzig, on his birthday saying, 'In some ways I envy you for being forty!'

There were plenty of invitations to Switzerland, Britain and America; but overseas travel required special permission and anything he did that brought the attention of the authorities to his case was dangerous. His father was influential enough to get some postponement, but not enough to get him out of trouble.

A Cry for Help

Bonhoeffer needed advice and he consulted the man he trusted most, who knew him and would not misunderstand his dilemma. In fact he needed the advice of an older man who understood the situation in Germany but was outside it. The registration and possible call-up were only part of his problem. He was beginning to feel his work in Germany frustrating. The collective pastorate, the encouragement of his 'illegal' students, the long debates with his fellow-churchmen who had disappointed him in their reactions to the terrible 'Crystal Night' and their inability to see the Jewish Question as something much bigger than whether Jews could hold office in the Church, all these things began to work upon his mind and suggest that perhaps he needed a period of service outside Germany to get his mind and conscience clear. Might there not be a call waiting for him outside and was it not necessary to get outside, just to hear that call clearly?

He wrote again to Bishop Bell,[1] who had so readily responded to his request to help the Leibholz family. Now it was for himself. The letter was a difficult one to write. He could not tell Bell everything, but he trusted him to read between the lines. The point he did make clear in this letter was that he wanted to escape from the call-up. His reasons were mixed and he needed advice. He was not at this stage a pacifist. It was only under 'these circumstances' that he could not fight. He was afraid that his actions might be taken as the attitude of the Confessing Church, 'which would be regarded by the regime as typical of the hostility of our Church to the state'. He also says that for him the worst thing about registering for military service would be the 'military oath'. This was an oath of allegiance to the Führer as well as to his country. He was patriotic enough, but an oath of allegiance to Hitler would be impossible for him. He wanted nothing more than the removal of Hitler from power. So he was puzzled and needed help.

There was another point which he did not include in the letter and which he had hardly formulated himself. How far can a Christian minister use violence? This was not only the pacifist issue. One detects that Bonhoeffer accepted the legitimate role of a Christian engaged in war. He had the 'conspiracy' still in mind. Initially, as we have seen, this was a plan to arrest Hitler and give him a legal trial. As Hitler's successes continued, something more drastic was in the air. It was probably Churchill who first made the conspirators face this fact. When he was approached for help, he said they could have all the help they wanted, but first, he added, you must bring me Hitler's head! If it came to it, would Bonhoeffer be able to satisfy his conscience and be party to an assassination? Could he square this with his theology? There were no Lutheran theologians with whom he could discuss this issue.

His whole family tradition was against such action and there was no help in the family, none of them except Hans von Dohnanyi could understand his dilemma. At no time in his life was Bonhoeffer more confused than at this moment when all these complex problems were reduced to an apparently simple matter of registration for military service, with the subsequent oath of allegiance. He had to get away. This was a flight from complexity. It could be looked upon as 'dodging the draft', or the need to breathe the fresh air of freedom outside Germany, or a fear of losing his twin sister, or an escape from the deteriorating quarrels of the Confessing Church, or even fear of involvement in the conspiracy. Bonhoeffer did not know.

Friends in England

On 10 March 1939, he and Eberhard Bethge took the night train to Ostend. Bonhoeffer could not sleep until they had crossed the German frontier. He had heard of the plans to attack Prague and knew that his journey could be interrupted at any point on German soil. They crossed the Channel to England and went at once to see Bishop Bell. He confided in the older man, who knew how to pray and also to demand what was right of him. He was prepared for a direct 'Yes' or 'No' and would have heeded what Bell said; but he also knew that after all the advice, he would ultimately have to take the decision alone.

There is no clear record of what they said, but it can be assumed that Bell assured him that he would be understood if he decided to leave Germany temporarily. There is no doubt also that they discussed the problems of the ecumenical movement and its attitude to the Confessing Church. The Provisional Committee that was to set up the World Council of Churches had already started work under the chairmanship of William Temple, while Bonhoeffer had already criticised the ecumenical movement for failing to develop a theology. But this time it was personal problems that dominated the conversation.

Bell's compassionate understanding helped and Bonhoeffer's letter of thanks is enough to show how much: 'Before returning to Germany I just wish to thank you once again for the great help you gave me in our talk at Chichester. I do not know what will be the outcome of it all, but it meant much to me to realise that you see the great conscientious difficulties with which we are faced.'[2]

Bonhoeffer had gone to England, officially, to visit relatives – this was considered a legitimate reason for travel abroad – but he did not need that excuse to visit Sabine, apart from his need of her, he had to clear up some financial difficulties with Gerhard Leibholz. They had reached the safety of England, but the restrictions on taking any money out of Germany prevented them from transferring their assets in Germany to England for a reasonably independent life there. The Bonhoeffer family, and in particular the father, Karl Bonhoeffer, had international connections and Dietrich could call upon these as well as his English friends to make life comfortable for the Leibholz family. He would certainly do this. Gerhard accompanied him as he travelled about England and he was able to establish a circle of friends for him. The Bonhoeffers were a close family who knew the importance of contacts.

Bonhoeffer also met Pastor Rieger, who was caring for German-speaking congregations in London – his own pastorate of a few years earlier. Leibholz and Rieger went with him on 3 April to see Reinhold Niebuhr, the American theologian who was holidaying at Bexhill. The conversation would be theological and each would want to bring the other up to date on their separated worlds. Bonhoeffer had known Niebuhr well in America and the last book of his he had received was *Moral Man and Immoral Society*, in 1933. There was obviously some catching up to be done on American theology, but there was also a need to inform Niebuhr of what had been happening in Germany. This Bonhoeffer did to some effect, and Niebuhr at once began to arrange engagements for him in America. This would give him a chance to inform America about the real issues in Nazi Germany and at the same time enlarge his understanding of theology in the USA. Niebuhr arranged invitations for Bonhoeffer to visit Henry Smith Leiper at the Federal Council of Churches in New York and Paul Lehmann at Elmhurst College. This laid the basis of Bonhoeffer's visit to New York later in the year.

The English Church's Failure to Understand

Apart from his own personal dilemma, Bonhoeffer was also deeply concerned with the representation of the Confessing Church in international meetings. He saw all too clearly that the time would come when only the officially recognised territorial Churches, largely in the hands of the German Christians or those so-called 'undestroyed Churches' which had worked out an agreement of non-intervention in one another's affairs with the state, would be able to travel overseas. He saw Leonard Hodgson, the General Secretary of the Faith and Order Movement in London, and pressed for a permanent representative of the German Confessing Church in London or Geneva to keep the international links open. Bonhoeffer had already failed to convince Schönfeld in Geneva and he had no greater success now. Geneva seemed to think that Germany was quite adequately represented by the officially appointed people already there.

Bishop Bell supported Bonhoeffer, but in vain. The World Council of Churches (in the process of formation) seemed unable to understand the Church struggle, or perhaps unwilling to involve themselves in what looked like a political decision. Bonhoeffer's worry was that the official Church's External Affairs Office was represented primarily by Heckel, who had come out in favour of the German Christian *Godesberg Declaration.* One quote from that declaration will show why Bonhoeffer was disturbed:

> [National Socialism continues] the work of Martin Luther on the ideological and political side [and thus helps] in its religious aspect the recovery of a true understanding of the Christian faith . . .
>
> The Christian faith is the unbridgeable religious contrast to Judaism . . .
>
> Supra-national and international churchism of a Roman Catholic or world Protestantism is a political degeneration of Christianity. A fruitful development of genuine Christian faith is possible only within the given orders of creation.[3]

The chairman of the Provisional Committee charged with setting up the World Council of Churches was William Temple, who for all his eminence was totally ignorant of German Church affairs. Thus Bonhoeffer had a hard job convincing the growing ecumenical movement, whose importance he saw, that they were becoming politically involved by accepting the representation provided by such official bodies. The only one of importance in England who really understood him was Bishop Bell, to whom he wrote in near despair: 'I am afraid that we shall very soon be cut off entirely from our brethren abroad . . . Frankly, and with all due respect, the German representatives in Geneva cannot represent the cause of the Confessing Church.'[4]

Waiting in London

Bonhoeffer stayed longer in London than he had planned – more than five weeks in all. He was again fascinated by what he saw. In particular he was impressed by the abrupt change in public opinion in London when, on 15

March, Hitler breached the Munich Agreement and invaded Czechoslovakia. At first he was so sure that war would break out almost at once that he toyed with the idea of letting himself be caught by the war while he was near his twin sister in Oxford. Using a code, he wrote to his parents about the imminence of war and his undecided state: 'The main question that is rather holding me back is whether I am to wait here for Uncle Rudi' (13 April 1939). They replied that things had not got as far as Uncle Rudi coming, i.e. the war.

While in London he saw the film, *Queen Victoria*, and confessed that when he saw the continuous history of this country that was now threatened, he could not keep back tears of anger. Finally he returned to Berlin on 18 April. He ran into the elaborate celebrations for Hitler's fiftieth birthday. He was sickened by what he read in the official Church papers and saddened by the *Junge Kirche*, a journal which had been so brave.

> It has today become evident to everyone without exception that the figure of the Führer, powerfully fighting his way through old worlds, seeing with his mind's eye what is new and compelling its realisation, is named on the few pages of world history that are reserved for initiators of a new epoch . . . The figure of the Führer has brought a new obligation for the Church too.[5]

The Decision to Leave for America

The first few weeks back in Berlin were taken up with trying to postpone his military call-up. This was not too difficult because the international tensions had relaxed a bit when it became obvious that Britain was not going to war for Czechoslovakia. Besides, Bonhoeffer had some very important invitations to America in his pocket and Germany was very anxious to keep relations with the USA as normal as possible. Reinhold Niebuhr had done as well as he had promised and there seemed to be no reason why Bonhoeffer should not leave at once for the security of America. But he had one more obstacle to overcome. It was of the greatest importance to him that he should have the understanding of his brethren and the official approval of the Council of Brethren of the Old Prussian Union. They nearly always acceded to Bonhoeffer's wishes, but he had to be sure that they would not regard his 'flight' as running away from the battle. They understood and saw both the significance of keeping the Confessing Church free from political involvement over Bonhoeffer's refusal to take the oath, and the importance of having someone in America who could persuade the Churches there of the seriousness of their struggle. The inability of most of the ecumenical leaders to understand the cause of the Confessing Church and the heretical state of the German Christians was clear to them when they heard of Bonhoeffer's arguments in London and

William Temple's statements. Reinhold Niebuhr had also assured Bonhoeffer that he was needed in America.

The month of May was therefore largely taken up with efforts to forestall the military authorities' order to report to the recruiting station and to convince the Council of Brethren that he would be of more use to them in America than as a threatened and silenced theologian in Germany.

When his aeroplane left Tempelhof airfield on 2 June, it looked as though his problems were behind him and he could relax. Everything had turned out well: he would see the Leibholz family in London and then sail on the *Bremen* with his brother Karl-Friedrich, who had an invitation to lecture at Chicago. But Dietrich Bonhoeffer was ill at ease. No one had yet been appointed to do his work with the collective pastorate at Sigurdshof and there he had left a sad note to the unknown successor: 'To my successor. He will find here: 1. One of the finest tasks in the Confessing Church . . .' He added something about the teaching the scattered students should receive, and urged the director, whoever he might be, '. . . to go on walking with the brethren as much as possible, or to be with them in some other way.'

He was clearly leaving behind a much loved work and still looked upon these students in the collective pastorate as his children. The fact that no one had been appointed yet to succeed him worried him at a time when he had very serious steps to consider. Hellmut Traub was eventually appointed, but he did not hear of that until weeks later, in New York.

As he was leaving, news came of further measures against the Confessing Church. Those pastors who were acting according to the rules of the Council of Brethren were accused of transgressing against the official plan to make collections and hand them over as instructed. Accordingly the grants towards their stipends were suspended on 1 June. On the day that Bonhoeffer left, he heard that Martin Niemöller, already imprisoned for two years, had been placed on the retirement list by the official Church authorities. He learnt that a minority within the Confessing Church was being deprived of its rights, but that a majority was trying to accommodate to the new regime. On 31 May, a Church leaders' conference endorsed a declaration signed by Marahrens, Wurm, Meiser and others (all Lutheran leaders and bishops) laying down the terms on which they would acquiesce in the Godesberg Declaration. In it the statement retained the important instruction to the Churches: 'to join fully and devotedly in the Führer's national political constructive work ... In the national sphere of life there must be a serious and responsible racial policy of maintaining the purity of the nation.'

So from the beginning of his journey Bonhoeffer was deeply worried about what he was leaving behind. On the day before his landing in New York he records in his diary: 'If only the doubts as to one's own way were overcome.' These doubts were not resolved when he arrived to a generous and affectionate reception in New York.

Misunderstanding in New York

Because of censorship in Germany it was never possible to be totally frank and clear in correspondence. The invitations had been issued with a view to obtaining Bonhoeffer's presence in America and some thought they were rescuing him. There were to be lectures and courses of study which he could conduct, but there was also one offer that could not be mentioned in letters that might be opened. It came from the Federal Council of Churches to employ Bonhoeffer to coordinate work among German refugees in New York and it was to last for three years. This he had not understood, and to the surprise of his hosts he reacted strongly against the notion. If he accepted the post with the 'American Committee for Christian German Refugees in the City of New York', it was obvious that he would never be allowed to return to Germany.

He had come with all his doubts and uncertainties: he wanted to leave Germany, but he did not want to slam all the doors behind him. Once he realised what the well-meaning Americans had planned for him, he had to say quite bluntly: 'My starting point for everything is that I intend to go back in one year. Surprise. But I am quite clear that I must go back.'[6]

For two weeks he fought out his inward conflict, as he sat in the 'prophet's chamber' (the guest room in Union Theological Seminary, where visiting speakers are comfortably housed), in the garden of Dr Coffin's house in Lakeville or in the streets of New York. The problems of his return worried him. He had no news from Germany, he was terribly homesick. The generous Americans provided him with every comfort, but Germany herself was lacking. He chided himself in his diary for being so homesick at his age and after so much overseas travel, but he knew the danger of being cut off permanently. He was not a refugee and he did not want to be rescued! He was deeply moved in American homes by the prayers for the German brethren, but they only made him want to go home and be among them even more. He began to feel the self-reproach of the wrong decision. At last he could bear it no longer and wrote a long letter to Dr Leiper, the Executive Secretary of the Federal Council of Churches, explaining his doubts and asking for a meeting on 20 June.

The Crucial Decision

On the evening before the meeting with Dr Leiper which was to decide his future, he wandered aimlessly round Times Square, wrestling with his lonely feelings. That night in his room he wrote up his diary:[7] 'No news from Germany all day, by any post; waiting in vain. It is no use getting angry . . . I want to know what is happening to the work over there, whether it is all going well or whether I am needed. I want a sign from over there for tomorrow's decisive talk; perhaps it is just as well it has not come.'

It was a difficult meeting. Dr Leiper had worked hard to get money for the refugee work and raised the first thousand dollars. When Bonhoeffer declined, Dr Leiper was disappointed and felt let down, in Bonhoeffer's words, 'perhaps a little upset'. It was not a clear decision and, after he had taken it, he continued to worry about what it really meant. He might still remain in America and lecture for an academic year, but his diary shows with what difficulty he wrestled with matters that never seemed to be crystal clear. He was not one of those who always knew the will of God for him, he had to agonise and decide, never quite sure whether he was right. His entry in the diary describing his visit to Dr Leiper reveals his state of mind at this time:

> It is strange that I am never quite clear about the motives that underlie my decisions. Is that a sign of vagueness, of intellectual dishonesty or a sign that we are led on beyond what we can discern, or is it both? . . . The reason that one gives to others and to oneself for an action are certainly inadequate. We can, in fact, justify anything; but in the last resort we are acting from a plane that is hidden from us; and we can only ask God to judge and forgive us . . . At the end of the day I can only ask that God may judge this day, and all the decisions mercifully.

Bonhoeffer continued to express his uncertainties in his diary, but he gradually came to see that he had to return. The date was not fixed because he still had a lecture course to prepare. Was it homesickness, vanity in thinking that the Confessing Church could not manage without him, a fear of being trapped and never able to get back to his homeland, incompatibility with America (he wrote to his parents that he could hardly bear the atmosphere in New York, 'full of hatred and horribly pharisaical') or some deep-seated inner urge? It was to Reinhard Niebuhr that he gave the clearest explanation:

> I have made a mistake in coming to America. I must live through this difficult period of our national history with the Christian people of Germany. I will have no right to participate in the reconstruction of Christian life in Germany after the war if I do not share the trials of this time with my people . . . Christians in Germany will face the terrible alternative of either willing the defeat of their nation in order that Christian civilisation may survive, or willing the victory of their nation and thereby destroying our civilisation. I know which of these alternatives I must choose; but I cannot make the choice in security![18]

'Do your best to come before winter'

The crucial decision was made. If Paul Lehmann had been in New York at the time he might have dissuaded him, but there were mightier forces at work than Bonhoeffer himself knew. He still had lectures to deliver at the summer school and enjoyed their preparation. His plan was to leave in the autumn, but news from Europe indicated that war would not be long delayed and he grew anxious lest he be trapped in America and the decision to return taken out of his hands. Throughout this period the daily readings, the *Losungen*, prepared every year by the Moravians and used by virtually all German Protestants, constantly guided and rebuked him. On 26 June the *Losung* was taken from 2 Timothy 4:21: 'Do your best to come before winter.' The text followed him around all day. He spoke of feeling like a soldier on leave who is summoned back to fight. It is not a misuse of Scripture, he says, to apply the text to myself, adding, 'May God give me grace to do it.' The news grew more ominous every day. In Danzig, Goebbels had issued threats and it was obvious that Germany would invade Poland before long. Then he heard that his brother had declined a professorship which had been offered to him and was going home on 8 July.

ELEVEN

Sharing the Trials and the Shame

When Bonhoeffer returned to Berlin on 27 July 1939 he had solved nothing. All the problems which led him to consult Bishop Bell, to accept an invitation to America, and to allow his friends to go to endless trouble to arrange a programme for him which would at least temporarily protect him, still remained. He had wasted many people's time and money and embarrassed his friends. He had taken a crucial decision, but it was negative. He had decided to refuse the safety of America. What he had chosen was by no means clear. His reasons for choosing were clearer than what he had chosen!

There was an element of the masochist in him when he allowed his favourite Psalm 119 to speak to him in a convincing way: 'It was good for me that I was afflicted, that I might learn thy statutes.' The puritan in Bonhoeffer rose to that word. It was all part of what Albrecht Schönherr described as 'a sound life'. That openness and integrity could face suffering and learn from it. From the child wanting to die a good death to the *Cost of Discipleship*, the life of Dietrich Bonhoeffer was all of one piece. Then something happened at the time of this American visit. He admitted that he had learnt more about America in that month than he had in a year on his previous visit. Mary Bosanquet, in her *The Life and Death of Dietrich Bonhoeffer* puts the change in somewhat overcharged words, but there is a measure of truth in her dramatic assessment:

> For as Bonhoeffer became more and more deeply enmeshed in the evil of his time, he was driven quietly to accept the loss of that particular personal treasure which he had many times struggled to abandon, but which yet had clung to him, wrapping its powerful tentacles round his inmost being; the sense of his own righteousness.[1]

Paradise Lost

The idea of staying in America was very attractive. Bonhoeffer had friends and he was greatly respected. Those who were trying to further the ecumenical movement saw in him an advocate of considerable strength. Those who agreed with him about the weakness and insularity of American theology saw a role for him. Paul Lehmann, who had written from Elmhurst College to nearly forty different universities and educational establishments commending Bonhoeffer as a speaker, tried to dissuade him from leaving, even at the last moment: 'I do know that it is unthinkable that you should return before America shall have had the fullest opportunity to be enriched by your contribution to its theological hour of destiny,' he wrote. Like many serious Americans he saw much good coming from the refugees who were flooding in from Nazi Germany: 'the widening of the American theological understanding by the cross-fertilisation with the continental tradition.'[2] Paul Tillich had fled to America as early as 1933 and he was already finding space to develop his theological and philosophical work. He was also beginning to attract a following and influence American theology. He was able to do that for many years, until his death at a ripe old age.

Staying in America was a very comfortable option for Bonhoeffer, compared with the majority of exiles. He could live out his calling there – doing theology, writing his *Ethics*, with freedom offered by the ecumenical institutions which welcomed him. Back in Germany, he was evidently an embarrassment to the Confessing Church. He could not have been blamed for seeking self-fulfilment where he was wanted instead of returning to where people found his frightening appeals and actions uncomfortable.

Had he stayed, he might have lived still, enjoying his eighties as a respected theologian with a whole library of books to his credit – to say nothing of innumerable honorary doctorates! But he did not.

The Loss of Righteousness

Instead of this clear and secure position, with an appointment which would enable him to help German refugees and play his part in educating America to the real situation in Germany, he abandoned security and righteousness for a devious life in a dangerous homeland. A little of the deviousness comes out already in his reaction to Paul Lehmann's friendly efforts. In his letters seeking invitations for Bonhoeffer to the universities Paul had included a sentence which was hardly diplomatic. In the part of the letter where he was giving personal details he said that since Finkenwalde had been closed by the authorities, Bonhoeffer's teaching activities had been going on privately in Pomerania. When Bonhoeffer learnt of this he insisted that Lehmann write another letter to all of them correcting it. Greatly embarrassed, Paul Lehmann had to write that he had misunderstood the situation and that Bonhoeffer had already returned to Germany.

But far worse still was to come. Bonhoeffer was inevitably becoming involved in the conspiracy. Little by little this Christian man became completely a man of his time. His involvement in the conspiracy would require the abandoning of much that Christian life demands – expert lying built up gradually into closely woven deception, and ultimately the willingness to kill. Not for a moment did he regard these evils as anything more than they were ? evil. But he saw them as necessary. The awful road that he had chosen must have seemed at times like the road to hell rather than to paradise regained. His own words, written a few years later from prison, express what he had chosen without fully knowing it at the time:

> We have been silent witnesses of evil deeds; we have been drenched by many storms; we learnt the art of equivocation and pretence; experience has made us suspicious of others and kept us from being truthful and open; intolerable conflicts have worn us down and even made us cynical. Are we still of any use?[3]

That was the road ahead.

Germany at War

Before Bonhoeffer reached Berlin, it was obvious to everyone that Germany was heading for war. He therefore stopped briefly in Britain to say goodbye to relatives and friends and there he learnt of Paul Schneider's death with great sorrow. He spent ten days in London with his sister and Franz Hildebrandt. There was no time to see Bishop Bell, but he wrote before he left London: 'My passport expires next spring; it is uncertain when I shall be in this country again . . . We shall never forget you during the coming events. '[4]

Reinhold Niebuhr was still active on his behalf. He persuaded John Baillie to invite Bonhoeffer to give the Croall Lectures in Edinburgh and Bonhoeffer accepted for the winter of 1939–40. He later wrote from Berlin giving as the theme for the lectures, 'Death in the Christian Message'.

A few days later, on 1 September, Germany invaded Poland and from 11 a.m. on 3 September a state of war existed between Britain and Germany.

Bonhoeffer seems to have expected more action after the declaration of war, but after Poland there followed a lull, what we came to call in Britain 'the phoney war'. For him there was an early tragedy. Theodor Maass, a former student at Finkenwalde, was killed in action. Bonhoeffer had taken up again his work of caring for the younger theologians and he wrote copious circular letters to them, giving news to keep them in touch with each other, raising theological issues for discussion and trying to encourage them in their preaching. In one such letter on 20 September he gave them news of their first casualty:

I have received the news, which I pass on to you today, that our dear brother, Theodor Maass, was killed in Poland 3 September. You will be as stunned by this news as I was. But I beg you let us thank God in remembrance of him. He was a good brother, a quiet, faithful pastor of the Confessing Church, a man who lived from word and sacrament, whom God has also thought worthy to suffer for the Gospel. I am sure that he was prepared to go. Where God tears great gaps we should not try to fill them with human words.[5]

He then in a very practical note added the address of Theodor's parents in Stralsund. This contact with the former students became an important task for Bonhoeffer.

The Last Things and the Things before the Last

The material for his Croall Lectures, which of course could not be given in Edinburgh, was written into the draft for his book, *Ethics*. The book was never finished, but two sections of the draft deal with 'death'.[6] He first attacks the 'idolisation' of death: 'The miracle of Christ's resurrection makes nonsense of the idolisation of death which is prevalent among us today.' He is referring to the Nazi philosophy and the popular support for Germany on the brink of war when he roundly condemns the idea of building for eternity, or the big talk of a new man, a new world or a new society – 'all that is new is the destruction of life as we have it'. This section is embodied in a part which deals with ethics as 'formation'.

Bonhoeffer prefers the word 'conformation' which, he writes, is achieved 'only when the form of Jesus Christ itself works upon us in such a manner that it moulds our form in its own likeness'. The full implication of this comes out when he adds a little later:

It is not Christian men who shape the world with their ideas, but it is Christ who shapes men in conformity with himself. To be conformed with the Incarnate – that is to be a real man. It is man's right and duty that he should be man. The quest for the superman, the endeavour to outgrow the man within the man, the pursuit of the heroic, the cult of the demi-god, all this is not the proper concern of man, because it is untrue.

At the end of this part of the book he adds:

What Christ does is precisely to give effect to reality. He affirms reality. And indeed he is himself the real man and consequently the foundation of all human reality. And so formation in conformation with Christ has this double implication. The form of Christ remains one and the same, not as a general idea but in its own unique character as the incarnate, crucified and risen God.

> And precisely for the sake of Christ's form the form of the real man is preserved, and in this way the real man receives the form of Christ.

With this powerful theological foundation there is no place for *theoretical* ethics. Human ethics must be concrete. This is the equivalent of Bonhoeffer's early statement to the ecumenical conference, when he said the Church should command in its utterance of the Word of God – not some abstract, 'War is wrong', 'But to participate in *this* war is wrong', not what is good or ill, once for all in eternal principles, but Christ taking form here and now and judging. When in a long section called, 'The Last Things and the Things before the Last',[7] he opens with 'Justification as the Last Word' and develops the concept of grace which justifies, as 'The Penultimate' he is not afraid to tackle the question of suicide head on. One of the most carefully reasoned passages in the book is headed 'Suicide'. Bonhoeffer has already asserted the 'right to bodily life'. This right is an innate right:

> Since it is God's will that there should be human life on earth only in bodily form, it follows that it is for the sake of the whole man that the body is to be preserved. And since all rights are extinguished at death it follows that the preservation of the life of the body is the foundation of all natural rights . . . the body does not exist in order that it might be sacrificed, it exists to be preserved, enjoyed.

In fact, he recognises the exalted right or duty to sacrifice one's life, but this must be seen in the light of a fundamental right to conserve the body. What then of suicide? Is it a despising of the bodily life? 'Man, unlike the beasts, does not carry his life as a compulsion which he cannot throw off.'

Bonhoeffer argues that he is either free to accept his life or destroy it. In this liberty to die man is given a unique freedom. He can avoid defeat and rob fate of its victory. The stoic argument for suicide is put clearly. But this does not mean that he approves of suicide, only that we may not arraign the suicide before the court of morality. Neither may we call it cowardice: 'If this action is performed in freedom it is raised high above any petty moralising accusation of cowardice or weakness.'

But for a Christian it can be arraigned before the court of God – it is not immoral, unethical, but it is a lack of faith. A man may give his life for his friend. That too is suicide. But when it is not a sacrifice, it is a refusal to believe that God is able yet to do something with what remains of life. He shows convincingly that a purely moral judgement on suicide is impossible: 'The right to suicide is nullified only by the living God.'

There is much more in *Ethics* to show that Bonhoeffer was at this time working on material that he might have delivered in the Croall Lectures.

More importantly, it shows that he was coming face to face with death once again as Germany plunged into war and his students were facing death day by day.

In the letter in which he tells of the death of Theodor Maass he lists the students serving at the front and writes of death: 'Death has again come among us, and we must think about it whether we want to or not.'

So long as he could operate from Köslin or Sigurdshof, Bonhoeffer was completely absorbed in his theology and the care of his students. In the loneliness of rural Pomerania he was fighting a battle of tremendous significance for the soul of Germany. The war in Poland interrupted the work for a while, although Bonhoeffer did not cease to write and keep close contact with all his students, past and present. That war was soon over and students were back in Köslin and Sigurdshof. The early confusions of the war left the Confessing Church in some disarray. It had been rumoured that Martin Niemöller had volunteered for military service from his prison. It was never fully established whether he did or not, but it was the kind of rumour circulated to encourage the tendency to rally together and forget differences in time of war. This put new strains on the Confessing Church and made Bonhoeffer more adamant in his insistence that Church could have no dealing with no-Church. There were also fears for Niemöller's life and those who were arrested for illegal gatherings heard with alarm of the death of Paul Schneider in prison.

Bonhoeffer began the circulation of theological papers to help his students preach more effectively at the various seasons of the year. He began with Christmas and a memorable opening: 'No priest, no theologian stood at the cradle in Bethlehem. And yet, all Christian theology has its origin in the wonder of all wonders that God became man. Alongside the brilliance of holy night there burns the fire of the unfathomable mystery of Christian theology.'

It is a theological paper, ancient thoughts and not original, what he calls minute fragments from the edifice of the Church's Christology. He says that he has written it not for them to admire the building, but that they might be led by one thought or another 'to read and to consider more reverently and more prayerfully the biblical witness of the mystery of the Incarnation of God, and perhaps also to sing Luther's Christmas hymns more thoughtfully and more joyfully.'

Shortly afterwards he develops similar thoughts to help his young ordinands to preach during the Epiphany season.[8] He was binding them closely to the Christian year and strengthening their Lutheran theology.

These theological papers were added as supplements to the circular letters and were sent monthly to the Brethren of the Confessing Church of Pomerania. The February letter raised a controversy. It was concerned with the *Abendmahl* (Eucharist or Lord's Supper). He had interpreted Luther and a protest came from Eberhard Baumann of the Reformed Church. The Confessing Church of Pomerania included both Lutheran and Reformed. Bonhoeffer refused to write a paper which would offend no one if that meant he could not clearly define the Lutheran position and express his own theological convictions. He was never obscure and only by obscurity can differences be covered up. The controversy raged, as it had in the days of the Reformation, but it did not divide the Confessing Church. Instead, it stimulated its theological awareness. Considering the role the Reformed Church had played in the epic Church struggle since Barmen in 1934, when the Confession was issued from a Reformed Church, it was not surprising that an attack on the Reformed attitude to the Lord's Supper met with protest.

Eberhard Baumann wrote from Stettin on 12 March to Superintendent Onnasch of Köslin, protesting against what he called Bonhoeffer's 'so-called greeting' to the Confessing Church. He feared for the future of the Protestant Church in Germany, he said, if this kind of controversy was to be encouraged in the name of 'brotherly greetings'. They were soon reconciled when Bonhoeffer explained that he was trying to make the Church aware of the importance of theological discussion. He would have no feeble Confessing Church, unable to express one or other tradition or pretending all to believe the same when there were profound differences among them. Not to express this clearly would be to erode truth. It was not the last time that Bonhoeffer was to cause controversy. He sought no monolithic structure of doctrine, but robust discussion of theological issues. Long before his time in the ecumenical movement he was urging those of different traditions to face squarely the consequences of baptism, eucharist and ministry in their faith and order.

Subsequent theological papers dealt with the Resurrection and the Ascension, but then something happened that changed his work, although it did not alter his absorption in theology. The last centre for a collective pastorate, Sigurdshof, was closed on 17 March by order of the Gestapo. The students had already left. Since the closing of Finkenwalde in 1937, Bonhoeffer had been a nomad, with no fixed abode and no desk or study he could call his own. He had oscillated between Köslin and Schlawe, so long as they were centres of the collective pastorates, then Sigurdshof (the last refuge to close) and Berlin. All now had to be done by correspondence and personal visits. He held his community of students together with news and theological papers, one vast pastoral and theological correspondence course.

Pastors on Military Service

His pastoral concern for the brethren had led him to see that under the conditions of military service another discipline applies. The young men of the Confessing Church were not chaplains and he urged them to accept their role as 'a soldier among soldiers'. In May 1940 he had received at home in Berlin 'words of thanks, greetings and long letters'. He set about answering them all, with a circular letter.[9] This letter is mostly addressed to those serving in the armed forces and at the end he apologises to those who are still struggling in their home ministry for his apparent neglect. But he is concerned primarily with the experience of those who have no preparation for the kind of ministry they are now expected to exercise. Where does the 'Cost of Discipleship' come in on the Polish front? Some had written saying that they cannot exercise their ministry and fear that they are untrue to their ordination, when all they can hope for is to be a 'soldier among soldiers'. Bonhoeffer wrestles with this problem. He has a high view of ordination, but he writes to them:

> I don't know now whether it is quite right to keep telling you that even at the front you are still 'in the ministry'. Certainly, none of us is ever released from the responsibility of being a Christian and no one may deny that he is a pastor. But isn't that rather different from saying so obviously that even at the front one is 'in the ministry'? In my view, you are not, and in that position you really cannot be.

Bonhoeffer is very aware of the peculiar burdens put upon his students, who feel that their indelible ordination imposes a commitment upon them. He warns against enthusiasm, talks of ordination as 'a grace and comfort for us, to make us certain of our ministry. It is not meant to trouble us.' The letter is very practical, urging them to write home rather than long letters to him, although he values these letters. He advises the more enthusiastic among them to be soldiers and discover what the Christian vocation means as soldiers. He deals sympathetically with their queries and problems, then turns them towards the work God is doing: saying, 'Let's look at his grace, which has preserved us so far through many dark hours . . . Let's look at his faithfulness, which has always been constant. God has begun with us and our Church and he will also carry things through to the end, so that all will be well for everyone.'

He sends to them his Meditation texts for the month, recommends the new Stuttgart Jubilee Bible, whose notes are particularly valuable on the Old Testament, bids them pray for one another. Dealing with the peculiar problems of wartime, he sees a great advantage, despite all the dangers and difficulties, of being able to share the lot of most Christians. This lesson learnt from his students was the germ of Bonhoeffer's 'secular holiness' of later letters.

I can well remember meeting a Baptist pastor in Hanover after the war whose church had been bombed and congregation scattered. I went to help him and express my sorrow. I found a man radiant with faith, saying, 'At last I am free – free to be a minister of Jesus Christ. I am no longer trammelled by church programmes.' These students at the front were experiencing, or could now experience, something of this liberation.

Interference and Protest

Relations between the state and the Confessing Church began to improve as Hitler's war proceeded successfully. In 1940, although there were some interferences and a few pastors of the Confessing Church were deprived of their livings, the intercession list grew shorter, fewer were in prison. Hitler, through the Ministry of Information, had given instructions not to interfere with the Church unless absolutely necessary. In wartime a country does not want internal squabbles. But there were still some serious interferences. An interesting letter of protest is preserved from one of Bonhoeffer's students, to the Disciplinary Board of the Brandenburg Consistory, dated 30 May 1940:

> As a front-line soldier who has to risk his life every day and is therefore used to speaking frankly, I must tell you plainly, gentlemen, what anger and disgust I feel at your conduct. Men whose merits and patriotism cannot be seriously doubted are to be hunted down while most of their friends are engaged in defence of the Fatherland and are therefore in no position to make effective protest . . . Like innumerable front-line soldiers, I am entirely on the side of the condemned pastors in this matter. With the 'judgement' that you gentlemen have now delivered from the security of your baize-topped tables, you have for one thing included me in your impudent and insulting challenge. You may as well be clear that by your decision you have wantonly injured the morale of countless soldiers . . . However helpless it may be, the Confessing Church is more confident and more certain than you in your unspiritual position of power.[10]

That young ordinand or pastor of the Confessing Church must have enjoyed writing to the officials of the National Church (German Christian) in this way. He was learning the attraction of being a 'soldier among soldiers'. The protest concerned the action taken by the Consistory through its Disciplinary Board in April and May against members of the Council of Brethren (Confessing Church) and in particular Albertz and Böhm. The letter of protest was written from the Belgian front.

But these were not the only interferences. Bonhoeffer was forbidden to speak in public on 4 September 1940 and this was bound up with the requirement of reporting to the police wherever he was living. In the following year, 27 March 1941, he was forbidden to print or publish any of his writings. There had long been a measure to prevent him from circulating his theological papers to his students at the front.

The Councils of Brethren of the Confessing Church were also greatly hindered in their work by the number who were called up.

Bonhoeffer's Protest

It was clear that Bonhoeffer was going to be silenced and that every effort would be made to render him useless to the Confessing Church. Meanwhile, rumours were coming through to him that 'euthanasia' was being practised on a wide scale and that Jews were being deported for elimination. In this situation he became more and more involved with the conspiracy against Hitler. His main informant, protector and confidant was his brother-in-law, Hans von Dohnanyi. Bonhoeffer had international contacts in neutral countries and could be used to convey information as a courier if he was officially registered as one who could serve the cause of Germany in the propaganda war.

In June 1940 Bonhoeffer was travelling in Königsberg, Danzig and on 17 June in Memel. He and Bethge were together at a small pastors' conference in the morning with Dr Werner Wiesner and had the afternoon free before an evening service. They took the ferry boat out to the peninsula, passed submarines, tugs, and mine-sweepers. The air was full of great events. Stalin had delivered an ultimatum to the Baltic States which, thanks to Hitler's non-aggression pact, he could take with ease. Germany cared little for this, because all attention was focussed on the war in France. While they were enjoying the sun in an open-air café, the loud speaker blared out a fanfare and then news of the surrender of France. There was great excitement and jubilation. Bonhoeffer raised his arm with the rest to give the regulation Nazi salute, while Bethge hardly knew what to do. Then he heard Bonhoeffer whispering to him: 'Put up your arm you fool! This thing is not worth dying for.' Bonhoeffer was not prepared to run risks for a mere salute.

About the same time that ghastly episode of transportation of Jews began, and of all places – from Stettin. Throughout much of July Bonhoeffer travelled. A brief message reads: 'I go today to Danzig, then to Frau von Kleist and should be in Berlin for Monday and Tuesday, where I must talk with Hans . . .'

He had fallen foul of the Gestapo and he needed the protection of Hans von Dohnanyi. A study conference which he had arranged for former students at Blöstau was dissolved on 14 July and Bonhoeffer protested. It seems to have been in connection with this that he was later, in September, forbidden to speak in public and required to report regularly to the police. With these clouds gathering around him, he spoke to Hans von Dohnanyi and General Hans Oster about the possibility of extra-parochial work with the Abwehr. His years of conspiracy were about to begin. Bonhoeffer had protested against the injustice of prohibitions. He addressed his letter to the Minister of National Security in Berlin.[11] It began with indignation that so loyal a patriot could be suspected of breaching security:

> On 9 September 1940, the State Police Headquarters at Köslin informed me of the National Security Office Order (IV A 4g 776/40) by which I am prohibited from speaking in public within the territory of the Reich. The reason given is 'disruptive activity'. I reject this charge. I am proud to belong to a family which for generations has earned the gratitude of the German people and state. Among my ancestors are Field Marshal Count Kalckreuth and the two great German painters of the same name, the Church historian Karl von Hase of Jena, well known throughout the academic world of the last century; and the Cauer family, the sculptors. Lieutenant General Count von der Golz, who liberated the Baltic is my uncle, and his son, Councillor Rüdiger, Count von der Golz, is my first cousin. Lieutenant General von Hase who is on active service, is also my uncle. For almost thirty years my father has been Ordinarius Professor of Medicine in Berlin and still holds distinguished public appointments; for centuries his ancestors have been highly respected craftsmen and councillors of the free city of Schwabisch-Hall, and their portraits are still proudly displayed in the city church there. My brothers and brothers-in-law have senior public appointments; one of my brothers was killed in the World War. It has been the concern of all these men and their families to serve the German state at all time, and to risk their lives in its service. In deliberate affirmation of this spiritual heritage and this inward attitude of my family, I cannot accept the charge of 'disruptive activity'. Any conduct which could be described by this charge is alien to my nature.

That was the main basis of his protest. He 'pulled rank', knowing that those who read this letter were lesser men. But he was also meeting the charge that the Confessing Church consisted of a group of rebel pastors. He represented the Church, the academic world and the leaders of military and civil life. It was an extraordinary opening to a letter of protest! He defined his work in the collective pastorates as fully within the meaning of the vocation of the pastor of a German Evangelical Church. He did not use the term Confessing Church. But he did describe the occasion which appears to have caused offence:

> On the occasion of a stay in East Prussia, I was invited to lead a Bible study and to give a lecture for a small meeting at Königsberg of students from different faculties. Three or four students met at Blöstau, near Königsberg, on

July 13 1940, and there were about as many members of the congregation. In the afternoon, I led a Bible study, followed by a short talk about the story of the rich young ruler (he appended an outline of his Bible study). On the Sunday morning I conducted worship for the Blöstau congregation and preached on the Gospel for the day. After the service I was sitting and talking with three or four students when a considerable number of officials of the secret police appeared and told us that we must stop. Our attention was drawn to an order of the end of June 1940 which none of us knew about because it had never been published, and which was not even produced for us despite our constant requests.

He pointed out that the officials were quite polite and said there was nothing to worry about and that they would not have bothered if they had known how small the meeting was. It looked as though an informer had sent the secret police, because this was supposed to be a 'confessional meeting'. He concluded by asking the meaning of this restriction on 'confessional activity'. Was he, for example, forbidden to explain the teaching of Luther on some aspect of Christian doctrine to a small group- He ended the letter with the regulation, Heil Hitler!

He received no answer. He had now to make up his mind about his future activities.

A Time to Think

The news of the surrender of France which Bonhoeffer heard on 17 June at Memel forced him to rethink his whole attitude to the 'unrighteous state'. Eberhard Bethge comments on that event that, 'It was then that Bonhoeffer's double life began, namely the pastor's engagement in the political underground movement'. Then he lost his 'righteousness'.

We may interpret this in various ways. Bonhoeffer knew of the seriousness of the change and, looking back, saw that it disqualified him from taking up his ministry later. It was a psychological change which affected all Germany. Since the rise of Prussia almost a century earlier, the two contenders for the dominance of continental Europe were Germany and France. The Franco-Prussian war lived in every German memory as Waterloo did in every British memory. In fact, even Waterloo was part of it, as I discovered when talking of the fall of Napoleon in Germany. They had never heard of Wellington and looked upon the victory as a German one. The humiliation of the First World War had been felt by every patriotic German, including the young Dietrich. The harsh terms of the Versailles Treaty were thought to be the work of France where they were written, and the author to be Clemenceau. When Germany could not meet the reparations without starving her people, France had occupied the

Rhineland. Now, the surrender of France to Germany. This was a turning point.

Wilhelm Niesel remembers that, shortly after these events, he was attending a meeting of the Council of Brethren of the Confessing Church of the Old Prussian Union when Bonhoeffer 'breezed in. To our utter amazement he made a speech telling us we had to change our attitude towards Hitler; events had proved that God was with him and we had to recognise it.'

Eberhard Bethge sprang to Bonhoeffer's defence and said that Niesel had misunderstood what he said:

> A capitulation of Bonhoeffer, even for a second, is out of the question. Something quite different happened to him. He wanted to make clear the significance and relevance of the fact that a successful tyranny was apparently going to last longer than they had all thought ... Bonhoeffer saw sorrowfully but clearly that there would never again be just a return to what had once been ... the road to something new would be far costlier and lengthier than they had assumed, and the shape of the goal was yet unknown.[12]

That does not completely alter Wilhelm Niesel's reading of what Bonhoeffer said, but it does put it in a wider context. The conspirators with whom Bonhoeffer was already in touch had expected Hitler to overstretch himself. At Munich they waited in 1938 for the failure which would be the signal for Hitler's arrest and his arraignment before a moral court. When he invaded the rest of Czechoslovakia, they expected a declaration of war and were ready for his defeat. In defeat he would be overthrown and a different government established. The war in Poland was sufficiently remote from the west to make it safe for him, but when France and Britain declared war, they were again ready for his defeat. The fall of Paris was the end of that way of thinking. They were talking of assassination now.

If Bonhoeffer was to undertake assignments for the Abwehr (a blend of MI5 and counter-espionage, closely in touch with the armed forces) he would have to appear as a double agent. He must support Hitler openly and subvert his regime among the neutral countries. He must also do what he could in such an official position to help the Jews.

The Theological Implications of Hitler's Success

Even as a conspirator, Bonhoeffer could not cease to be a theologian and the course he was about to embark upon was in need of theological undergirding. While he was making up his mind about the extent to which he could accept a position on the Abwehr, he went to the estate of Frau von Kleist in Klein-Kössin and spent four weeks working on his *Ethics*. There is a very important chapter in that book which Bethge says he worked on at this point. It is the treatment of 'Success'.[13]

In a passage which describes the current reaction in Germany to Hitler's success against all odds, and which might well have been relevant at the Nuremberg Trials of the defeated, he writes of the successful man: 'The world will allow itself to be subdued only by success. It is not ideas or opinions that decide but deeds. Success justifies wrongs done. Success heals the wounds of guilt . . . The successful man presents us with accomplished facts which can never again be reversed.'

That sounds a little like what Wilhelm Niesel heard at the Council of Brethren in the house of Pastor Hasse in Nowawes, from the lips of Bonhoeffer. No doubt discussions of this view with Frau von Kleist, and even his future fiancée who lived not far away, led him to analyse various reactions to the facts. He saw three possible attitudes which may be adopted towards the facts of the successful man:

a) the majority give way to the idolisation of success.

b) when the wounds of guilt are healed, then success is simply identified with good. 'This attitude is genuine and pardonable only in a state of intoxication.'

c) the continuance of success is then assured by the proposition that 'only good is successful'.

Bonhoeffer continues with this third attitude in a way that shows its attraction for him, if only briefly:

> The competence of the critical faculty to judge success is reaffirmed. Now right remains right and wrong remains wrong. Now one no longer closes one's eyes to the crucial moment and opens them only after the deed is done. And now there is a conscious or unconscious recognition of a law of the world, a law which makes right, truth and order more stable in the long run than violence, falsehood and self-will.

But he concludes that this optimistic thesis is misleading. Either the historical facts have to be falsified to establish it in order to prove that evil has not been successful, or conversely that success is identified with good. He rejects pharisaical criticisms of the past that complain that all success comes from wickedness, and insists that the Crucified invalidates all thought which takes success for its standard.

> Christ confronts all thinking in terms of success and failure with the man who is under God's sentences, no matter whether he be successful or unsuccessful. It is out of pure love that God is willing to let man stand before Him. In the

cross of Christ God confronts the successful man with the sanctification of pain, sorrow, humility, failure, poverty, loneliness and despair (this list is no rhetorical flourish – it is Bonhoeffer in those lonely days of decision). This does not mean that all this has value in itself, but it receives its sanctification from the love of God ... But the unsuccessful man must recognise that what enables him to stand before God is not his lack of success as such, nor his position as a pariah, but solely the willing acceptance of the sentence passed upon him by the divine love.

The Benedictine Abbey of Ettal

By November 1940, Bonhoeffer had ended his travelling between Klein-Kössin and Munich. His mind had been made up and he accepted a place in the Abwehr. That kept him safe from military call-up and arrest. But he was not immediately thrown into a field of espionage. He found a home with the Benedictines at the Abbey of Ettal in Bavaria. The headquarters of the Abwehr were in Munich. His prolific correspondence with Bethge during this period helps us to follow the movements of his mind.

He visited the abbey for the first time to make arrangements on 31 October. A few days later he writes from a hotel in Munich, envying Bethge's parish work, especially his preparations for Bible Week, 'A pity we can't prepare it together once again.' That letter tells of contacts that he is making and of the way in which he finds it easier to work with the Catholics than the Lutherans! He also reports on the hindrances put in the way of Church activities (remarkably similar to what the Russians imposed after the war in their East Zone!); a ban on bookstalls in the churches; pre-military training on Sundays, 8–11 a.m.; after an air-raid, no service before 10 a.m., no bells before 1 p.m. In the same letter he talks of a holiday at Christmas with Bethge and the unexpected luck of finding a 200 mark note in his pocket. He writes of seeing his publisher, then a few days later of a visit to Berlin and then to Jena to see Wolfgang Staemmler, a man whom he had greatly admired when he discovered how close they were in their view of the need for discipline and sacrifice in preparation for the ministry. At the time of this visit, Staemmler was chairman of the Council of Brethren, holding the Confessing Church of Saxony together, but within a few days of Bonhoeffer's visit he was arrested, for speaking out too boldly. Bonhoeffer had some important decisions to take which he needed to discuss with Staemmler, whom he completely trusted. He just had time before the provost was put in prison for a year.

Writing on the train back to Munich, what he calls an illegible letter to Bethge, he describes that visit:

The visit to Staemmler was very good. He began by telling me how well you had put my case in a touching and friendly way, so that they now all have a bad conscience about me. I certainly didn't intend that, but thank you for setting things rolling. They have decided that I can continue as head of the training centre of the Confessing Church and keep myself in readiness for that. Meanwhile I am to continue my academic work. Staemmler was very sceptical about a pastorate . . . So for the moment I am free . . . What shall I do now?[14]

In that letter he discusses where he should live over the next four or five months of waiting. Naturally he says nothing about the Abwehr, but as it turned out he had no engagement from there until the following February. In the same letter there is an interesting section on 'The Catholic Question' in which he points out that Lutheran and Reformed had managed to get together in the Confessing Church, despite considerable differences in theology.

We have managed to work together on the basis of two things: the guidance of God (Union, Confessing Church) and the recognition of what is given objectively in the sacraments: Christ is more important than our thoughts about him and his presence. Both are theologically questionable bases for unity ... and yet the Church decided in faith for eucharistic communion. Would not these two things also be possible with respect to the Catholic Church?[15]

He points out that over the eucharist it will be easier for the Lutherans to understand the Catholic point of view than it was for them to accept the Reformed view.

He does not answer all his questions, but he has clearly pondered the two earlier unions and their evident success. In 1817, the Churches of the Old Prussian Union had joined Lutheran and Reformed in what is still called *Unierte* (United), and more recently the Confessing Church had taken both Lutheran and Reformed into its Church, united by the guidance of God and the eucharist. It had not been easy and Bonhoeffer himself had maintained the right of division over the Eucharist as we have seen. Clearly his visit to Ettal had set him thinking about the Catholic Church and a prospective stay of several months at the abbey there made the issue a live one.

He arrived in Ettal on 17 November and wrote to Bethge next day: 'I've been here since yesterday – a most friendly welcome; eat in the refectory, sleep at the hotel, can use the library, have my own key to the cloister, had a good long chat with the abbot yesterday, in short, everything that one could want. All I need is the desk! Many changes have taken place in my attitude to Catholics over the last six years.[16]

Apart from the new contacts he made with Catholic organisations, he was able to compare the value of this community life at Ettal with what he had seen in England and tried to put into practice at Finkenwalde. Writing to his parents he says of the monastic life:

> This sort of life isn't strange to me, and I find the regularity and silence conducive to work. It would indeed be a loss (and it certainly was a loss at the Reformation) if this form of common life, which has been preserved for fifteen hundred years, should be destroyed, as is thought possible here. I think that a great deal of friction, which must inevitably be felt in such a close life together, is avoided through stern discipline. This provides a very sound basis for work.[17]

He found some things strange – the reading of historical material at lunch and supper in the singing tone of the liturgy! He had tried straight reading during meals at Finkenwalde, but never attempted to intone the material. Bonhoeffer approved of the food!

Inevitably his attitude to the Catholics changed while he was at Ettal. Writing to Bethge he envies his busy life, but does not complain, or tries not, about his own inactivity, which for some he admits would be 'a foretaste of paradise!' To illustrate this paradise and his growing awareness of the value of the Catholic Church he adds:

> I've just come from a quite marvellous mass. With *Schott* in one's hand one can still pray a great deal and be utterly affirmative. It's not simply idolatry, even if I find the way from our own sacrifice for God to God's sacrifice for us, with which the mass is concerned, a hard and apparently perverse one. But I must learn to understand it better. I'm still a guest. The ordered life suits me very well, and I'm surprised at the similarity to much of what we tried to do of our own accord at the seminary. Moreover, the abbot and a number of the fathers have read *Life Together*! We're going to have a discussion soon. The natural hospitality, which is evidently specifically Benedictine, the really Christian respect for strangers for Christ's sake, almost makes one ashamed.[18]

He continually urges Bethge to visit him at Ettal.

The Advent Sermon

Bonhoeffer could not let Advent pass without preaching, but that was forbidden. He therefore wrote what he called *A Meditation for Christmas in the form of a Sermon.*[19] His text was: 'To us a child is born . . .' (Isa. 9:6,7).

His opening words echoed the state of Germany as well as Judea in the time of Isaiah:

Amidst the calamitous words and signs, which the divine anger and a terrible punishment announces to a fallen people whose end is near, amidst the deepest guilt and distress of the people of God, a voice speaks, softly and mysteriously, but with a sacred assurance, of redemption by the birth of a divine child. It will not be fulfilled for 700 years, but the prophet is so deeply steeped in the thoughts of God and his decisions that he speaks of the future as though it were already here. He talks of the hour of redemption as though he stood already in worship before the manger: 'To us a child is born'. What will happen is in the eyes of God already real and certain.

As he expounds the two familiar verses in Isaiah, he marvels that God's redemption is not by power, nor by might, not by wisdom or clever strategy, but in a helpless child. The titles given to the child are too heavy for the shoulders of a Hercules, but not for the divine child. As he waxes lyrical, we hear the strains of Hitler's thousand years Reich shattered like Wagner's *Twilight of the Gods*. We also catch glimpses of Bonhoeffer's uncertainties about the machinations of the Abwehr. We might also catch the sound of a Church which needs to be judged and repent before God can use it for his purpose. The sermon closes with words whose meaning is advanced by the conditions of the time – and yet they are timeless. This is his last Advent sermon:

> With justice and with righteousness, Jesus governs his kingdom. The congregation of believers does not escape his judgement. No, the strictest judgements are on them. They acknowledge themselves to be his Church in that they do not fly from his judgement, but bow before it. Only when Jesus condemns the sinner can he give a new righteousness. His kingdom shall be a kingdom of righteousness, not self-righteousness, but God-given righteousness, established only by the judgement of sin. Right is stronger when it rests upon justice and righteousness. The endurance of this kingdom will be based upon the fact that wrong will not go unpunished in it. A kingdom of peace and righteousness, the unfulfilled longing of the human race, breaks through with the birth of the divine child. We are called to this kingdom. We can find it when we receive the sacraments of the Lord Jesus, in the church, in the congregation of believers. We find it when we accept his Lordship, when we recognise our Saviour and Redeemer in the child in the manger and when we let him give to us a new life in love. From this time forth – that is from the birth of Jesus – and forever more this kingdom will last. Who defends it that it is not shattered and destroyed like all other kingdoms by the storms of world history? The zeal of the Lord of hosts will do this. The holy zeal of God himself will guarantee that this kingdom will remain for ever. When it comes to its ultimate fulfilment, it will have overcome all human guilt, all the attacks of human pride. Whether we are

there or not it will come to pass. God himself carried through his plan to its conclusion, with us or against us. But he wants us to be with him, not for his sake, but for ours. God with us – Immanuel – Jesus – that is the secret of this Holy Night. We rejoice: 'To us a child is given, to us a child is born'.

I believe in Jesus Christ, born truly man from the Virgin Mary, and also born in eternity, truly God from the Father. He is Lord!

At Ettal, he continued to work on his *Ethics*, wrestling also with the possibility of a different title: 'Preparing the Way and Entering upon it', corresponding to the two parts of the book - the things before the last and the last things.

It was a strange life that he was living, although of course he kept in touch with friends in Munich and visited Berlin. He seemed to be away from the real battle. He wrote constantly to Bethge and worked hard at his book. Once he had an assignment from the Abwehr he was happier, but that was not until February and in the nature of things he could not talk too much about it. While some of his students were dying at the front and others were imprisoned or suffering various persecutions, he seemed to be ideally settled, able to concentrate on his work as rarely ever before, able to visit Berlin and indulge in his music, playing quartets with his friends. Several were anxious about him, wondering why he was not in the thick of it. Even those who knew about his work with the Abwehr wondered if it were more than an excuse for keeping him safe.

His letters in the early days of 1941 showed that he was himself worried about this. But by the end of February, activity started along with a quite new kind of life. He would be in the centre, where active resistance to the unrighteous state was possible. To use his own simile of the mad driver, he was now able to 'put a spoke in the wheel'.

The Meaning of the Change

Events had changed a man of peace, an admirer of Gandhi, an advocate of the condemnation of war, some would say a pacifist, into a man deeply involved in the resistance and prepared to collaborate in plans to assassinate Hitler. Many have been troubled by this change. Before we can describe it in the next chapter, let me close this with a quotation from Willem A. Visser't Hooft,[20] the architect of the World Council of Churches. He acknowledges that 'One of the most difficult decisions in Bonhoeffer's life was whether he should actively engage in the resistance against National Socialism and in the preparation of a *coup d'état*.' Such action was contrary to all his upbringing and his Lutheran theology, but when he saw that there would be a war, he knew that he could not deny what he had said about 'concrete discipline'. He was not the man to stop halfway in his action.

172

To reject the political system of that time in theory, to reject it by withdrawing into a spiritual realm, was not enough for him. Such an attitude was schizophrenia, it meant that the challenge was not taken seriously, it meant just talk not action. That in the first instance the Church fought for its own preservation filled him with sorrow. In a situation where millions of people were threatened in their very existence, it was not a question of saving the Church. But it was mankind that had to be saved. The very conviction which had made him a man of peace, led him into resistance.

Visser't Hooft quotes three sentences from different periods in this time of resistance which sum up Bonhoeffer's mind as he enters upon it:

> 'If we claim to be Christians, there is no room for expediency';
> 'Our action must be understood as an act of penitence';
> 'Only in defeat can we atone for the terrible crimes we have committed against Europe and the world.'

TWELVE

The Abwehr

Probably the best translation of the word 'Abwehr' when used as the name for that strangely official and yet subversive organisation to which Bonhoeffer was now attached is 'counter-intelligence' – but that tells you very little about it. The staff of Abwehr was a group of senior military men with civilian advisers in all fields of German life. They had extraordinary powers and they concealed from the highest authority in the land their continuing efforts to overthrow Hitler and the National Socialists. They had access to information which was denied to high ranking officials and they were expected to gather information and disseminate it. Many of their activities come under the heading of espionage. A person assigned to their staff might travel abroad to learn what the world was thinking of Hitler's regime and also to inform foreigners about 'the truth' of events. So long as so many countries were neutral it was important to keep them on the side of Nazi Germany, just as it had been important before the war to isolate one's enemies. If loyal to the regime, it is easy to see how valuable such a department would be. MI5 is important in Britain, and similar departments exist in all countries, although each has its own way of deploying the counter-intelligence service. Inevitably there are defections, like Burgess and Maclean in Britain, but in Germany during the whole of the Nazi period the Abwehr was subversive of the regime. This was due to the character of its leadership, Admiral Wilhelm Canaris, and more particularly, General Hans Oster. The recruitment of staff was also carefully watched and there was little infiltration. The department proved useful enough to the regime and was given a great deal of freedom until the subversion was eventually discovered.

The Involvement of the Confessing Church

Bonhoeffer's brother-in-law, Hans von Dohnanyi, was in constant touch with the Abwehr and became its principal legal adviser. He encouraged its use as a means of protection for endangered pastors of the Confessing Church. It was possible to assign a pastor to the staff of the Abwehr and thus keep him free from call-up or arrest. If he became involved in any activity which might look suspicious, they could rescue him from the police. On the surface it looked as though this was what it was doing for Bonhoeffer. He was clearly endangered and his work in Pomerania was hindered by his constant reporting to the police. When the Abwehr assigned him to their staff headquarters in Munich, his reporting to the police became an office routine and he could travel anywhere without local reporting. When he was first approached, he was told that his travels in Pomerania would be useful for information-gathering, so near to what was to become the Eastern Front.

Bonhoeffer agonised long about the rightness of such activity. Two things eventually decided him.

First, his growing dissatisfaction with the Confessing Church and its pietism. As early as 1934, he had said in a letter to Erwin Sutz, 'Hesitations about expressing a view of the state's actions must be broken. It's only fear, anyway! "Open your mouths for the dumb". Who in the Church still knows that this is the demand put to us in the Bible for such times.'

Second, a conviction that some political action must be taken, particularly after the collapse of France and the deportation of the Jews. When the actions of the state had become horrendous and the full horror of the 'final solution' was beginning to emerge, and many of his friends had seen the inside of the concentration camps, he saw inactivity or silence as personal guilt staining the body of Christ. He was writing his *Ethics* in 1940 when beginning his work for the Abwehr and the agony of his mind comes clearly through in his confession of guilt:[1]

> Even the most secret sin of the individual is defilement and destruction of the body of Christ (I Cor. 6–15). From the desires that are in our bodily members come murder and envy, strife and war (James 4:1ff). If my share in this is so small as to seem negligible, that still cannot set my mind at rest; for now it is not a matter of apportioning the blame, but I must acknowledge that precisely my sin is to blame for all. I am guilty of uncontrolled desires. I am guilty of cowardly silence at a time when I ought to have spoken. I am guilty of hypocrisy and untruthfulness in the face of force. I have been lacking in compassion and I have denied the poorest of my brethren. I am guilty of disloyalty and apostasy from Christ. What does it matter to you whether others are guilty too? I can excuse any sin of another, but my own sin remains guilt which I can never excuse.

What he says about the apostasy of the Church and its timidity is read in the light of this personal confession of guilt. And he is powerful in his condemnation of the Church.

The Extent of the Conspiracy

One must be careful not to exaggerate Bonhoeffer's role in the Abwehr. He was quite a small unit and effective over a very short period. The conspiracy was going on years before he even knew about it and it continued after his arrest for more than a year, until that fatal failure to destroy Hitler in the Wolf's Lair on 20 July 1944. Bonhoeffer's part and the difficulty he had in accepting such an involvement is better understood when we look at the extent of the Abwehr's commitment and the major figures involved.

The conspiracy goes back to 1933, when the elite of the German army, or its General Staff, was prepared to use Hitler, but intended to get rid of him as soon as convenient. Admiral Wilhelm Canaris became the head of the Abwehr in 1935. He was a consummate master at covering up his tracks. So much so that Paul Leverkühn, who worked very closely with him in military intelligence, writes in his book that Canaris was never involved in the conspiracy nor even wittingly allowed his organisation to be used by the conspirators! Others equally close to him are sure that he was deeply involved. In the nature of things this was very secret work and you were not always sure who your friends were! Constantine Fitzgibbon concludes from a careful study of all the evidence that:

> Canaris, engaged in a duel of wits with the British, American and Russian intelligence services and simultaneously fighting the Nazi Party Intelligence Service, gave at least his benevolent protection to men within his own organisation who were actively engaged in plans to overthrow the government and later to ensure a victory for the Western Allies.[2]

There is no doubt about the deputy head of the Abwehr, General Hans Oster. Oster was born in 1888, son of a Lutheran pastor of Alsatian extraction, brought up in Saxony and educated at Dresden. He served in the Saxon artillery regiment throughout the First World War. He was decorated for gallantry and in 1917 transferred to the General Staff. After the First World War he continued as a staff officer and was present in Dresden during the revolutionary excesses of the communists, who drowned the Saxon Minister for War in the Elbe. He supported his superior General Schleicher who wanted to use the army to suppress both Nazis and communists and set up military rule. When Oster joined the Abwehr, its head was Colonel von Bredow, a convinced anti-Nazi. Bredow and Schleicher were murdered by the SS on 30 June 1934. From that night, Oster's single aim was the overthrow of the Nazis. Once Canaris was appointed he had an ideal instrument for this purpose. Canaris resisted all interference from the Nazi secret service. The Abwehr had its own network of agents and means of communication within Germany which could not be tapped by the Nazis. Its central office had direct communication with all the senior military headquarters, because it was administered by the Supreme Command of the Armed Forces.

In 1938, a false charge of homosexuality was brought against Colonel General von Fritsch, Commander in Chief of the Army, because he was not sympathetic enough to the party. This was the point at which Dohnanyi, Bonhoeffer's brother-in-law, was first involved in the conspiracy. Hitler wanted to eliminate von Fritsch because he had objected to the Führer's remarks to the commanders-in-chief of the three Armed Forces on 5 November 1937, 'Every generation needs its own war, and I shall take care that this generation gets its war.'

Hitler ordered Gürtner to investigate the case of Fritsch, adding, 'You will know yourself which end of the rope to pull.' With the same words Gürtner handed the papers over to Dohnanyi. For a time he was freed from all other duties to work at the defamation of Fritsch. He consulted with Oster and plans were drawn up for a *coup d'état*. The army would not submit to the defamation and Dohnanyi prepared papers for Fritsch to challenge Himmler. General Beck, chief of the General Staff, joined them. Fritsch hesitated and Hitler's triumphant march into Vienna halted the plan to confront him. However it brought Beck into the conspiracy. What looked like being a successful *putsch* was off. Nevertheless Dohnanyi and Oster worked closely together, gathering details of Nazi crimes for an indictment of Hitler when the time came. They made themselves knowledgeable about what happened in Dachau and Buchenwald and later in Poland and the other occupied countries.

After Munich Oster, using the machinery of the Abwehr, kept Britain informed of Nazi intentions. With his knowledge, Freiherr von Schlabrendorff was sent to London to inform Churchill of Hitler's plans to invade Poland. He later revealed the plans to occupy Norway to the Norwegian government; he told the Dutch attaché of the proposed operation in the West, giving the exact date for the invasion of the Netherlands. The Dutch and British intelligence services ignored the information because they were sure it was a plant! Dr Josef Müller, the Abwehr man in the Vatican, kept Oster in constant contact with the British through the first two years of the war. The support in Germany for the resistance which at one time seemed adequate to overthrow the Nazi regime weakened, when it became evident that the British were only interested in them for the purpose of espionage and had no intention of treating with them or lending any support. Many of the generals were content to make the best of a bad job and were clearly influenced by Hitler's repeated victories. The clearest account of these abortive attempts is contained in John Wheeler-Bennett's *Nemesis of Power*. I recall a review of the book by Hanns Lilje, then Bishop of Hanover, for the Third Programme of the BBC. His scheduled twenty-minute talk overran to forty minutes! He was deeply moved as he talked about and lived again those terrible years in Germany when the best men lost hope. But Oster and the Abwehr did not lose hope. From now on they had but one objective, the elimination of Hitler. With the help of British explosives they made many attempts, but Hitler's erratic timetable and last minute changes defeated them. The nearest they got to success was the attempted assassination on 20 July 1944 and that was the end.

The Influence of Geneva

Bonhoeffer was now able to travel on a Foreign Office permit, issued at the request of the Abwehr, to neutral countries. He made use of this to spend one month in Switzerland, 24 February–24 March 1941. Permission to leave he had, but he also needed a guarantor in Switzerland to allow him entry. He named Karl Barth, who hesitated to endorse his entry. Barth said later that he was very dubious, because he could not understand how Bonhoeffer could get permission to travel unless he had gone over to the other side! Eventually he agreed and Bonhoeffer spent four useful weeks in Switzerland, first with Erwin Sutz, to hear news of the Leibholz family in Oxford and to renew an old friendship. Then he also saw Siegmund-Schultze, the former ecumenical leader in Berlin, who because of his strong peace emphasis was now living in exile. But Bonhoeffer's main objective was Geneva. He spent only a week there, partly because everybody was so busy on relief work for prisoners of war that they had no time for him. Except Visser't Hooft, who gave him all the time he wanted. Bonhoeffer collected information in Geneva and told Visser't Hooft of the situation in Germany. He listened carefully to Bonhoeffer and recognised that he was hearing one of the most authentic descriptions of the attitude of the Confessing Church. He wrote to the Bishop of Chichester, first giving news of this exciting meeting and then reporting in greater detail after digesting what he had heard:

> Inside the Confessing Church there is a certain difference of conviction with regard to the stand which the Church should take. There is, on the one hand, a group which believes that the Church should stick to what is called 'the inner line', and concentrate exclusively on the building up of its own spiritual life . . . There is, on the other hand, a group which believes that the Church has also a prophetic and ethical function in relation to the world and that it must prepare for the moment when it can again fulfil that function.[3]

After that, Visser't Hooft reports that Bonhoeffer thought most of the Confessing Church regarded a victory for Germany to be fatal for the

Church in their own country, as well as elsewhere in Europe. On the other hand, he did not disguise the fact that they knew a defeat for Germany would be the end for them as a nation. Either way a disaster, but Visser't Hooft added, obviously putting Bonhoeffer's own point of view: 'One hears, however, also voices which say that after all the suffering which their country has brought upon others they almost hope for an opportunity to pay the price by suffering themselves.'[4]

On his return to Germany, Bonhoeffer found that he was barred from all activity as a writer. The next few months were disturbing ones for Bonhoeffer and his friends. In May, twenty-three leaders of the Confessing Church were arrested; on 22 June Hitler invaded Russia. His references to these events in his letters are few; he talks instead of enjoying peaceful days and carving himself a cross and liking country life. In July he talks with incredulity of those who think the war will end soon. He does, of course, write to the brethren and his letters are much appreciated, but he seems not to be involved. Frau von Kleist senses that something is wrong when writing to Bethge. First she expresses an appreciation of Dietrich's 'splendid and appropriate letter to the brethren' and then her concern for him: 'I'm sometimes rather worried about him, as it can't be good for him to be so unoccupied.'[5]

In reality, he was much involved in the conspiracy. Based at Ettal, he spent a few days in Berlin, talking of it as a visit to the family; then Munich, which always meant the Abwehr. At the end of August he was back in Geneva.

The Church and the New Order in Europe

This time there were many who wanted to talk with him, but again his main discussions were with Visser't Hooft. In July, the SCM Press in London had published a book by William Paton, Secretary to the International Missionary Council, on *The Church and the New Order*. Hugh Martin, the Director of the press, had sent it to Visser't Hooft for his comments. Bonhoeffer saw it on arrival and recognised its importance. In fact, Visser't Hooft thought that it helped Bonhoeffer to resolve most of his problems about cooperation with the conspiracy. The book set out the kind of peace terms that should be offered to Germany once the National Socialist state had been overthrown and outlined the nature of the new Europe that might emerge from the war. It was a brave and confident book considering that Britain, with the Commonwealth, was standing alone against the Nazi masters of Europe, who had launched an apparently successful attack upon the Soviet Union. The USA had not yet entered the war and an impartial observer could hardly anticipate the British victory over so triumphant an opponent. Bonhoeffer saw in the book the hope for a Germany purged of Hitler and his monsters. He and Visser't Hooft discussed the book in detail and sent to Hugh Martin and William Paton comments which jointly, they agreed might be brought before responsible people in Britain. Visser't Hooft specifically mentioned the Bishop of Chichester as one who knew them both.

Side by side with the book they read an issue of *The Christian News Letter* by Dr Oldham on the same subject of post-war problems. As two continental Christians on opposite sides in the war they felt able to say things that are not always too clear to the 'insular' British. They pointed out that a strong apocalyptic trend had revived among Christians living under Nazi rule in Germany and in the occupied countries. This trend could become other-worldly, but it could also lead to a realisation that the Kingdom of God has its own history which does not depend upon political events, and that the life of the Church has its own God-given laws which are different from those which govern the life of the world. Paton had pointed out that the Church does not depend upon victory in the war. This does not mean indifference to the post-war order in Europe, quite the contrary. And Bonhoeffer points out in his comments that it is necessary to recognise the different attitudes of the occupied countries and those of Germany to the peace. The occupied countries looked for a British victory to liberate them; those who resisted in Germany looked to see if Britain would treat with them (if their country were freed from National Socialism) in some other way than 'unconditional surrender'. The Church cannot and should not elaborate detailed plans for post-war reconstruction, but it should remind the nations of the abiding commandments and realities which must be taken seriously if the new order is to be a true order.

Much of Bonhoeffer's argument was to plead for encouragement to those who were prepared to risk their lives – indeed were doing so already – to overthrow Hitler. Without this encouragement, support for the conspiracy, especially from the military, would dwindle away. He asked through these comments whether it was possible for the British government to offer such terms of peace to Germany that a new government composed of non-Nazis would not be discredited. Quite bluntly, Bonhoeffer was asking – and he would ask again – whether the present resistance movement could set up another regime in Germany and still survive. The shadow of the Versailles Treaty still hung over him. If the object of the Allies was to destroy Germany as a nation, then the most powerful elements in the resistance would put up with the Nazi regime and go ahead and win the war. In 1941 that looked a reasonable attitude.

Bonhoeffer was also concerned with Soviet Russia and that part of his comments is worth quoting. At this point, Germany was winning the battle on the Eastern Front too. Her armies were moving victoriously towards Smolensk. He understood that Russia was an enigma, and too little was known about what effect the war would have upon the Soviet system. But, if the resistance he knew of in Germany was successful, it would operate on the Eastern Front too, and he was worried about the effect of letting the Russians into Germany:

> Even though we may consider the British – Russian alliance a justifiable and unavoidable political decision, we must not minimise the danger which Russia still represents for all that we hold dear. Unless the war calls forth very fundamental changes in the structure of the Russian state, Bolshevism may well become a tremendous menace to those countries who find their fascist systems discredited by a German defeat. This, then, is one more reason for strengthening the hands of those non-Nazi elements in Germany which would be able to form a new government in that country.[6]

Visser't Hooft, who worked with him on these comments and sent them on to London, expressed his opinion that this period of thinking about post-war problems pushed Bonhoeffer into abandoning the quiet of his theologian's study to move into a political resistance – what Bonhoeffer would later call, 'coming out into the tempest of living'. These comments may well have helped him to clarify his ideas and resolve on certain actions, but the decision came slowly and was influenced by many different factors: the hindrances placed in the way of his work, the mounting casualties in the Russian campaign, serious doubts about any other way to be rid of Hitler than by assassination, the development of his own theology, particularly in the field of ethics, all pointed to involvement. He had not returned from America to be protected. As his former students died in Russia he was led deeper into the conspiracy which involved the military plot. On 22 June, the invasion of Russia had seemed so utterly stupid that the conspirators took heart; but the incredible successes undermined their will. For Bonhoeffer, it was the mass deportation of the Jews that made him decide.

Operation 7

The first clear evidence of his active involvement in the conspiracy is his connection with an Abwehr plan called 'Operation 7'. It was a small affair; but after it, he was committed to the conspiracy. The idea was to get a few Jews away from the horrors of the mass deportation. The Abwehr claimed that they needed Jews for their propaganda work in Switzerland. A handful of trusted Jews were to be sent there to assure the Swiss and, through them, all neutral countries that there was no persecution of Jews, only the punishment of criminals which British propaganda had represented as racial persecution. At first some of the Jews selected refused to cooperate and they needed to be told that it was a counter-plot. This in itself opened it up to danger. Then the Swiss had to be persuaded.

Wilhelm Rott, a pastor belonging to the Reformed tradition, from the Rhineland, who had formerly been an assistant to Bonhoeffer in the seminary at Zingst, was chosen as the best man to approach the Reformed churches of Switzerland. 'It is a question of the extreme distress in which our non-Aryan brothers and sisters have been for weeks,' he wrote. 'Since about the middle of October, the practice has started of transporting to the east non-Aryans from Berlin to other towns.'[7] He tactfully pointed out the problems. The Swiss laws did not permit reception of threatened non-Aryans, for Switzerland was neutral and terrified of being compromised. Rott pleaded that 'the door might possibly be opened for just a few'.

Although a small affair, it took quite a long period of careful negotiations and was not successfully completed until the summer of 1942. Then seven Jews were taken to safety and in no way served the propaganda purposes for which they were officially sent. The Gestapo were very suspicious, but the conspiracies were growing thick and fast and those who tried to discover who was against Hitler had their hands full. The military aristocracy in particular was deeply offended by Hitler's methods. His deportation of the Jews was far more than the slightly anti-semitic German leaders could sanction. He also disregarded the military code in issuing commands to his generals to shoot prisoners. One group of dissidents gathered around the figures of Helmuth von Moltke and Peter Yorck. These two Silesian landowners, both of whom had studied law in Germany, formed the core of the *Kreisau* group, together with their wives. Another lawyer in this group was Adam von Trott, a Rhodes Scholar at Oxford, who had worked both in China and in the USA. In 1939, he joined the Foreign Office in Berlin and was well aware of the anti-Nazi conspirators. It was he who informed London of the Nazi-Soviet pact in advance, but failed in his attempts to enlist British support for the democratic opposition in Germany. When war broke out he went to America and tried to enlist American support. The British embassy appears to have warned Roosevelt, who was at first favourable, against taking any action. British intelligence regarded Trott as a Nazi agent! Trott was in touch both with the Moltke Group and those to whom Bonhoeffer attached great importance – Beck and Goerdeler. In all these comings and goings, Bonhoeffer saw quite a lot of his brother, Klaus, and his brother-in-law, Hans von Dohnanyi.

Sabine and Gerhard Leibholz

Dietrich had kept in touch with Sabine and Gerhard as long as it remained possible, then his association with the Abwehr also gave him some freedom of movement to neutral countries where he could write letters to Oxford even in war time. Many of these letters are quoted in Sabine's book, *The Bonhoeffers: A Family Portrait*. They had only been in England a very short time before Dietrich was writing with contacts and telling of the peculiarities of the English way of life: 'Once one has become a little more accustomed to life there one feels more favourably disposed towards it than during the first few days! For instance, the ill-heated rooms are a curse of English life which one never escapes.'[8]

But as the months passed by and he could freely write to them from the neutral countries in wartime he became concerned for them. Internment worried him, as well as the religious upbringing of his nieces. A little before April 1942, Sabine sent him photographs of Marianne and Christine and he managed to reply during his visit to Scandinavia or Switzerland:

> You can hardly imagine what a joy the photos were for me and the rest of the family. Marianne had such an open, good and most intelligent face. There can be no doubt that she will make her way and be a great help to you. Christine is still the same lovely friendly girl she has always been . . . What about Marianne's confirmation? . . . I hope she will have a good rime with your Methodist minister. It is so important that she finds her way to Christianity and to the Church. There are so many experiences and disappointments which lead to nihilism and resignation, especially for sensitive people. So it is good to learn early enough that suffering and God are not a contradiction but rather a unity, for the idea that God himself is suffering is one that has always been one of the most convincing teachings of Christianity. I think God is nearer to suffering than to happiness, and to find God in this way gives peace and rest and a strong and courageous heart. I was moved so much by what you wrote me about Marianne and the verse she liked so much from the 90th Psalm: 'Wait upon the Lord . . .' How much I would like to talk to her about all this! As my godchild she is particularly in my heart and prayers.[9]

Norway

Switzerland and in particular Geneva had proved useful for restoring old contacts with the ecumenical movement and for staying in communication with Britain. The next overseas visit was of a very different kind. From 10 – 18 April 1942, he was in Norway, an occupied country. The man who had given his name to a traitorous attitude, Quisling, had been appointed puppet prime minister. Quisling's first act was to forbid the Dean of Trondheim to hold services in his cathedral, and when the Dean was dismissed from office, all the Norwegian bishops laid down their office too. That was 20 February 1942. The following month, a decree that established a Norwegian equivalent to the Hitler Youth Movement was met by a mass resignation of teachers. On Easter Day (5 April) all the pastors laid down their office. Bishop Berggrav, Norway's senior bishop, had been put under house arrest a few days earlier, and it was expected that he would be imprisoned.

The Abwehr acted at once. Two emissaries were sent to prevent the conviction, arguing that if the whole Norwegian Church was put in disarray by the sentencing of Berggrav, it would have serious military effects. The two emissaries were Helmuth von Moltke and Bonhoeffer. It was a sudden decision and Bonhoeffer had not expected it. He was working at his *Ethics* in Klein-Kössin, expecting to make a third visit to Switzerland. Dohnanyi summoned him to Berlin and he went gladly to Oslo with von Moltke. What interested him at once was the Norwegian Church struggle. They were doing exactly what he had proposed several years before to the Confessing Church in Germany. When a senior churchman was dismissed for refusing to comply with the instructions of the government, all clergy laid down their office and went on strike. Berggrav was not imprisoned and this could have had something to do with the presence in Norway of these two officials from Germany. They were not able to see Berggrav, but they talked with several Church leaders and, perhaps most important of all for Bonhoeffer, they talked with each other. Basically they had the same objectives. Von Moltke wanted a more just government in Germany, but he was not prepared to resort to violence. He could see that it would be good for Hitler to be removed and he was prepared to work for the overthrow by legitimate means of the National Socialist government. As a Christian he found that its actions violated his conscience. Bonhoeffer, by now, was convinced that Hitler had to be removed by any means and was in favour of assassination if that were the only way. Von Moltke had not yet started his subversive group on his estate at Kreisau, but a meeting was planned to which Bonhoeffer was invited, although he could not attend.

The visit to Norway gave them both a clear picture of an occupied country and the effective resistance of a Lutheran Church. While in Scandinavia, they spent two days in Sweden, a neutral country like Switzerland, but with a Lutheran Church structure much nearer to that in Germany. Bonhoeffer took the opportunity to write to Bishop Bell while he was in Sweden.

They returned by way of Copenhagen, briefly passing through another occupied country with a Lutheran Church. Back in Berlin, their first task was to report to the Abwehr.

Switzerland Again

Within three weeks of his return to Berlin, Bonhoeffer was in Zurich, writing letters to his sister in Oxford and Bishop Bell in Chichester, renewing contacts with his old friend Erwin Sutz, and then hurrying to his main objective – Geneva.

Bonhoeffer arrived in Geneva on 14 May and was disappointed to find that Visser't Hooft had left already for England, for he was anxious to share his experiences of Norway with him. Visser't Hooft's mission to England had been partly to take a memorandum from the enigmatic Adam von Trott. He succeeded in seeing Stafford Cripps and passing the memorandum on to Churchill. At this point, many of the resisters in Germany were anxious that their resistance should be recognised by the resistance movements in the occupied countries, particularly in Holland (Visser't Hooft was himself a Dutchman) and Norway. The key to this recognition was in the various Church struggles. Much of the German resistance, in so far as it was known at all outside Germany, was seen as the revolt of the old officer class. Bonhoeffer was thus quite crucial in an operation that gave credence to the 'conspiracy'. In fact the four key figures involved in convincing the occupied countries and Britain were Von Moltke, Adam von Trott, Visser't Hooft and Bonhoeffer. They were not always in good communication with each other, but the pattern was emerging.

In Geneva Bonhoeffer learnt that Bishop Bell was due to visit Sweden soon, which meant there was an opportunity of meeting. Plans were afoot for a dramatic *coup d'état*, to which Bonhoeffer was privy. Its success would depend upon having the right support in Germany and this support would be forthcoming if some word of encouragement came from the British.

An argument and a message had to be communicated to the highest authority in Britain – Churchill, or at least Anthony Eden. Bonhoeffer saw the possibility of doing this through the Bishop of Chichester, a member of the House of Lords, with ready access to Anthony Eden. The information he gleaned in Geneva came from a telegram from Bishop Bell to Visser't Hooft, while Bonhoeffer was there. It read simply, 'Visiting Sweden for three weeks commencing May 11th'. Further enquiries showed that Bell would be in Sweden rather longer. Bonhoeffer cut his Swiss visit short. He hurried back to Zurich, made the necessary enquiries concerning the progress of Operation 7 and returned to Berlin.

Peace Feelers in Sweden

What lay behind that short telegram in Geneva was a British government policy to keep good relations with neutral countries during wartime. The British were as anxious as the Germans to keep the neutrals friendly! Kenneth Clark and T. S. Eliot were both sent to Sweden in the cause of art and poetry. Bishop Bell, who had long-standing contacts with Sweden, going back to 1925, was sent to encourage good relations with the

Churches. Part of his description of that wartime journey is worth quoting to set the scene for Bonhoeffer's activity:

> I arrived a little before 3 a.m. on 13 May, at the airport of Stockholm, in an aeroplane with a Norwegian pilot and two crew, and no other passengers. During the first fortnight I travelled to different parts of Sweden, and met many old friends and saw many new faces. In the course of my travels I learnt far more of what was happening in the world than there was any possibility of learning in Britain. But the first fourteen days, enthralling as they were, did nothing to prepare me for my dramatic encounter with a German pastor.[10]

The German pastor was Dr Hans Schönfeld, who had come directly from Berlin. Bell was suspicious because he represented the official German Church. Bell was informed enough, largely through Bonhoeffer, to recognise that this meant the enemy of the Confessing Church. But Schönfeld was a brave man and had taken considerable risks in his travels between Berlin and Geneva. He was clearly under strain when he met Bell in Student Movement House in Stockholm. He gave the bishop information about what was being done for English prisoners of war in Germany, about the work of the YMCA and the SCM. He then came to the main purpose of his visit. He told him of plans for a *coup d'état* and Bishop Bell asked for details in the form of a written document. Schönfeld provided this, although it would have been very dangerous in the wrong hands.

The document explained that there had been many diverse groups working in Germany in opposition to the Nazi regime, but until recently they had operated separately and with no communication with each other. During the winter of 1941–42 they had crystallised into coordinated centres of opposition throughout the whole European continent. There were three main sections, all now working together: high ranking army officers and senior civil servants; former leaders of trades union and other workers' organisations, officially banned; the Churches, including Evangelical under Bishop Wurm and Roman Catholic led by the Fulda Bishops' Conference. It went on to say that these coordinated centres were prepared 'to eliminate Hitler, Himmler, Göring, Goebbels, Ley and Co'. They could, at the same time, put the Gestapo, the SS and the SA out of action. This would lead to the formation of a new kind of government in Germany which could be closely associated with Great Britain. There were detailed proposals for a Federation of European States. It concluded with a section on how to deal with Russia!

Before any revolution was possible, however, the army had to be sure that the Western Allies would treat with a Germany purged of Hitler and Himmler. All this needed checking, but the bishop had remarkable confirmation when he met Bonhoeffer on Whitsunday, 31 May.

Bonhoeffer's Meeting with the Bishop of Chichester

On that Whitsunday, Bishop Bell was in Sigtuna, a town some miles from Stockholm, famous for its educational settlement. Without Schönfeld's knowledge, Bonhoeffer had travelled to Sweden in his role as courier for the Abwehr and sought out Bell to give him similar information. This confirmation was decisive. Bell had many doubts about Schönfeld, but none about Bonhoeffer. Here was one person he had known for nine years and whom he completely trusted as a Christian of integrity who could not be in the pay of the official German Church. Bell calls him, 'an uncompromising anti-Nazi, one of the main springs of the Church opposition, entirely trusted by the Confessional (sic) Church leaders and deeply disliked by Bishop Heckel and all tolerators or supporters of the Nazi regime.'[11]

Bell had a long discussion with Bonhoeffer before Schönfeld also arrived in Sigtuna. The authenticity of the proposed revolution was thus fully confirmed. Bonhoeffer also gave him the names of the conspirators and these were appended to Schönfeld's document which Bell presented to Anthony Eden on his return.

From June until August, the Bishop of Chichester tried to argue the case for the opposition in Germany, but no word of encouragement could be squeezed out of the war machine which was only interested in the total destruction of what Churchill called 'the monstrous tyranny'. In 1942, the Vansittart policy held the field and this was interpreted in Germany as the annihilation of the German state. Anthony Eden showed some interest at first, but on 17 July wrote to Bell, 'am satisfied that it would not be in the national interest for any reply whatever to be sent.' Bell pressed further, asking that at least some clear statement be made to allay fears and suspicions in Germany that all Britain wanted was the annihilation of Germany. Could the Allies not say that they have no desire to enslave a Germany which has rid itself of Hitler and Himmler? That had an effect upon Eden, but not enough. On 4 August he wrote: 'For the present I do not think it would be advisable for me to go any further in public statements.' He was aware of the risks the conspirators were running, but adds, 'they have so far given little evidence of their existence and until they show that they are willing to follow the example of the oppressed peoples of Europe in running risks and taking active steps to oppose and overthrow the Nazi rule of terror I do not see how we can usefully expand the statements which have already been made.'

In due course, Bonhoeffer and Schönfeld learnt through their own channels that the British government was not prepared to take any steps or make any commitments which would encourage them. They were on their own. After this the conspirators lost a great deal of support.

Italy

Meanwhile, Bonhoeffer had returned to Berlin and been sent on another foreign assignment, this time to Italy and with Hans von Dohnanyi. They made contact with the Italian resistance and waited in Rome for an answer to the peace feelers. They had hoped to be able to strengthen the hand of the Italians by encouraging news from the British. Bonhoeffer never lost an opportunity to write to his sister. In Rome, the head of the German College, Dr Zeiger, was able to send a letter to Sabine by means of the Vatican post.

Bonhoeffer and Dohnanyi left Italy on 10 July with no news from London. This meant that the support of the army officers was waning, particularly in view of Rommel's successes in North Africa. It was Dohnanyi who received the disappointing news at the end of August when he was in Switzerland, this time without Bonhoeffer. Meanwhile, Bonhoeffer had been reading English books which he collected in Geneva. He read Oldham's *Christian News Letter*, writings of the *Peace Aims Group*, Temple's *Malvern Conference*, books by William Paton and Bell. All of them seemed to assume that after the war it would be very easy to pick up the threads with the Confessing Church. He was impressed because of what they planned to do with the help of the Confessing Church, but he was also frightened because he knew the appalling limitations of that Church. Bell in particular seemed to see the problems much too simply. He felt that the Churches on both sides could influence the peace treaty and avoid the mistakes of a dictated Versailles Treaty this time. Bonhoeffer, who had grown gradually disillusioned with the Confessing Church in Germany, was concerned about its moral fibre. He had seen it duck every important issue and watched it protecting itself rather than being a 'voice for the dumb'. There were very serious indications that the Confessing Church too had been influenced by Hitler's victories.

The Italian visit had been short and mostly to Germans in Italy. His contacts had been largely with Catholics, but he saw some hope in the growing discontent with Mussolini and the resistance to Italy's involvement in the war. Italy was already beginning to realise that she was a second class partner. The victories in Libya, which should have been hers, were German victories. The Church resistance was of a different kind and Bonhoeffer must have seen the strength of an independent base in the Vatican, which was not under the control of the fascists and was in the heart of the capital. No such base existed in Berlin, except the Abwehr.

The short visit to Italy included Venice, Florence and Rome. Its purpose had been to explore the possibility of a link between German and Italian resistance when the time came. He wrote little or nothing about this one visit to Germany's principal ally.

The Necessary Reform of the Evangelical Church

Those who planned the overthrow of the Nazi regime did not give up when they learnt that Britain was still not prepared to take them seriously. After all, that had been Britain's attitude since the early thirties. What they had to do was provide evidence that they were able to pull off a coup, that they were ready to sacrifice and take risks, that something was already happening. The second half of 1942 was one of the busiest periods for the conspirators. It was then they planned the assassination that never succeeded and began to look seriously at the kind of government which would replace Hitler's. Bonhoeffer was asked to draft a document on the reform of the Church. He did this in July 1942[12] with great care. It began with two clear principles – making good what the Evangelical Church has done wrong, and the independence of the Church. No steps could be taken to reform the Church until the Church struggle was over. When this happened, there were seven theses to be considered:

1. The Church struggle was not essentially against the Nazis, but against those who perverted the Church life of the nation. It must continue until these intrusions are done away with.

2. The Confessing Church had set up, as emergency structures, certain organs, such as synods and councils of brethren, which enabled the Church to survive persecution, imprisonment and discrimination. This had been a shadow organisation to the German Christian national Church. The structures of the Confessing Church must form the basis of the new reformed Church after the overthrow of the Nazi regime.

3. The official structures have been so intertwined with the violence of the Nazi regime that they are devoid of spiritual power.

4. The Church struggle can only come to an end with the full support of the Confessing Church, including both its emergency structures and all the congregations and pastors who stood by it at great sacrifice. The resistance of these local Churches could not be broken by violence and it is from these pastors that the true leaders of a reformed Evangelical Church must come.

5. A resistance from the German Christian side is to be expected, but while the unity of the Church is a precious thing, it may be necessary to allow a small group to break away as a Free Church, which will be doomed sooner or later to dissolve.

6. The German Christians have divided the Church. There will be need for a new leadership, recognised by the different Confessions. The resistance to this unity by the various traditions of the provincial Churches and differing confessions will soon be overcome by an accepted and strong leadership.

7. It would be a backward step to allow the forces of reaction to

reestablish the old bureaucratic relationship between Church and state. A new relationship must be worked out by the younger pastors and laity who have proved themselves in the Church struggle.

Bonhoeffer proceeded on the basis of these theses to outline a pattern and propose structures for the Churches in post-war Germany. Some of his proposals were taken up after the war, but the old Confessional rivalries, the persistence of habits learnt in the Nazi period, together with the failure of all four occupation forces to recognise the real problems, led as Bonhoeffer feared to the reestablishment of a reactionary Church. If Bonhoeffer had lived it might have been different.

The Engagement

It was not the first time that Dietrich had fallen in love, but earlier he had set his face against marriage. The early years of the Nazi rule seemed inappropriate to begin a family. His own family life had been happy and something of that must have been revived as he watched the admirable families of the Pomeranian Junkers. In particular, the home in Klein-Kössin, where he spent such peaceful and inspiring times with Frau von Kleist-Retzow and her family turned his mind to the happiness of family life despite the uncertainty of the times. There were two granddaughters who had visited Finkenwalde as children. The older attracted him at first and he hardly noticed the younger sister, Maria von Wedemeyer. Seven years after the visits to Finkenwalde Maria had grown into a very beautiful eighteen year old, and he could not fail to notice her. Something of his change of attitude, since the grim conclusion that marriage must be postponed until the crisis is over, comes out in a letter written to his Swiss friend, Erwin Sutz, on the occasion of the latter's marriage in 1941. He had written many letters on the occasion of marriages of his students and preached at many weddings. Now, writing to Erwin Sutz, he outlines the confidence which underlies the decision to marry in 'times like this'. He refers to these times as the 'last times' and insists that he does not mean this altogether apocalyptically! Marriage is making an affirmative gesture to the world and the world's future. To marry is to assert a faith in God's mercy:

> for by this act, in the midst of general destruction, a man desires to build; in the midst of a life lived from day to day ... he demands a future; in the midst of our exile from the earth, he demands some living space; in the midst of the general misery, some happiness. And the overwhelming fact is, that to this improbable desire, God says Yes, that here God confirms our will with his, when one would expect the opposite. And so marriage becomes something quite new, majestic, glorious – for those of us in Germany who seek to be Christians.[13]

Dietrich was twice her age and he was involved in a dangerous conspiracy. It looked a most inappropriate union. His friends and her family were surprised and Dietrich was uncertain. Then Maria's father was killed on the Eastern Front. Dietrich wrote to her mother the kind of letter that was appropriate for the widow of a Junker. He wrote of the qualities of her late husband and extolled the blessings the father had bestowed upon the children, the immeasurable value of a Christian home. Recalling the contacts he had had with Hans von Wedemeyer in Finkenwalde seven years before, he added this tribute:

> The spirit in which he lived will be the spirit in which you and your children are together. The same earnestness with which he then spoke to me about his son's Christian upbringing will now inspire you to help your children to a Christian mourning for their father; the same love that was given to him for the Word and Sacrament will unite you with each other and with the community in heaven; the same spirit of sacrifice and obedience to the will of God will cause you to accept in quietness and thankfulness what God has sent to you. How God can be praised for such a Christian mourning by a whole family for the father who has been called home to God.[14]

After the husband's death Bonhoeffer visited Klein-Kössin for a few days before his Italian trip and there he saw Maria again. It is clear from a letter written to Bethge when he was on his way to Rome that the meeting had disturbed him more than he cared to admit – 'the delightful thought of a few minutes of high tension will no doubt melt once again to the realm of unfulfilled phantasies'.

But there were two people in this love affair and Maria did not leave Dietrich to do all the running. They contrived to meet several times in Berlin and in Klein-Kössin and fell deeply in love. The decorum of the class to which he and she belonged did not allow them the privacy of being alone together except in public places, but they talked of their love. Her mother, Ruth von Wedemeyer, greatly respected Dietrich Bonhoeffer as a distinguished pastor who had been of great strength to her in her bereavement. She was aware that her late husband also had confidence in his judgement to the extent of entrusting his son to him for Christian teaching. However she did not look to that kind of marriage for her daughter. The difference in age worried her and the dangerous enterprises in which Dietrich was involved made her fear for her young eighteen year old. When her consent was sought for the engagement, she did not refuse it, but insisted upon a year's delay, during which time they should not see each other. This was intolerable to Dietrich and he persisted until she agreed to the engagement, although she did not want it announced publicly. On 17 January 1943, Dietrich Bonhoeffer and Maria von

Wedemeyer were engaged. It was not announced publicly until his arrest some months later.

The Unmasking of the Abwehr

The winter of 1942–43 was a disastrous one for Germany. Hitler had been proved right so many times, against the advice of his most experienced generals, that he believed he could 'walk on water'. The attack on Russia had been sheer folly and yet his armies advanced to Smolensk with victorious ease. The order to advance on Stalingrad was also given against the advice of his generals, but he dismissed those who disagreed and went on to his own destruction. The conspirators could see what was happening and frantically tried to stop it. In defeat, Germany needed a different government to talk with the Western Allies, even though they appeared not to want to talk. It would be far better if Germany could keep itself intact before the end, and perhaps even force the Allies to treat with them. The need to eliminate Hitler became urgent. The various centres of resistance, now coordinated, hatched plots of daring and carried them out with courage. There were a few protests publicly against the Stalingrad venture, such as the *White Rose* pamphlet which brought the students of Munich out, only to be tried by the People's Court and put to death. It was then, in March 1943, that the conspirators felt they were nearest to their objective. A plot to assassinate Hitler on the Eastern Front and subsequent plans for a take-over by General Olbricht, chief of the General Staff, seemed sure to succeed but failed. Plot after plot staggered to unbelievable failure. Hitler was thought to have divine protection and it looked to be true!

Bonhoeffer was involved in all these plans, constantly waiting for news of success and ready to play his part in the reconstruction of Germany. He always knew there was a danger that the conspiracy would be discovered and summary executions follow. Maria's mother was not wrong in seeing him as a most unsuitable husband for her young daughter, however much she admired him. After the failure of 'Operation Flash', when the bomb taken by General von Tresckow on to Hitler's plane failed to ignite, the conspirators might well have been discovered or discouraged. They went on.

Their undoing, however, came from quite a different quarter. They had survived so far because the Abwehr insisted that to do its job it needed complete secrecy. The Reich Security Office was not able to investigate. This 'no-go' area for the Gestapo led to jealousy and efforts were made to discredit Admiral Canaris. The Gestapo's intention was to prove that the Abwehr were misappropriating funds. When they began to investigate the use of Swiss currency they discovered more than they expected and were soon on the trail of 'Operation 7'. They had always suspected the plan to send selected Jews into Switzerland as agents; they suspected the misuse of funds for them and discovered that the plan had been a hoax. Then they began to investigate who was responsible. The Abwehr had covered its tracks so well that it was difficult to pin the crime on any one person, even more difficult to show that the Abwehr itself was engaged in subversive dealings. At no point did they suspect that it was plotting the assassination of Hitler. The person they thought most likely to be vulnerable was Hans von Dohnanyi and this meant that Bonhoeffer was close to scrutiny.

The atmosphere in which Bonhoeffer lived during these last months before his arrest is vividly described by Mary Bosanquet in her book. She tells how Dietrich was rehearsing the cantata, 'Lobet den Herrn', with the family in preparation for his father's seventy-fifth birthday. Among those singing was Hans von Dohnanyi, who was urgently waiting for a telephone call to say that Hitler had been assassinated and he must come at once to the Abwehr office. Dietrich was also aware of the plan and Dohnanyi s car stood at the door with the engine warmed. Mary Bosanquet writes of Dietrich:

> No one looking at [his] broad, cheerful face would have guessed that he was listening for anything more dramatic than the balance of voices. The hours went by; the singers worked diligently. No sound came from the next room where the telephone stood. And when at last the family folded up their music and dispersed, three of them knew that another attempt on Hitler's life had failed.

Amidst this uncertainty, the details of Operation 7 were being discovered by the Gestapo and charges were prepared against Dietrich and Hans von Dohnanyi for accepting bribes from the Jews who escaped through the operation to Switzerland.

On 31 March, both men were at Karl Bonhoeffer's birthday party. A few days later, Dietrich telephoned his sister Christine (Hans' wife) and was answered by a strange voice. He at once realised that Hans and Christine had been arrested. In fact the Gestapo were ransacking the house. Dietrich said nothing to his parents, but went next door to his sister Ursula and asked her to prepare him a large meal! He went through his papers and destroyed any incriminating evidence, leaving some false papers deliberately for the Gestapo to find. He then ate a good meal and waited. At four in the afternoon, two men arrived and took him in a black Mercedes to Tegel prison.

THIRTEEN

Awaiting Trial: The First Year in Prison

On 5 April 1943, three of the Bonhoeffer family were arrested following house searches. They went to different prisons. Dietrich was taken to the interrogation prison in Tegel, north-west of Berlin; his sister Christine to a similar prison in Charlottenburg, west Berlin; her husband Hans von Dohnanyi, to the Moabit Military Prison, Lehrter Strasse in central Berlin. There would be other prisons and other prisoners.

Conditions were not too bad at first. As soon as he could, Dietrich wrote to his parents to tell them not to worry. He was getting enough to eat and did not find the physical discomfort hard to bear. The mental upheaval was worse and it gave him the opportunity to review his whole situation. This was good for him and he even describes it as 'a good spiritual Turkish bath'. He began to read and learn by heart the hymns of Paul Gerhardt, he had his Bible with him and there was a library in the prison. He was soon sending for books and acquiring some writing paper. He recalls the birthday party for his father and hears again in his head the chorale they sang for him: 'Praise to the Lord, the Almighty, the King of Creation . . . Shelters thee under his wings, yea, and gently sustaineth.' The words and the music comforted him. His mind is on his family and particularly the wedding preparations for Renate, his niece, who married Eberhard Bethge a few weeks later. He avoids self-pity, but is deeply disappointed that his own wedding to Maria von Wedemeyer is now indefinitely postponed – 'If only I could have a few words with her!' But he seizes upon little things that give him pleasure – a thrush singing beautifully in the morning and then in the evening too. His long period of waiting, reassessing, thinking and struggle is beginning. At the time of the arrest, he had no idea that he would be in prison for two years and that at the end he would be executed. He had high hopes of acquittal. The interrogations were hopeful and when a charge was formulated it seemed that he could easily refute it. He was charged with 'subversion of the armed forces'.

Hans von Dohnanyi was worried by the thought that he had been responsible for all the trouble that had come upon the Bonhoeffer family. He was well treated by the prison staff, as was Dietrich, and the commandant was almost a friend to him, but this did not help him in his self-accusation. As soon as he could he sent a message to Dietrich – that was Good Friday, 23 April – from Sacrow near Potsdam. His wife, Christine, was still in prison, although she remained there only a few weeks more. After recalling the rich memories of worshipping together, sparked off by the sound of the bells ringing for Good Friday services, he admits his sorrow to Dietrich:

> You cannot know how much it oppresses me that I am the cause of this suffering that you, Christine, the children, our parents now undergo; that because of me, my dear wife and you have been deprived of your freedom. 'To have had companions in trouble is a comfort, but to *have* them in trouble is a burden.' And that mistrustful question, 'Why?', keeps forming itself on my lips. If I knew that all of you, and you in particular, were not thinking of me reproachfully, a weight would be lifted from my spirit. What wouldn't I give to know that the two of you were free again; I would take everything upon myself if you could be spared this testing.[1]

All three saw each other occasionally during the interrogations, but they were not allowed to speak to each other. This letter comes from a troubled heart, made worse by that silent confrontation. Dietrich did all he could to let Hans von Dohnanyi know that he understood and in no way blamed him.

Looking Back Ten Years

Before his arrest, Bonhoeffer had worked on his *Ethics* and part of the material for that book was cast into an essay which he gave to Hans von Dohnanyi, Hans Oster and Eberhard Bethge at Christmas 1942. One copy was left under the beams of his parents' house in Charlottenburg. It was clear that he was aware of the danger of arrest and ready for it when it came. That essay, which was the necessary prelude to his *Ethics*, looks back over the first ten years of Hitler's rule: 1933–43. It is of great importance in assessing Bonhoeffer's attitudes at the beginning of his imprisonment. He tries to examine what he and his friends have done during these years. They had not been idle, but they had often been confused. The old truths had not really sustained them in the hours of trial. Some other lessons, learnt by past generations, had been forgotten and only by first-hand experience could they be regained. He therefore sets out, not to write something original, but to explain what had come home to them in their experiences of the past ten years. They had been extraordinary experiences, for which they were not prepared by the lessons of past generations. He compares their efforts to combat the evil of their day to those of Don Quixote and realises that they had the wrong weapons. Those old swords had been honourable in their day and effective, but with the monstrous dimension of evil they had met, the old swords were rusty and useless. They were like men leading a cavalry charge against sophisticated fire power. He asks whether in the whole of human history there have ever been people with so little ground under their feet – 'every available alternative seemed equally intolerable, repugnant and futile'. They had to look beyond all the existing alternatives for the source of their strength.

In turn he examines and finds wanting the qualities that had sustained earlier generations – reasons, conscience, duty, freedom, enthusiasm, private virtue. The only one that can stand fast now is the one who can sacrifice all this 'when he is called to obedient and responsible action in faith and in exclusive allegiance to God'. The civil courage which is called for in such times is hard for a German brought up to obey his superiors and to suppress personal preference. They have now had to learn a new kind of freedom. 'Civil courage,' he writes, 'can grow only out of the free responsibility of free men. Only now are the Germans beginning to learn the meaning of free responsibility.' He then adds one of his most perceptive insights, by which he was able to sustain himself in view of his acceptance of assassination as the only solution to Hitler. 'This free responsibility depends on a God who demands responsible action in a bold venture of faith, and who promises forgiveness and consolation to the person who becomes a sinner in that venture.'

This is an insight which he illustrates in many different ethical situations. He deals with success, with folly, with the temptation to contempt for humanity, confidence, sympathy, suffering, optimism, insecurity and death. It is in fact the sketch for his book on the new *Ethics*. How different it reads from those writers who have deduced from his letters, 'The New Morality'. It is in this essay that he asks the question, 'Are we still of any use?' He was aware of the loss of his 'righteousness', the evil deeds he had witnessed, the deceptions he had learnt and practised, the intolerable conflicts that had made them suspicious of all men and even reduced them to cynics. There is a deep personal anguish in the question he asks of all his friends in the conspiracy – and in that lonely prison cell, of himself: 'Will our inward power of resistance be strong enough, and our honesty with ourselves remorseless enough, for us to find our way back to simplicity and straightforwardness?'[2]

On Trial

The importance of Bonhoeffer for the prosecution was the information that he might give to incriminate Hans von Dohnanyi who was the main target. So far, the Abwehr had not been incriminated and Admiral Canaris was still in command with all his protected status. It was important for him to remain there and he therefore gave every pretence of having Dohnanyi fully investigated. The trial began with charges amounting to high treason and gradually dwindled down to trivia of procedure. A code card was discovered, which might have incriminated Dohnanyi, but Hans Oster was able to show that it was a standard instrument of procedure for counter-espionage. The letter 'O' which caused the prosecution so much bother was shown to be a cipher for Hans Oster. Then, the prosecution investigated Operation 7, but while the project could be condemned as too expensive and ineffective, no subversion could be detected. Then Bonhoeffer's travels abroad were investigated and here he became important.

He was frequently interrogated and obviously found it difficult to think of the right answers in the heat of the moment. Some time in June, he wrote to the prosecuting judge[3] – Dr Roeder, to explain his difficulties. He defends himself at great length in that letter. Its tone is that of wronged innocence, but throughout he is trying to show that he and Dohnanyi were acting in a most patriotic way. In the course of that letter, he refutes the suggestion that he was only taken into the Abwehr to protect him from the Gestapo and/or to dodge the draft. He argues logically and then personally with indignation that he could ever be accused of disloyalty to the Fatherland. The final paragraph of that letter shows something of the game he is playing and the duplicity into which he had advanced:

Finally, a couple of personal remarks on the matter. It certainly cannot have the force of proof for you – but perhaps you will believe me personally, and this is the hope in which I speak, that it is hard for me to see how earlier conflicts with the Gestapo, which as I profoundly believe, have arisen from a purely Church attitude, have now led to the point when I can be thought capable of such a severe failing in the obvious duties of a German towards his people and nation. I still cannot believe that this charge has really been made against me. If this had been my attitude, would I have found my fiancée in an old officers' family, all of whose fathers and sons have served as officers since the beginning of the war, some with the highest distinction, and have made the greatest sacrifice? My fiancée has lost both her father and her brother at the front. If that were the case, would I have cancelled all the engagements which I had made in America and have returned immediately upon the outbreak of war to Germany where I had to expect to be called up straight away? Would I have offered myself as an army chaplain immediately after the outbreak of war? If anyone wants to learn something of my conception of the duty of Christian obedience towards the authorities, he should read my exposition of Romans 13 in my book, *The Cost of Discipleship*. The appeal to the subjection to the will and the demands of authority for the sake of Christian conscience has probably seldom been expressed more strongly than there. That is my personal attitude to these questions. I cannot judge how far such personal arguments have any legal significance, but I cannot imagine that one can simply pass over them.

Other letters followed[4] dealing with points he says he forgot to mention at the interrogations. His letters usually end with 'Heil Hitler'.

There were ups and downs, but during the first months in prison his confidence grew that the charges would be withdrawn and both he and Dohnanyi would soon be free. He had confidence in Dohnanyi and it was well placed. He was therefore prepared to forget all his Lutheran training on personal integrity and keep to the rules as agreed. He played his part well and deceived many. He was afraid at one point that he might break down under interrogation or torture. For this reason he exercised regularly and ate any nourishing food that his family and friends brought him. From April to July, the plan succeeded. He was healthy, he convinced his prosecutors and Dohnanyi disposed of one charge after another, by taking full responsibility upon himself. He then defended himself skilfully and Dr Roeder, the Judge Advocate, had to be content with minor charges.

Letters to and from the Family

It was at first difficult for the family to visit Dietrich in prison, but they could write letters and he was allowed to send one every ten days. He delighted in the writing of these letters, mostly to his parents. They were opportunities to share his life with those he loved. They are so vivid and detailed that as we read them we can almost look into his cell. He tried to live with the family and share their experiences, although he knew that they could never totally share his – 'I read, meditate, write, pace up and down my cell – without rubbing myself sore against the walls like a polar bear!'

He soon learnt that it was best to concentrate on what you can do and try not to think of what you are prevented from doing. He had time to think and study. He took full advantage of the permission he'd been given to have books sent in to him and tried his hand at all kinds of writing – poems, drama, even a novel. Quite early on he did a little study on 'The feeling of time', and noted that an earlier occupant of his cell had scribbled on the wall, 'In a hundred years it will all be over.' That attitude was obviously not satisfactory to him. He wanted to discuss 'prison psychosis' with his father who had done much work with prisoners in his professional capacity as a psychiatrist. He found the Psalms gave some help and two texts in particular recur: 'My time is in your hands', and 'How long, O Lord?' Maria is mentioned in every letter. He is concerned about how she is bearing up, and takes comfort from the fact that she had behaved so well when her father died. Then he learns that she has come to stay with his parents in Berlin in order to visit him whenever permission is given.

The marriage of Renate Schleicher (daughter of his sister Ursula) to Eberhard Bethge was a great joy to him, and he sternly refused to countenance a suggestion that they should postpone the wedding because of the times.

All this made his longing for Maria more intense and her eventual visit precious, but painful.

The Wedding Sermon

Dietrich wrote a sermon for the wedding of Eberhard and Renate in May.[5] Its theme is the astonishing freedom and responsibility which enable human beings to say 'Yes' to life and take the helm in their life's journey.

'The children of earth are rightly proud of being allowed to take a hand in shaping their own destinies.' He urges them not to talk too quickly about God in this matter. It is their own decision and their own very human wills that have brought this about. The course they have taken is of their own choosing. Marriage is not in the first place a religious thing, but secular, 'you yourselves, and you alone, bear the responsibility for what no one can take from you.' Having made that abundantly clear with a little male chauvinism mixed in — 'you, Eberhard, have all the responsibility for the success of your venture' and 'you Renate will make it easy for your husband' — Bonhoeffer provides the God context:

> God adds his 'Yes' to your 'Yes' — he is guiding your marriage;
> God makes your marriage indissoluble;
> God establishes a rule of life by which you can live together in wedlock;
> God has laid on marriage a blessing and a burden;
> God gives you Christ as the foundation of your marriage.

Within that context, he insists upon the secular character of marriage: 'From the first day of your wedding until the last the rule must be: "Welcome one another . . . for the glory of God".'

His youngest sister, Susanne, brought him detailed news of the wedding, although she was not allowed to visit. She simply left the things outside for him, but that proximity and the news she received from the prison staff that he was well seemed to her like a visit — 'Simply being near to you means a great deal,' she wrote.

The family were very concerned for Dietrich and hopeful that he would not be in prison long. At the end of May, his eldest brother, Karl-Friedrich, wrote of meeting Maria and how much the whole family liked her and admired her courage and self-sacrifice. In that letter he writes, 'I hope that this really is the last letter that I shall have to write to you in prison.'

Dietrich is, of course, very frustrated that he cannot introduce Maria to the family himself and constantly asks for more news of her. In between details of his reading and new ideas about time, he throws in sentences about Maria which show where his mind constantly dwells. He has to stop himself thinking too often of the happy times he has had with her, the memory becomes too painful for him.

Maria von Wedemeyer

Nothing disturbed Bonhoeffer more than the absence of Maria. For some time he could only read her letters and hear about her from other members of the family. Then, quite unexpectedly, he came face to face with her at the time of one of his interrogations. Roeder thought that the sudden shock of seeing her would weaken his will and he would reveal something he had been keeping back – preferably about Hans von Dohnanyi. She was brought into the room with practically no forewarning and Dietrich was visibly shaken. He was silent at first and then carried on a normal conversation, expressing his emotions only by the pressure of his hand. It was a traumatic meeting, but the prelude to many more. Roeder obviously concluded that Bonhoeffer had little to tell. Permission was given for her to visit almost every month and his ten day interval between letters was shortened to four. Thus, he was able to write alternate letters to his parents and Maria. She treasured those love letters until her death and then gave orders that they should not be published. Private letters of that kind are not for public eyes. A letter every eight days was too slow and he soon persuaded a friendly guard to smuggle extra letters past the censor. Dietrich frequently told Maria that she had made it possible for him to continue, for her presence in Berlin strengthened him. Dietrich was reluctant to express his emotions, but the floodgates opened at times in smuggled letters and when the attending officer tactfully left the room on some of her visits. She says of those times, 'he expressed his emotions with an intensity that surprised him more than it did me'.

They planned their future with confidence. As the months went by, he did not lose heart, but it was becoming a greater strain. The first few weeks were treated as tiresome, but temporary. He and his family talked of forgetting all about these times for they would soon be over. Everyone expected that the interrogation might last one or two months, but no longer. Dohnanyi was so clever and he seemed to be running rings round Roeder. They even enjoyed the news of the trials. But as the weeks lengthened to months dark shadows came over the mind and times of depression surfaced. It was at these moments when the thought of Maria kept him from slipping into the abyss.

He wrote to her on 12 August 1943, a letter which she quotes:

You cannot imagine what it means in my present situation to have you. I am certain of God's guidance here. Everyday, I am overcome anew at how undeservedly I received this happiness, and each day I am deeply moved at what a hard school God has led you through during this last year. And now it appears to be his will that I have to bring you sorrow and suffering . . . so that our love for each other may achieve the right foundation and the right endurance. When I also think about the situation of the world, the complete darkness over our personal fate and my present imprisonment, then I believe that our union can only be a sign of God's grace and kindness, which calls us to faith. We would be blind if we did not see it . . . Our marriage shall be a 'Yes' to God's earth; it shall strengthen our courage to act and accomplish something on the earth. I fear that Christians who stand with only one leg upon the earth also stand with only one leg in heaven.[6]

Although one must respect Maria's desire to keep Dietrich's love letters to herself, it makes us realise how much we are missing of this remarkable man by not having access to them. She did not destroy them and they are preserved in the Houghton Library at Harvard – thirty-eight of them – but they are not accessible to the public.

In an Appendix to the later edition of *Letters and Papers from Prison* (SCM Press, 1971) there is an article written by Maria von Wedemeyer in which she quotes from some of these letters. The above is one such quote. She calls the article, 'The Other Letters from Prison' and pays tribute to Bethge's monumental *Biography*, but she might have called the article, 'The Other Bonhoeffer'. The picture she gives is of a passionate man, deeply in love, longing for his beloved and impatient for the full expression of their love. He is tender and concerned for the awful strain he is putting, not only upon himself, but also upon this lovely young girl. For she is still only a teenager. At nineteen, she is being called to bear the responsibilities of a much older woman. At first, his frustrations are those of any lover and her visits a delight. She appears older than her years and he younger than his. But then he talks to her like a father, reminding her that he was brought up in a strict family where emotions were not easily expressed. Gradually the strain begins to tell and later we shall read in his poems and letters of the loss of hope that they would ever be united. But at this stage, during the early months of his imprisonment, he is merely frustrated and impatient. Preparations for his marriage go ahead, but she has to do all the practical work. They talked of the furniture in their future flat in detail, discussed ways in which they should live, walks, the beach, music and all the everyday things of a normal married life. Dietrich thought he was the better cook. He urged Maria to learn English, although she couldn't see the point. She did not share his delight in music, but he tried to get her to practise the violin with some hope of playing with her. He took a dim view of her interest in mathematics! All the little things that might have been their daily conversation if he had not been in great danger and imprisoned. He also chose the text for the wedding and worked on the menu.

As the older and better read individual he advised on her reading, not always sharing her tastes. They disagreed about Rilke. She tried to read his books, but he knew that she would find them frustrating and said that the only one she should be concerned about was *Life Together*, but he wanted to be around when she read that! There was humour and all the interaction of happy lovers, frustrated only by their separation. Of course, he went up and down, as month succeeded month. When he thought he would soon be out because the trial was over, he discussed dates for the wedding or asked Maria to look out for musical instruments. He was a bit puzzled by the religious ceremonies in her home town of Pätzig where they would be married and by the Berneuchen Movement to which her family belonged. He thought that if there was a good chance that he would not be called up for several months after his release they should marry at once; if he was likely to go into the army within a few weeks, they should wait until the war was over.

Life in Prison

Bonhoeffer soon accustomed himself to the physical inconveniences of prison and they were much reduced by his friendship with the prison warders and the generous parcels of food and clothing brought to him by his family. The inactivity was the worst part; he wanted to be out into the storm of living. The trial was dragged out and took very little of his time. One result of this was that he frequently got the dates wrong on his letters. To avoid this and to pattern his life, he lived by the Christian year, meticulously keeping its seasons and festivals. He expected letters written in connection with the great religious festivals and complained when a letter was not sent from family or Maria at Whitsuntide. He listened to the church bells and arranged both his worship and his devotional reading to correspond with the Church's year. Advent, always his favourite season for preaching, was specially marked. He opened the Christian year with the pomp and ceremony of a prison cell and even learnt from his situation. Maria tells us that he wrote about Advent to her: 'A prison cell, in which one waits, hopes, does various unessential things and is completely dependent upon the fact that the door of freedom has to be opened *from the outside*, is not a bad picture of Advent.'[7]

One of the hardest things to bear was being shut away from the sun. He had always loved the warmth of the sun and records, in a letter to Maria, how once in Cuba when he had to prepare a sermon, 'coming from the ice cold of America into the blooming vegetation' he almost succumbed to the sun cult and hardly knew what to preach. That too was Advent. What made him remember that was a special privilege once granted to him to be allowed to sit in the warm sun of the prison yard to write his letter.

Much later, in the famous poem, *Who am I?*,[8] he describes his own estimate of himself as:

> restless and longing and sick, like a bird in a cage,
> struggling for breath, as though hands were compressing my throat, yearning
> for colours, for flowers, for the voices of birds.

He would not use such words at this stage, but already the shadows were shutting out the sun . . . and shutting out his Maria and his family. He enjoyed the social life of a big family, although he liked to be able to withdraw from time to time. Maria never taught him to dance, nor did she really try, because she thought him a hopeless case, but he was a good party man and he missed those happy, carefree days. After months of solitude, he longed for company. With his usual contrast of moods, he wrote: 'I have a real hunger for people. I am afraid, however, that at first I shall have trouble in enduring long gatherings of many people. Even in times past I could endure family festivities, which in fact I love dearly, only if I could escape into my room for half an hour from time to time.'

Then he wrote that he began to dream of that half hour of escape, but now with Maria. He did not trust himself to dwell too long on being alone with Maria and wrote to her on those lines, probably many times. But the letter she has let us see reveals much of those feelings:

> It would be better if I succeeded in writing to you only of my gratitude, my joy and my happiness in having you and in keeping the pressure and impatience of this long imprisonment (this was about four months after his arrest) out of sight. But that would not be truthful, and it would appear to me as an injustice to you. You must know how I really feel and must not take me for an ascetic saint . . . I can't very well imagine that you would want to marry one in the first place – and I would also advise against it from my knowledge of Church history.[9]

He tries to see in the unusual conditions of this strange engagement certain advantages. They have grown together in a way that would not normally have been possible. Occasionally he is troubled that they have lost so much time that they might have enjoyed together, discovering their love and its expression in new ways. If they had met a year earlier and known their love for each other while there was time to cultivate it in freedom, life would have been simpler and easier for her. But he dismisses the thought. She would have been too young then. In this way, she has grown marvellously and their love has matured. He does not talk of God bringing them together, because that would have been to belie his wedding sermon to Renate and Eberhard. Instead he reaches the conclusion that for each of them it was the right moment to fall in love. Conditions have given them access to a level of happiness which is denied many who have grown together in easier times. What attracted Maria to him was his zest for life, his masculinity, and both of them looked for a challenge in life.

Bonhoeffer read a great deal in prison and like many others at that time discovered the power of Adalbert Stifter's writing. He recommends his writings to Maria and suggests his book, *Aus der Mappe meines Urgrossvaters* (*From great-grandfather's portfolio*). It was from that book that he picked out the phrase, 'pain is a holy angel' and commented upon it. The full quote was 'Pain is a holy angel, who shows treasures to men which otherwise remain forever hidden; through him men have become greater than through all the joys of the world.' He began to ask his family to look for books by Stifter and was delighted when he found his *Witiko* in the prison library.

Gradually, Bonhoeffer enjoyed the company of other prisoners in Tegel, especially foreign prisoners, and he hoped to make long friendships after his release. He kept in touch with Hans von Dohnanyi and was eager for any news of him. He grieved at his illness. Then came the air-raids in the winter of 1943–44. His fellow-prisoners were encouraged by his calm during the worst raids and felt safer when he was at hand. In prison, he took a continuing interest in what was happening at home and even advised about the air raid shelter and the protection of pictures. For several months he writes optimistically about being out soon and it is clear that the possibility begins to recede into anxiety. He remembers Schlatter's lectures on ethics when he said that it was one of the duties of a Christian to be patient if he were held for interrogation. Then he begins to dream more and more of being released and back home with his parents.

At the end of July, Bonhoeffer was allowed to write to his father about a lawyer for his defence. He makes a few suggestions, asking that it be a lawyer not concerned with Church politics, but he leaves the choice to his father. The trial, he thinks, will take about three days and he clearly looks forward to being released fairly soon. He is also delighted that he is now permitted to write more often.

The Long Hot Summer

The summer of 1943 was very hot and Bonhoeffer's letters were much concerned with Hans von Dohnanyi, who suffered from the heat, and with precautions he had taken to make his cell more comfortable. Bonhoeffer was moved to a room just under the roof which made the heat more intense, which he seemed to accept, but gave him more privacy. His family sent him far more provisions than the other prisoners received, and although he shared some he did not like to appear as a privileged prisoner. His parents had suggested that because of the heat he should ask to be moved to a lower floor, but he obviously valued the privacy and felt that Spain, Cuba, Mexico etc. had prepared him for enduring such heat. There is a little of the bravado in his 'it does not make much difference whether the temperature in the cell is 34 or only 30!' Yet his mixed motives come out in the words, 'I don't want to ask to be moved to another floor, as that would not be fair to the other prisoners who would have to come into my cell, probably without such things as tomatoes.' He felt able to stand the heat as well as anyone and he did not want to be disturbed in a world he had created in that cell.

He had an orderly routine, he was well looked after by his parents and he could have visitors. In fact, prison was becoming a little like a monastery to him and he found some satisfaction in living under these conditions. That is how the letters seem to present it, with the occasional outburst of longing for Maria, impatience at the delays, concern for others whom he could not reach, etc.

It is, however, in his poems that his deepest thoughts emerge and his life in prison cannot be understood without a careful entering into that famous poem, *Who Am I?* Although written rather later than this first year in prison, it depicts a struggle which had been going on for a long time. His fellow-prisoners, his warders, his visitors saw a man who had mastered the limitations of his cell and constructed a meaningful life from the bits and pieces. To them he speaks from his cell 'like a squire from his country house', he seems to be in charge of the warders, giving them orders, he seems to 'bear the days of misfortune equably, smilingly, proudly, like one accustomed to win'. But that is not how he feels inside. He longs for a friendly word, he trembles with anger, he is unable to sleep because he is always expecting something to happen, he is tired and suffering from 'prison psychosis', he cannot pray, he is tempted to suicide and he is at times utterly confused and asks who he is – the one his fellow-prisoners admire for his calm or the contemptible, woebegone weakling he feels himself to be. His faith does not give way. Whatever else he may doubt, he does not doubt the wisdom of God and he resolves his conflicts with the simple affirmation: 'Whoever I am, thou knowest O God, I am Thine.'

Hopes and Disappointments

It was not until 25 September 1943 (i.e. more than five months after his arrest) that an official warrant was made out for his arrest. Bonhoeffer had already been alerted to this and plans were well advanced for the provision of a good lawyer to defend him. He was expecting the trial by the 17 December, which would be too late for him to be out for Christmas, but at least he could contemplate being home for Easter 1944. His high spirits were a little dampened by the news that because of Dohnanyi's illness the trial had to be delayed. He hoped not for too long, for he was eager to be done with it all and confident of acquittal.

Advent in Prison

Over the years, Bonhoeffer had associated the Advent season with music and preaching. Advent 1943 was severely restricted and we can gather from his letters how much he longed to be free to preach. Almost all his letters during that season contained fragments of sermons!

In one dated 28 November 1943,[10] he describes his prison celebrations that Advent. He hummed Advent hymns, adorned his Advent *Kranz* with a reproduction of Lippi's *Nativity* and feasted on an ostrich egg! He discusses the tunes to which the Advent hymns should be sung – 'not in the dull four four time, but in the expectant swinging rhythm which suits the texts so much better.' He is excited by new insights into the doctrine of the restoration of all things in Christ, as promised in Ephesians and developed by Irenaeus. He criticises the sentimental music offered to the prisoners by kind visitors and suggests that good sermons would be much better for them. One letter to Bethge contains a mini-sermon for Christmas Eve in which he makes four relevant points:

a) Nothing can fill the gap when we are separated from those we love;
b) The dearer and richer our memories, the worse it is;
c) Times of separation are not total loss – they can strengthen fellowship;
d) Any concrete situation can be mastered – it is fear and anxiety before that magnify the conditions.

And then, a theme on which he must have pondered much in those days: 'From the moment we wake until we fall asleep we must commend other people wholly and unreservedly to God and leave them in his hands, transforming our anxiety for them into prayers on their behalf.'

FOURTEEN

Conspiracy, Love and New Theology

By Easter 1944, Bonhoeffer had been in prison for one year and he was beginning to feel that only the overthrow of the régime, from within or from without, could release him. He prayed for the defeat of Hitler's Germany, but probably even more earnestly for the success of plans he knew to be afoot for the assassination of Adolf Hitler and the take-over of his rule. When he had first been admitted to prison, his influential connections were not known and he was therefore treated like any other prisoner. For twelve days he suffered this humiliation and he did not forget it. Later he observed closely the treatment of his fellow-prisoners with no such connections as his. His account of *Prison Life after One Year in Tegel* reads like an official report for some society concerned with prisoners' welfare. And it most certainly was.

It begins with a vivid description of his reception:

> The formalities of admission were correctly completed. For the first night I was locked up in an admission cell. The blankets on the camp bed had such a foul smell that in spite of the cold it was impossible to use them. Next morning a piece of bread was thrown into my cell; I had to pick it up from the floor. A quarter of the coffee consisted of grounds. The sound of the prison staff's vile abuse of the prisoners who were held for investigation penetrated into my cell. When I had to parade with the other new arrivals, we were addressed by one of the jailers as 'blackguards', etc.[1]

This changed for him, but he watched the treatment others received and wrote his complaints. The food was bad and prisoners did not receive the rations due to them; there was no work organised, games were prohibited. He comments that there were no air-raid shelters, but they could have been constructed by the 700 prisoners in Tegel. Lighting was meagre and prisoners had to sit in the dark for hours each evening because what light there was was not switched on. Few precautions were taken to protect prisoners during air-raids. Prisoners who were investigated appeared in chains.

He observed all this humiliation and complained with little permanent effect except to alleviate his own conditions.

Yet, after a year, he was so beset by visitors that he had to apologise to Bethge and also to Maria for not writing at Easter. His greatest deprivation by then is expressed as his lack of intelligent conversation.

Anticipation of Great Events

Bonhoeffer and his circle were fond of semi-coded messages in their writing, necessary to allow freedom of expression in a police state. For example, they referred to the outbreak of war in terms of 'Uncle Rudi'. At this time, with Dietrich and others in prison, it was even more important to understand what each was writing about without making it too evident to the censor. Thus, when he writes to Bethge on 11 April about Maria's birthday on 23 April and regrets that she must celebrate it without him, he adds, 'I have the impression that the two of us – I mean you and I – will only get back home at the same time.' Bethge is on military service in Italy and the 'same time' referred to is 'after an overthrow of Hitler or the end of the war'. The whole paragraph is full of hidden references to that great event, ending with, 'I must just make the best of it, and go on hoping for Whitsuntide.' Bethge picks this up after a reference to Catholics among his army comrades who pay a great deal of attention to laws and regulations. Then he adds, 'By the way, Whit Sunday plays a great part in their consciousness . . . I hope all goes well with you. Don't lose courage about the final date.'

Through all these references it is clear that both are expecting something to happen at Whitsuntide. Bonhoeffer even pretends to an interest in graphology in order to convey his thoughts. More seriously, he reacts to Bethge's suggestion that his prison experience will have changed him and given him much to report when they meet. In an extraordinary passage, he confesses that while, of course, he has learnt a great deal, he doesn't think that he has changed much. This is after a year in Tegel. 'I don't think I've ever changed very much,' he adds, 'except perhaps at the time of my first impressions abroad and under the first conscious influence of my father's personality.' He admits self-development, but not change. There is a continuity in his life. He opens up the question of different experiences of Christ, contrasting 2 Tim. 1:3a, 'I thank God whom I serve with a clear conscience as did my fathers', with the experience of sudden conversions from a life of sin, I Tim. 1:13. He does not spend his time regretting things that have happened in the past, wondering what it would have been like if he had acted differently. But he has a sense of confidence that everything has taken its natural course, 'determined necessarily and straightforwardly by a higher providence'.

This sets him free to think more clearly and almost at once he poses a question which has been much on his mind – something he has had to ask during that first year in prison: 'Why do we grow accustomed to hardship in the course of time?' He is not content to put it down to nature's self-protection; he is inclined to see it as the result of a clearer and more sober estimate of one's limitations and possibilities. This also enables him to take a calmer view of other people, their predicaments and needs. He can help them more easily and really love his neighbour. There is a little digression for Bethge on the way in which we change in self-development with our feelings growing cooler and calmer. This does not mean we become insensitive, but rather that we see things more clearly. A warm heart and a cool head are called for. He has freed his mind from any regrets or questioning about the past, placed himself firmly in the hands of a higher providence and caught glimpses of great events on the horizon. To his parents, he writes that he 'got used to things' and only queries, as with Bethge, 'which has been greater, the growth of insensitivity or the clarification of experience'. He already knows the answer. A prisoner learns to be insensitive to certain things that have little significance, but there are other things, 'which we have consciously or unconsciously assimilated and cannot forget. Intense experience forges them into convictions, resolutions and plans, and as such they are important for our lives in the future'. He contrasts the short stay in prison, which is largely annoying, with a long stay of a year or more and gives his alternative explanation of what Bethge had described as 'a great change': 'One absorbs not only an interesting or intense impression, but a radically new style of life.'

In his next letter to Bethge, at the end of April, there is a powerful attempt to understand events he is sure are about to take place. He uses all his biblical insights to grapple with this, stating, 'I'm firmly convinced that, by the time you get this letter, great decisions will be setting things moving on all fronts. During the coming weeks we shall have to keep a stout heart . . . We shall have to keep all our wits about us.'[2]

He uses texts from the Bible freely to clarify his mind about the way in which this can be done. There is no mistaking the exciting anticipation of great events in that letter at the end of April.

People Cannot be Religious Any More

It is in that same letter that he begins his new theological thoughts. His practice of reading the Bible, morning and evening, 'and often during the day as well', keeps his thinking close to that of its writers, from whom he quotes widely. He tests out the traditional theology of his Church against the experiences of men in prison with him; he takes his soundings constantly in biblical texts. Gradually he comes to the opinion that very little can be taken for granted. When assuring Bethge that he is 'getting on uncommonly well' and that fellow-prisoners keep telling him that he is 'radiating so much peace' and 'always so cheerful', he confesses a different world of feelings within himself: his poem *Who am I?* accentuates that contrast. He begins to use his letters to Bethge and his poems as his study and pulpit.

There are his writings too. It is not only *Ethics* which he is still working on, but that unwritten book on the future of the Church and its relation to people of the present day. He tries out ideas in these letters, but not casually. Much thinking and prayer and study of the Bible has preceded the remarks apparently thrown off in a personal letter. Bethge is the only one to whom he can write about these things, because for ten years they have shared the changing theology of a Christian in Nazi Germany, and they have discussed matters endlessly. Bonhoeffer is aware that he is going beyond Bethge, and expects him to be surprised, even worried. Yet, he must go on, because he knows that the time is past when people can be told everything in theological or pious words. The monstrous evil that had beset his country and the poison which it had injected into the Church had made 'inwardness and conscience' obsolete. These are the 'rusty swords' of which he writes eloquently in *Ethics*, and with appreciation for the role they have played in the past. Perhaps, religion too is obsolete. He detects that they are moving towards a 'completely religionless time' and that people as they now are, 'cannot be religious any more'. This he deduces from observation of those who call themselves 'religious' – the German Christians, the Confessing Church, the monks at Ettal, for all their differences, come under this heading of 'calling themselves religious'. But they do not act up to what they call religious, they live by other means. He can only conclude that they must mean something quite different from what an earlier generation meant by 'religious'. There are echoes of the boldness of his very first sermon in this letter.

He observes that the war is not calling forth any 'religious' reaction, as other wars have done. He questions whether Christianity is right to assume that humanity is basically religious. For nearly two thousand years, we have made the claim that Christianity represents the highest form of religion and Bonhoeffer does not doubt that. He questions whether religion itself is essential to modern man. In sweeping terms that have more than a ring of truth in our day, he outlines the way people have left the Church:

> The foundation has been taken away from all that has up to now been our 'Christianity', and there remain only a few 'last survivors of the age of chivalry', or a few intellectually dishonest people, on whom we can descend as religious. Are they to be the chosen few? Is it on this dubious group of people that we are to pounce in fervour, pique or indignation, in order to sell them our goods? Are we to fall upon a few unfortunate people in their hour of need and exercise a sort of religious compulsion on them?[3]

These are rhetorical questions. He is really trying to find what is left, 'now that the preliminary stage of Christian civilisation is over and we are entering a new era with a complete absence of religion – as we have known it.'

Out of this analysis come his crucial questions. He has already said, earlier in the letter, that what is bothering him incessantly is what Christianity really is, or indeed who Christ really is for us today. Now his questions are direct. He assumes an irreligious civilisation, a Europe in which Christianity was a necessary preliminary to a religiousless age, saying, 'How can Christ become the Lord of the religionless as well? Are there religionless Christians? If religion is only a garment of Christianity – and even this garment has looked very different at different times – then what is religionless Christianity?'[4]

These are questions, not statements. Karl Barth had started on this line of investigation, but instead of carrying it through to completion, arrived at a positivist statement about revelation. Bonhoeffer is critical of this and thinks it prevented him from a more radical theology which would be relevant to the contemporary situation. The question Barth never posed or, if he did, never seriously answered, was: What do a church, a community, a sermon, a liturgy, a Christian life mean in a religionless world? Barth had certainly rejected the *deus ex machina*, which meant God coming in from the wings to rescue us from the consequences of our own stupidity. But Bonhoeffer wanted to find out how to talk in a secular way about God. He posed the situation that we are secular-religionless Christians, claiming to be 'called forth' (which is the meaning of 'church' in Greek), 'not regarding ourselves from a religious point of view as specially favoured, but rather as belonging wholly to the world?' Questions, but they have implications for our understanding of Christ, who is no longer an object of religion, but rather the Lord of the world. Bonhoeffer queries what that really means. He is aware that too often we answer our deepest questions with religious phrases that cover up the answers.

The letter breaks off when he has raised the question of the role of the arcane discipline which had meant so much to him at Finkenwalde. He also throws in a question about the difference between the ultimate and the penultimate. A disappointing ending, but fortunately he discovers that he has time to add a page.

Freedom from Religion

The extra page explores the meaning of the debate over circumcision which takes up so much of the New Testament. The equivalent of freedom from circumcision in our day, he suggests, is freedom from religion. He notes that he feels a great deal more at home – the word he uses is 'brotherhood' – with non-religious people than with religious people. He admits that he does not like speaking about God with religious people, because they always bring in the boundary of human knowledge or resources. It's the old *deus ex machina* again. But with non-religious people he can mention God by name quite calmly and as a matter of course. The little diversion about the boundaries of human knowledge and resources leads him to a question which he has long pondered: 'Is even death (which people now hardly fear) and is sin (which they now hardly understand) still a genuine boundary today?' He reverts to something he developed at length in his Christology lectures in Berlin during the summer of 1933: 'I should like to speak of God, not on the boundaries, but at the centre, not in weakness, but in strength; and therefore not in death and guilt, but in a man's life and goodness.'[5]

He has some memorable phrases about the inadequacy of a theology of the boundaries. After saying that it is better to leave the 'boundaries' in the silence of mystery, he almost preaches at Bethge: 'Belief in the resurrection is not the "solution" of the problem of death,' 'The church stands, not at the boundaries where human powers have given out, but in the middle of the village.'[6]

This is emphasised in the Old Testament and Bonhoeffer is convinced that we read the New Testament far too little in the light of the Old. His task now, and he threatens to write more about it, is to find out what religionless Christianity looks like and what form it should take in Germany after the war.

Understanding in a Secular Sense

A few days later he was writing again, continuing the same theme. He had been thinking about Bultmann's essay, *Kerygma and Myth*, which had been circulated in the form of a paper before his arrest. It dealt with demythologising, and the unravelling of mythological concepts such as miracle, ascension, and so on in the Gospels. Bonhoeffer maintained, not that he went too far, but that he did not go far enough. It is not only the 'mythological' concepts which are problematic, but the 'religious' concepts. The heart of his criticism of Bultmann is put in one sentence: 'You cant, as Bultmann supposes, separate God and miracle, but you must be able to interpret and proclaim *both* in a non-religious sense.' This leads him to ask what he meant by 'interpreting in a *religious* sense'. It means, he concludes, to speak metaphysically and individualistically. Neither of these is relevant to the biblical message or to man today. He uses a battery of texts to substantiate his view that 'the question of saving one's own soul' does not occur in the Old Testament and that even Romans 3:24ff is not an individualistic doctrine. In that chapter, the conclusion is simply that 'God alone is righteous'.

Again, he acknowledges the great merit of Barth's criticism of religion and again criticises his positive doctrine of revelation. Bonhoeffer stands by the Old Testament and John 1:14: 'And the Word became flesh and dwelt among us.' He is not prepared to have the virgin birth, the Trinity or anything else boldly stated as revelation – without relating their meaning to the present world in a fully incarnational Christology. It is thus, not only mythological concepts based upon the matrix of thought in the first century that trouble him, but the need to reinterpret in a secular sense the concepts of 'repentance, faith, justification, rebirth and sanctification'. This venture into the secular understanding of religious terms is to take him much further than Bultmann. He detects that Bultmann remains a liberal at heart. Such weak fare is not for him.

Meanwhile he continues to write to Eberhard Bethge and occasionally also to Renate. He writes to Bethge about his new insights in theology, about 'selfless self-love' and gives little lectures on how mothers-in-law should behave. The writing was important, both to keep him in contact with the everyday problems of family life and to clarify his own theological thinking: 'I can't help sharing my thoughts with you, simply because that is the best way to make them clear to myself.'

The Baptism of Dietrich Wilhelm Rüdiger Bethge

He was disappointed not to be able to baptise the first child of Eberhard and Renate, but he did write the sermon[7] for that christening in the form of a message addressed to the child, with special reference to the three names he bears. He points out that they represent three houses and outlines the values they embody, from a country parsonage to a sophisticated middle class culture. These are worlds from which he can draw strength although in his lifetime they will disappear: 'the old country parsonage and the old town villa will belong to a vanished world'. But he assures the child that the spirit that imbued them will, 'after a time of misunderstanding and weakness, withdrawal and recovery, preservation and rehabilitation' find new forms. The past may at times seem to hang around our necks and make life harder, but it will also make life richer. A great deal of the 'sermon' is taken up with the value of a secure home and a good family tradition, abiding values which do not change, and then at the end comes a passage addressed to this little boy as he grows into the future. It is Bonhoeffer thinking of his struggle to understand the great Christian verities in a new age. He does not abandon them, but knows that they must be reinterpreted.

> Today, you will be baptised a Christian. All those great ancient words of the
> Christian proclamation will be spoken over you, and the command of Jesus
> Christ to baptise will be carried out on you, without your knowing anything

about it. But we are once again being driven right back to the beginnings of our understanding. Reconciliation, and redemption, regeneration and the Holy Spirit, love of our enemies, cross and resurrection, life in Christ and Christian discipleship – all these things are so difficult and so remote that we hardly venture anymore to speak of them. In the traditional words and acts we suspect that there may be something quite new and revolutionary, though we cannot as yet grasp or express it. That is our own fault.

He goes on to explain why. He points out that in the struggle of his day, the Church has been fighting for its own preservation. Therefore the use of these traditional words lose their force. This has limited the role of the Christian in his day to two things – prayer and righteous action among men. A new form will be born for the Church out of this prayer and action. But the time is not yet – 'We are not yet out of the melting pot.' Any premature attempt to reorganise the Church would be fatal, but he is sure the day will come when the Church in its new form will find a way to understand the great Christian verities in terms of its contemporaries in the world. Until that time comes, the Christian cause will be a silent and hidden affair, praying and doing right, waiting for God's time. His hope is in the child: 'May you be one of them.' And finally, a word of life for Dietrich Wilhelm Rüdiger Bethge: 'But the path of righteousness is like the path of dawn, which shines brighter and brighter until full day.' (Prov. 4:18).

In a very real sense, Bonhoeffer was there at the baptism. A friend who was a good musician took the sermon and a present and was able to report to the family on Dietrich and his life in prison. What was more important to Dietrich, however, was that he should be told everything about the baptism so that he (Corporal Linke was his name) could report back to the prisoner: 'Just tell him a great deal and let him make notes, so that I can learn everything.'

Dietrich as Counsellor

While Dietrich was in prison, his deep affection for Eberhard (Bethge) brought them very close in correspondence and in visits. He felt concerned when Eberhard was in danger and during one of the visits Eberhard had shared with his friend the experience of the Italian front and his fear of death. He was a little ashamed at this and Dietrich wrote a private letter – 'Intended only for you', i.e. not for Renate to see – defending his right to want to live happily and naturally with his wife Renate. He used the analogy of polyphonic music to describe the Christian life. What Bonhoeffer had heard from Bethge deeply disturbed him and he put all his theological insights into his letter. That Eberhard had been able to confide in him he took as 'a confirmation of our friendship'. He recognises a tension in

Eberhard which he cannot get rid of and Dietrich tries to help him like a brother. 'There is always a danger in all strong, erotic love that one may love what I might call the polyphony of life.' He goes on to explain that what he means is that we should love God with our whole heart, eternally, and that this provides the *cantus firma*, to which all the melodies of life can relate as counterpoint. One of those counterpoint themes is earthly affection. 'Where the *cantus firma* is plain and clear, the counterpoint can be developed to its limits.' He recognises the agony Eberhard is experiencing as a result of his separation from Renate, one he himself is experiencing in his separation from Maria. He tries to help Eberhard, and himself, to realise that the desires of earthly love are not gross or to be contrasted with a spiritual love. 'Eberhard, do not fear and hate the separation, if it comes again with all its dangers, but rely on the *cantus firma*.'

On the following day, the day of the baptism, Bonhoeffer wrote again, as the siren sounded and bombs fell, 'Perhaps you were surprised that yesterday's letter was on the one hand intended to say something to *you* and on the other was itself so helpless, but isn't that what happens? One tries to help and is oneself the person most in need of help. What I said was more for Renate's sake than for your own; i.e. for the sake of your shared life rather than because I felt you didn't know it all well enough. The image of polyphony is still pursuing me.' He feels the joy of sharing in the baptism and the pain of not being there – perhaps pain and joy are also part of life's polyphony. There is a continuous conversation about this letter written on the day of the baptism recording alerts and all-clears. He tries to assure Eberhard that although it is safer in prison than at the front, and he would gladly change places, Eberhard has more than he realises: 'I want you to be glad about what you have; it really is the polyphony of life.'

Whitsun 1944

The festival of Whitsun had always meant a great deal to Bonhoeffer and it is referred to often in relation to Finkenwalde: 'Eberhard, is the recollection of Whit Sunday morning at Finkenwalde, as splendid and important for you as it is for me?' He does not often use the word 'blessed', but this Whitsun he wishes Eberhard and Renate, with their new baby, 'A blessed Whitsun, a Whitsun with God and with prayer, a Whitsun on which you feel the touch of the Holy Spirit, a Whitsun which will be a rock (a *rocher de bronce* are his words) in your memories for the coming weeks and months. You need days whose memory is not painful, because of something which is lacking; but a source of strength, because of something which endures.'

His words are practical and natural, sending him also a letter which he can use if he is taken prisoner by the Americans, and wishing him good weather and much joy in little Dietrich. He is considerate, saying that he will understand if there is no visit because of the air-raids, but all the same he complains a little later about having no Whitsun letter: 'At first I was a bit disconcerted and perhaps even saddened, by not having a letter from anyone this Whitsuntide. Then I told myself that perhaps it was a good sign, and it meant that no one was worrying about me. It's a strange human characteristic that we like other people to be anxious about us – at least just a trifle anxious!'

His new theological thinking was occupying much of his time and he found some support in a book on physics by Weizsäcker, *The World-View of Physics*. It confirmed his view that science was pushing back the frontiers of knowledge and that if we left to God only the bits we did not know, he would become the God of the cracks, jumping from one place of incompleteness in our knowledge to another. It was this book that led him to write a very significant passage in his letter of 29 May a few days after Whit Sunday:

> We are to find God in what we know, not in what we don't know; God wants us to realise his presence, not in unsolved problems but in those that are solved. That is true of the relationship between God and scientific knowledge, but it is also true of the wider human problems of death, suffering and guilt. It is now possible to find even for these questions, human answers which take no account whatever of God.

He adds that people have always dealt with these problems without reference to God and that the Christian answers to them are not particularly significant, saying, 'It may be that the Christian answers are just as unconvincing – or convincing – as any others.'[8]

In this field too he resists the idea of the God of the cracks – needed for our so far unsolved problems, the areas of life where we cannot cope. God must be recognised, he insists, at the centre of life, 'not when we are at the end of our resources'. And he continues: 'It is his will to be recognised in life, and not only when death comes; in health and vigour, and not only in suffering; in our activities and not only in our sin.' And this he bases upon the revelation of God in Jesus Christ.

Bonhoeffer gradually came to see the importance of these 'theological letters'. At first, when Eberhard Bethge suggested sending copies to others for comment, he was uncertain, even though Eberhard only suggested the Finkenwalde men. Bonhoeffer felt that he was talking aloud and could only do that with Bethge. Later, he asked him to keep the letters and send them to Renate for safe keeping, so that he could work on them when he was out. He was finding that he could think more freely in letters to Eberhard than he could when consciously writing a book. That Whitsun was a turning point for him.

216

For the past two years, since his meeting with the Bishop of Chichester in Sweden, he had committed himself to a resistance in Germany which was proceeding from plot to plot, haltingly at first, headlong towards the end, culminating in the failure of 20 July 1944. Bonhoeffer had already said in 1942 that the resistance was an act of penance. He never moved from his conviction that the overthrow of Hitler would lead to chaos, not victory. Christians, he had said, must not try to escape repentance, or chaos, if it is God's will. Whitsun passed and no news came. Whether he knew of the date of Stauffenberg's assassination attempt or its postponement, he waited.

The Longing for Maria

In the long warm evenings, Bonhoeffer was aware of his longings to be free and to enjoy life to the full. He liked food, drink, good company and he was in love with Maria, to whom he was engaged. Summer had come round for the second time in prison and he began to question himself about his endurance. If I were not so reasonable, he confessed, I might do something foolish. It was not surprising that the old temptation to suicide returned. In his eloquent passage in *Ethics* justifying a man's freedom to take his own life, he had insisted that humanly speaking 'suicide is the ultimate and extreme self-justification of man as man'. He had also said that 'it cannot be contested that through this deed a man is once again asserting his manhood'. Often, in prison, separated from Maria and all that made life human, he must have recalled words that he had also written in that section, 'If a man cannot justify himself in his happiness and his success, he can still justify himself in his despair. If he cannot compel the world to acknowledge his right, yet he can still assert this right himself, in his last solitude. Suicide is a man's attempt to give a final human meaning to a life which has become humanly meaningless.'

Towards the end of May, he confessed to Bethge his deep longing for Maria. Deliberately suppressed desire may after a time lead to one of two bad results. It either burns you up inside or, being bottled up for too long, there is a terrific explosion. He admits that conceivably one might react by becoming completely selfless, but adds, 'I know better than anyone else that that hasn't happened to me.' He must suppress his desires, although he recognised that Bethge might well have advised otherwise. He comments, 'But look, this evening for example I couldn't dare to give full rein to my imagination and picture myself with Maria at your house sitting in the garden by the water and talking together into the night. That is simply self-torture.'

Every sound he hears torments him. From the sick bay comes the music of *Solveig's Song* and he is moved by it – to wait loyally a whole lifetime. 'Don't you think,' he asks Bethge, 'that such loyalty is the only way to happiness, and that disloyalty leads to unhappiness?'

Even in his writing of love he involves Bethge in theological speculations. He proposes writing to him while he is serving in Italy about the 'Song of Songs' and comments that he would much rather read it as a straight love poem, 'that is probably the best "Christological" exposition.'

For some time he had been writing poetry as all lovers do, but he had hidden this from Eberhard and even Maria, whom the poems mostly concerned. Then on 5 June,[9] he wrote to Eberhard confessing his poetry, 'I should be behaving like a shy boy if I concealed from you the fact that I'm making some attempts here to write poetry.' He then encloses an exquisite and deeply moving poem about the last visit by Maria and the agony of her retreating footsteps. 'I hear your steps depart and slowly die away.'

He calls his poem, *The Past*, which is personified in Maria herself:

> Close to you I waken in the dead of night,
> and start with fear –
> are you lost to me once more? Is it always vainly that I seek you,
> you, my past?
> I stretch my hand out,
> and I pray –
> and a new thing now I hear:
> The past will come to you once more,
> and be your life's enduring part,
> through thanks and repentance.

It is a long poem and should be read in its entirety but these lines suffice to show his longing and feel his hope mingled with despair.

Klaus Bonhoeffer

Although most of the family tried to keep in touch with Dietrich, either by writing or visiting or sending messages, Klaus seemed to be keeping aloof. He was much involved in the plot which was to fail so disastrously in July, and therefore avoided drawing attention to himself, so he did not keep in touch with his brother. Sadly, Dietrich misunderstood this. He writes warmly to Eberhard about Karl-Friedrich and the good letters he writes, encourages Eberhard to conversation with him. But he worries about Klaus, saying, 'It's probably hard for Klaus to find a starting point after so long. I really know that it isn't a lack of warm-heartedness ... Klaus has inherited mother's tendency to complicate things.' He would like a conversation with Klaus again, but if he had known how involved he was he would have rejoiced.

'There is hardly anything more stimulating than a conversation with him, and I can't think of a more kind-hearted and generous, more distinguished character than he is, but he is not the man for the simple decisions of life,' he writes. Perhaps after all he did know. Klaus had always known that the family would suffer for his resistance. He had once said to Gerhard Leibholz, 'You will see, we shall all come to the scaffold yet.' Looking ahead we can see something of the character of the man in his behaviour when that gloomy prospect became true for him. He did not flee when he knew that he was about to be arrested, although an aeroplane was ready to take him to safety. Klaus feared that if he escaped reprisals might be taken against his family. He contemplated taking his own life, but was dissuaded by his sister Ursula, who later regretted her advice when Klaus was tortured by the Gestapo. Dietrich was misjudging him.

The Autonomy of Man

Bonhoeffer could not be involved much in the conspiracy, although he eagerly sought news from whoever might know. That may be why he most wanted to see Klaus, as it was the reason why Klaus kept away! It was inevitable that he would use his long imprisonment to read widely and rethink his theology. In these long hours, questions arose which led him on to new ideas and the reexamination of old, accepted concepts. He was not changing ideas for the sake of change, but radically examining his own assumptions and those of his Church. Bethge showed a lively interest and pressed him forward. In a letter of 8 June, Bonhoeffer protested: 'You now ask so many important questions on the subjects that have been occupying me lately.' He does not have the answers, but Bethge's questions lead him into new areas of thought. He was aware that new growth was evident in his theology, but it was 'all very much in the early stages'. He was led on more by an instinctive feeling for questions that would arise later than for any conclusions. In this uncertain state, he attempted to give Bethge a summary of where he seemed to be going. It was not a theological treatise, but some thoughts that might lead to important ideas.

A germinal idea that came out of this was the concept of 'man come of age'. He saw from his reading that something radical had happened to thinking man about the thirteenth century. A movement began then towards the autonomy of man. The discovery of laws by which the world lives and deals with itself in science, social and political life, art, ethics and religion set mankind free from a state of tutelage, particularly to the Church: 'Man has learnt to deal with himself in all important questions without recourse to the "working hypothesis" called "God".' In matters of science this has become obvious. We do not need God to solve scientific problems. We can do that on our own. But, he now maintains that 'for the last hundred years or so it has become increasingly true of religious questions also; it is becoming evident that everything gets along without "God" – and in fact, just as well as before. As in the scientific field, so in human affairs generally, "God" is being pushed more and more out of life, losing more and more ground.'

The Church has resisted this – both Protestant and Catholic – thus forcing the movement for the autonomy of man to consider itself anti-Christian. He detects a self-assurance in the world, able to handle failures and false developments without giving up. They are accepted with fortitude and detachment as part of the bargain. 'The attack by Christian apologetics,' he writes, 'upon this adulthood of the world I consider to be in the first place pointless, in the second place ignoble, and in the third place unchristian.'

The Church had first met the exuberance of the Renaissance with prohibitions and then tried to come to terms with it, limiting its range as far as possible. Even today, he claimed, the Churches were trying to push the adulthood of the world back into its adolescence. Scientific humanism and communism could be seen as the supporters of the mature man against the obscurantism of the Churches. This pointless and ignoble attitude to the coming of age of humanity, he also attacks on theological grounds as 'unchristian'. It confuses Christ with one particular stage in humanity's religious development. His thinking had much further to go, but it was already an openness that would enable him to examine 'religion' from the point of view of human development.

At this stage, he found it necessary to look at what had happened so far in Protestant theology – German theology, in particular. He was still too much a follower of Karl Barth, however critical, to align himself with the liberals, stating, 'The weakness of liberal theology was that it conceded to the world the right to determine Christ's place in the world; in the conflict between the Church and the world it accepted the comparatively easy peace terms dictated by the world.'[10]

He saw the strength of liberalism, particularly in Troeltsch, in that it did not try to put the clock back. Liberalism accepted the battle, even though it ended with its defeat. And defeat was followed by surrender.

He then looks at the three attempts made to rescue something after the defeat by going back to fundamentals and the Bible, in Germany particularly also going back to the Reformation. These three attempts are linked with three theologians – Karl Heim, Paul Althaus and Paul Tillich.

Heim, following the lines of German pietism, sought to convince the individual that he was faced with the alternative of Jesus or despair. He won the 'hearts' of many, but only the hearts without tackling the intellectual problems, thus separating life into compartments. Althaus, following the modernist direction, but with a strong Lutheran emphasis – Reformation tenets and the Confessions – tried to wring from the world a place for Lutheran ministry and worship. Having achieved that, he was prepared to leave the rest of the world to its own devices.

Tillich, using philosophical tools, set out to interpret the evolution of the world in a religious sense. And, Bonhoeffer adds, 'against its will'. He tried to give the world a religious shape. Bonhoeffer admits the courage of this attempt, but he was not accepted – 'the world unseated him' – because he presumed to understand the world better than it understood itself. Bonhoeffer does not quarrel with this. The world *must* be understood better than it understands itself but not in a 'religious sense', as the Christian socialists had also tried to do and failed.

He acknowledges again that Barth was the first to see that all these attempts to accept terms that would leave a space for religion in the world or against the world were doomed to failure. In his *Epistle to the Romans*, (despite what he calls 'the neo-Kantian egg-shells') Karl Barth had brought in the God of Jesus Christ against 'religion'. Later, in his *Church Dogmatics*, he had enabled the Church to recognise this distinction all along the line. But he failed in that, 'in his non – religious interpretation of theological concepts he gave no concrete guidelines', and this applies both to ethics and dogmatics. Karl Barth is not rejected, but seen as a pioneer.

Bonhoeffer goes beyond him, but regrets that the Confessing Church appears to have forgotten what he taught them. It has even lapsed from the Barthian 'positivism of revelation' to a conservatism which is only to restore. He sees that the great achievements of the Confessing Church are that it 'carries on the great concepts of Christian theology', but he comments that this task seems to be gradually exhausting it. There are genuine elements of prophecy in the Confessing Church, notably in the claim to truth and mercy, and also genuine worship, but all is undeveloped and there is a failure to interpret. He turns to other movements – Schütz, the Oxford Group, the Berneuchen Movement, which had so strongly influenced Maria's family. These are reactionary 'because they go right behind the approach of the theology of revelation and seek for religious renewal'. He finds little hope in any of them, but does say in an aside – 'the Oxford Group would have the best chance if they were not so completely without biblical substance'.

Once again he looks with approval on Bultmann's attempts to deal with the limitations of Barthianism, but he fears that he is following the old liberal path of reductionism. 'My view,' Bonhoeffer comments, 'is that the full content, including the "mythological" concepts, must be kept.' He is a little unfair to Bultmann, who does not suggest doing away with the mythological concepts, but interpreting them. In fact, the difference comes more in the way in which they are 'interpreted'. Bultmann demythologises and his process does justice to the mythological concepts; Bonhoeffer wants the interpretation done in such a way that religion is not made a precondition of faith.

Redemption Myths

Bonhoeffer was beginning to recognise the extent of the theme he was dealing with and widened his reading. There are some interesting notes at the end of June which he made after reading and thinking about the Greek myths. Then he began to compare these and other myths with the Old Testament. He started work on an exposition of the first three commandments.[11] He eventually called this paper 'The First Table of the Law', and it fills fifteen pages of the *Gesammelte Schriften* (*Collected Works*). The commandment which gave him the greatest trouble was the second against 'idolatry'. He rejects the usual interpretation of idolatry as 'wealth, sensuality and pride'. Idols are worshipped and this commandment implies that people are worshipping something. Then he adds, 'But we don't worship anything now, not even idols.'

Every theological task that he undertakes leads him directly to a consideration of the difference made by the religionless state of the contemporary world. He sees that the Old Testament is unique among the ancient religions in that the faith it demonstrates is not that of a religion of redemption. Admittedly, a crucial place is given to redemption, but always from a situation and into a world task, never from the world. Delivery from Egypt and later from Babylon is historical, not mythological. The oriental religions of Egypt and Babylon have redemption myths, but they are setting people free from the limitations of earthly life. Not so the Old Testament. We separate Christ from the Old Testament when we try to make Christianity a religion of redemption. The Christian hope of resurrection sends a person back to his life on earth in a wholly new way. Unlike the devotees of the redemption myths, the Christian has no last line of defence or escape available, which takes him away from the tasks and difficulties into the eternal. Like Christ, he must drink the earthly cup to the dregs. It is only if there is no escape that he can claim to be crucified with Christ. This world must not be prematurely written off – the Old and New Testament agree about this. Bonhoeffer's thoughts constantly returned to this theme. He watched in vain while the Church contended against those who should have been its allies. Looking back over the lamentable record of theology in conflict with Darwinism he writes, 'God is being increasingly pushed out of a world come of age, out of the spheres of our knowledge and life . . .'

He caricatures the pastoral counsellors who sniff around, like investigative journalists, to find out what is wrong with a person who is happy! 'If he cannot be brought to see that his happiness is really an evil, his

222

health sickness, and his vigour despair, the theologian is at his wits' end.' Of course Jesus cared about people on the fringe of society, harlots, tax-gatherers, but not only such; He didn't question a person's health, vigour or happiness. Bonhoeffer summarises what he is really concerned about with the words, '. . . the claim of a world that has come of age by Jesus Christ.'

The Visit of Uncle Paul

While Dietrich Bonhoeffer was in prison in Tegel, the Military Governor of Berlin was General Paul von Hase, his mother's brother! This curious circumstance caused quite a stir in the prison. The governor's nephew had special treatment. One day, the governor came to visit him. You can imagine the nervousness of those in authority. Bonhoeffer wrote, 'A few hours ago, Uncle Paul called here to enquire about my welfare. It's most comical how everyone goes about flapping his wings and tries to outdo everyone else in undignified ways. It's painful, but some of them are in such a state now that they can't help it.'[12]

That is just an interjection before he gets down to the more important matter of theology, but he returns to the visit in the same letter. The general behaved in a rather extraordinary way. It was obvious that he too was expecting something to happen soon. He was involved in the conspiracy and was executed on 8 August 1944, but at this point he was not suspect. Had he been a civilian, however exalted, he could never have behaved in the way that he did. He arrived at the prison, had Bonhoeffer brought downstairs to meet him at once and he stayed five hours! He ordered champagne – four bottles – and surely created a precedent in that dismal place. A unique event and almost a celebration before the event. Bonhoeffer was surprised to find him so kind and generous. With the warders present they could hardly discuss what was afoot, but both knew. He made it clear to everyone that he was on good terms with 'prisoner Bonhoeffer'. It was an extraordinary occasion and both expected to be able to joke about it later when Hitler's rule and the war were over.

Bonhoeffer was not always writing theology to Bethge. In fact much of his writing is about his concern for his friend in the uncomfortable conditions of the Italian front. After receiving a cheerful letter from Bethge he writes on 8 July: 'If I could assume that you were continuing in the cheerful and contented mood which was expressed by your last letter, I would be really glad.' He rejoices at Bethge's progress and, after a diversion about the heat and some experiments he has been trying, he returns to what absorbs his attention, the theological work.

He had not had time to marshall the biblical evidence for his views but tries some profound 'preliminary remarks' on the displacement of God from the world and in particular from public life.[13] This, he claims, has led to an attempt, like a rearguard action, to keep his place secure in the private sector – 'the secrets known to a man's valet'. He means the full range of his intimate life, from prayer to his sexual life. This is a revolution from below. Just as in journalism there are those who sniff out scandal, so in the religious sphere, they are not satisfied until they have shown the most saintly person guilty of hidden sins. 'They grub around in the flower garden only for the dung on which the flower grows.'

He is hard on the clergy who sniff around after people in order to catch them out. It is the mood of the age – novels, biographies, films and plays, must all seek out the secret scandals of a life. No character is depicted in any of the modern literature or media without a bedroom scene or undressing scenes in films. 'Anything clothed, veiled, pure and chaste is presumed to be deceitful, disguised and impure.' There is something of the offended taste of the puritan in this – 'people here simply show their own impurity' – but that is not all. He detects a social malaise of which the banishing of God from the public part of human life is the cause and the privatising of God the effect. 'A basic antisocial mistrust and suspicion' is what he calls 'the revolt of inferiority'. So much for his observation, and no doubt much of it comes from the books he had found in the prison library. But what are the theological errors lying behind it? He describes them as two-fold. The first is that to call a man a sinner is to declare that you have found him out; the second is that man's essential nature is his 'inner life' and God is to have his domain in these secret places.

Man is certainly a sinner, but his sin lies not in those weaknesses which can be spied out, but in his strength. Goethe and Napoleon were sinners, not because they were unfaithful husbands, but because of the use of their strength. The Bible never spies out little sins, it deals with more serious issues than the scandal columns of the newspapers. What are these sins of strength? Bonhoeffer attempts a few hesitant examples: 'in the genius, *hubris*; in the peasant, the breaking of the order of life; in the bourgeois, fear of responsibility.'

And on the second error he writes: 'The Bible does not recognise our distinction between the outward and the inward.' The Bible is always concerned with the whole man. When Jesus presses home the 'inward discipline' of the Decalogue in the Sermon on the Mount, he does not abandon the outward obedience of the Law. From the biblical point of view, and this is always decisive for Bonhoeffer, it is quite wrong to think that the essential nature of man can be understood only from 'his intimate spiritual background'.

There follows what is a crucial paragraph in these 'preliminary remarks':

> I want to start from the premise that God shouldn't be smuggled into some last secret place, but that we should frankly recognise that the world, and people, have come of age, that we shouldn't run man down in his worldliness, but confront him with God at his strongest point, that we should give up all our clerical tricks, and not regard psychotherapy and existentialist philosophy as God's pioneers . . . The Word of God is far removed from this revolt from below. On the contrary, it reigns.

Anticipation

It is in this letter that Bonhoeffer tells Bethge that he is working on a novel, although not getting very far with it. Keith Clements makes use of this novel in his book, *A Patriotism for Today* and shows how Bonhoeffer was wrestling with some of his basic ideas in the novel, which he never finished. Bonhoeffer refers also to two poems – *Who am I?* and *Christians and Pagans*. He sent both these poems with the letter. I have already referred to *Who am I? Christians and Pagans* refers more to his theological struggles. It is a short poem of three stanzas. A third poem to which he also refers, although he does not at this point send it to Bethge, is a long poem about life in the prison: *Night Voices in Tegel.*[14] At the end of the letter there is a semi-coded, but very clear, reference to the forthcoming attempt on the life of Hitler: 'We shall very soon now have to be thinking a great deal about our journey together in the summer of 1940, and my last sermons.' This reference is to the prohibition against Bonhoeffer preaching during the visit to East Prussia in 1940 and is a coded message for Hitler's headquarters Wolfsschanze (called the Wolf's Lair) in East Prussia, where the attempt is to be made.

On 16 July, a letter from Bonhoeffer contains many details about what he is reading, writing, listening to on the radio and how he is occupying his thoughts during the last days of waiting.[15] Dostoievsky's *The House of the Dead* impresses him with the thought of the non-moral sympathy that those outside have for its inhabitants and leads him to the question: 'May not this amorality, the product of religiosity, be an essential trait of these people, and also help us to understand more recent events?' He is composing as much poetry as his strength allows and he is listening to a lot of music on the radio. Then a little coded remark tells Bethge that he is able to hear the BBC: 'I've probably told you before that I often get down to a bit of work in the evening as we used to.' There then follows one of the clearest indications that the events are about to take place which will restore life to normal. After a reference to Hans Dohnanyi, whose health is suffering, he shows that he now knows what Klaus is doing: 'I'm glad that Klaus is in such good spirits; he was so depressed for some time. I think all his worries will soon be over; I very much hope so for his own and his family's sake ... I'm now having my books sent from Pätzig to Friedrichsbrunn. I often have to think of grandmother Kleist now; she has become so immobilised.'

This last clause refers to the penetration of the Soviet armies into Further Pomerania which he had probably heard reported on the BBC. But there is no coding in his eager anticipation of his marriage to Maria: 'Perhaps we shall be able to celebrate our wedding in Friedrichsbrunn. Maria, too, can't travel anymore after the new restrictions. Perhaps it is a good thing for her, but it's a shame for me. Unfortunately she was quite depressed the last time I saw her; I can well understand it ... It's time that we were able to be together.'

The Weakness of God in the World

In that same letter he is not able to finish without returning to his absorbing theme. He is working at the non-religious interpretation of biblical concepts and realises this is to be a big job, but he looks forward to having time to continue it with more access to books. Continuing with the non-religious interpretation of the world, he recalls how historically this has been creeping up upon us in various fields: Lord Herbert of Cherbury had maintained that reason is enough for religious knowledge; Montaigne and Bodin, in the field of ethics, had substituted rules of life for commandments; Machiavelli detached politics from morality and later Grotius set up natural law as international law, 'even if there were no God'. In philosophy, Descartes built his system on the model of a mechanistic world, running by itself with no interference from outside. The pantheism of Spinoza equates God with nature; Kant is a deist, while Fichte is a pantheist, as is Hegel. 'Everywhere,' he concludes, 'the thinking is directed towards the autonomy of man and the world.'

If this is so, then we must be honest and drop the concept of God as a working hypothesis in morals, politics, science – perhaps even, as Feuerbach has done, in philosophy and religion too. The natural reaction of the anxious soul who sees God pushed out of his world is to deny the whole development. There are all kinds of emergency exits out of this dilemma, but Bonhoeffer cannot approve of any. The death leap back into the Middle Ages or the longing to return to the simple knowledge of childhood are not possible unless we abandon our mental integrity. The only way is that of the New Testament and he quotes Matthew 18:3: 'Truly I say to you, unless you repent and become like little children, you will never enter the kingdom of heaven.' At first you think he must have got the reference wrong, but no! This way he describes as 'through repentance, through *ultimate* honesty'. The key paragraph in this whole letter follows:

And we cannot be honest unless we recognise that we have to live in the world *etsi deus non daretur* (as though there were no God). And this is just what we do recognise – before God! God himself compels us to recognise it. So our coming of age leads us to a true recognition of our situation before God. God would have us know that we must live as men who manage our lives without him. The God who is with us is the God who forsakes us (Mark 15:34). The God who lets us live in the world without the working hypothesis of God is the God before whom we stand continually.

Before God and with God we live without God. God lets himself be pushed out of the world on to the cross. He is weak and powerless in the world, and that is precisely the way, the only way, in which he is with us and helps us. Matthew 8:17 makes it quite clear that Christ helps us, not by virtue of his omnipotence, but by virtue of his weakness and suffering.[16]

It is in this way that Bonhoeffer contrasts Christianity with other religions. Other religions seek God's help because he is strong and all-powerful, able to rescue man from unknown forces and the consequences of his own mistakes. The whole apparatus of religion is designed to persuade God to come to our aid in his strength. The Bible directs us to God's powerlessness and suffering. Bonhoeffer sees that his description of the coming of age of man has helped to restore the biblical picture of God. It does away with a false conception of God and opens up a way to see the God of the Bible, 'who wins power and space in the world by his weakness'. This is to be Bonhoeffer's starting point for a secular interpretation.

A day or two later, he shows some anxiety about the letters and poems he has sent to Bethge. He is going to need those papers soon, he feels, when he is released and able to work freely on his new ideas. The poems are also most helpful in this new development and he particularly mentions the poem about Christians and pagans. Jesus asks his disciples in Gethsemane, 'Could you not watch with me one hour?' That is not what the pagan expects of God. It is a reversal of roles. 'Man is summoned to share in God's suffering in the world.' The letter is taken up mostly with this theme, quoting many biblical texts to support the thesis. He also develops something of the nature of a Christian life in the world – not to be religious in a particular way. It is not being religious that makes a Christian, but 'participating in the sufferings of God in the secular world'. He promises that the next time he writes he will look at the nature of this life, this 'participating in the powerlessness of God in the secular world'. He adds that it will be much easier when they can talk at length as once they did. And he clearly expects this to be soon. Two days later an attempt was made on the life of Hitler and the consequences were horrific – not for Hitler, but for some of the finest leaders of thought and action in Germany, including many of Bonhoeffer's family. There was little chance of Bonhoeffer surviving after that.

FIFTEEN

The Last Months

Perhaps the most tragic day in modern German history is 20 July 1944. On that day, a daring attempt was made on the life of Adolf Hitler and it failed. The failure led to the uncovering of the conspiracy, the exposing of the conspirators and many others who were against Hitler, but not involved in this particular conspiracy. It meant eventually that the flower of German military, diplomatic and cultural life was destroyed. Had there been no attempt, the war would have pursued its course and many of those who died would have lived to help reconstruct a defeated Germany after the war.

Bonhoeffer might well have survived. The reactions to this attempt vary widely. Hitler himself sent his blood-stained uniform to his mistress, Eva Braun, with the words: 'I have sent you the uniform of that wretched day. Proof that Providence protects me and that we no longer have to fear our enemies.' To the public he said in a 1 a.m. broadcast that he would be revenged and that this 'very small gang of criminal elements will now be ruthlessly exterminated'. He was as good as his word.

The only Church paper still being printed, *Pfarramt und Theologie* wrote:

> The frightful day. While our brave armies, courageous until death, are struggling manfully to protect their country and to achieve final victory, a handful of infamous officers, driven by their own ambition, ventured on a frightful crime and made an attempt to murder the Führer. The Führer was saved and thus unspeakable disaster averted from our people. For this we give thanks to God with all our hearts and pray, with all our church congregations, for God's assistance and help in the grave task the Führer has to perform in these most difficult times.[1]

For Winston Churchill, it was simply a case of 'the highest personalities in the German Reich murdering one another'.

Dietrich Bonhoeffer wrote to Eberhard Bethge the day after the attempt with no specific reference to the event, although he must have known that Hitler lived and vowed revenge. It is a quiet letter, putting the theological arguments to one side. He cannot quite forget his theological thoughts, but on this sad day he is 'content to live the life of faith without worrying about its problems'. He refers to the daily readings – 'in particular those for yesterday and today'. This is his only reference to 20 July. The readings were:

> July 20 – 'Some boast of chariots and some of horses; but we boast of the name of the Lord our God' (Ps. 20:7), and 'If God is for us, who can be against us?' (Rom. 8:31).
>
> July 21 – 'The Lord is my shepherd, I shall not want' (Ps. 23:1); and 'I am the good shepherd; I know my own and my own know me' (John 10:14).

It is a very personal letter, in which Dietrich writes to Eberhard as he could write to no one else. Living the life of faith means living completely in this world, not trying to make something of oneself, but 'living unreservedly in life's duties, problems, successes and failures, experiences and perplexities'. This means throwing ourselves completely into the arms of God, taking seriously not our own sufferings, but those of God in the world. 'Watching with Christ in Gethsemane – that is faith, that is repentance, that is how one becomes a man and a Christian. How can success make us arrogant, or failure lead us astray, when we share in God's sufferings through a life of this kind?'

These are thoughts he cannot yet share with Maria. In fact he can share them with no one but Eberhard. His final comment on the debacle of 20 July is probably the simple words of piety: 'May God in his mercy lead us through these times; but above all may he lead us to himself.'

Stations on the Road to Freedom[2]

At the same time he wrote a four-stanza poem which he sent to Eberhard, still unrevised, hoping to have time to polish them later. The stanzas deal in turn with the search for freedom by means of discipline, action, suffering and death. The last two lines make a climax to the search: 'Freedom, how long we have sought thee in discipline, action and suffering; dying, we now behold thee revealed in the Lord.'

In 1966, when I published the second volume of Bonhoeffer's letters, lectures and notes from the *Collected Works* (Collins), I called it *The Way to Freedom* and was able to find the four stages of his life marked in those papers by his discipline, action, suffering and readiness to accept death as the 'greatest of feasts on the journey to freedom eternal'. In 1968, when Mary Bosanquet published her, *The Life and Death of Dietrich Bonhoeffer*, she divided her story into these same four parts (Hodder & Stoughton). In 1986, when Otto Dudzus published an anthology of *Bonhoeffer for a New Generation* (SCM Press), he collected the most important passages around the structure of these four stations on the way to freedom. Thus the importance of that poem as a summary of Bonhoeffer's life and thought has been recognised by almost every student of his writing and also by those who knew him. And it was written at this crucial moment of the failure of the plot to kill Hitler.

The Debacle of 20 July 1944

Details of the coup and its failure filtered slowly into Tegel prison. It was not until several days later that Bonhoeffer learnt what had happened and he could never have learnt the whole story. He knew enough, however, to realise that he had little chance of survival except by escape. Before we come to the details of the escape plan, let us take a look at what happened on 20 July. Many attempts had previously been made on Hitler's life, all unsuccessful and none of them fatal for those who planned them. The conspirators had survived. Eventually a perfect plan was worked out with Colonel Count Claus Schenk von Stauffenberg as the key figure. In June 1944, at the age of thirty-seven, he had been appointed Chief of Staff to General Fromm, Commander of the Reserve Army, whose headquarters were at the War Office in Berlin. Stauffenberg had direct access to Hitler as Fromm's representative on many occasions. He was a war hero of considerable repute and insisted upon serving his country even though he had lost his right forearm, two fingers and an eye in action. Such disabilities spared him the usual search. He volunteered to carry a bomb into Hitler's conference. This he did in a briefcase which he placed at or near Hitler's feet during the mid-day conference on 20 July. The conference was at Rastenburg and after placing the bomb Stauffenberg left. He was flying back to Berlin before anyone realised how the explosion had taken place. But Hitler was spared, because another officer had moved the briefcase. Stauffenberg arrived in Berlin about 5 p.m., convinced of his success. He had heard the explosion as he drove away. Hitler was badly shaken, but able to get out of the hut where the conference was held. He immediately shut down all communication with the outside world. The conspirators, waiting in the War Office, were unable to receive the pre-arranged signal to take over Berlin. Everything was in chaos. Stauffenberg was identified as the officer responsible for the bomb. Hitler communicated with Goebbels, who was in Berlin and, before the night was out, Stauffenberg and his closest associates had been shot as traitors. Beck had been forced to commit suicide and the whole network of conspirators was hunted down for the great public trial which Hitler intended to stage as a major act of recrimination.

At 1 a.m. he spoke on the radio and vowed revenge. Hitler was angry and elated. Mussolini who came that afternoon to Rastenburg was shown round the wreckage of his map room with an air of triumph. 'It is not the first time

I have escaped death miraculously,' Hitler told him, and he was immensely impressed. He continued his boasting to the Duce who was already defeated at home, 'I am now more than ever convinced that the great cause which I serve will survive its present perils, and everything will be brought to a good end.' Later at the crowded tea party in the afternoon, he shouted in rage: 'I will crush and destroy the criminals who have dared to oppose themselves to Providence and me.'

Hitler was lucky to escape so lightly. His injuries were more psychological than physical. His hair had been singed, his right arm partially paralysed and his right leg burned, his eardrums damaged and his buttocks bruised. But four officers had been killed and two severely injured.

During August and September, Roland Freisler presided over the Nazi People's Court in Berlin, while hundreds of officers and civilians were interrogated and condemned. The victims were bullied and humiliated, and many were cruelly executed, their hanging filmed, so that Hitler might see that his vengeance had been fully exacted. It was a horrible time in Berlin and the war continued with its fearful bombing. Bonhoeffer makes frequent reference to this bombing in his letters from Tegel.

The Last Three Months in Tegel

It soon became dangerous to smuggle letters in or out of Tegel to Bonhoeffer. Hans von Dohnanyi, who had been ill with diphtheria for some time, was taken to the concentration camp in Sachsenhausen. The arrests in August exposed the conspiracy and it was feared that all would soon be known. The only hope for Bonhoeffer was escape. This was carefully planned, with preparations made to receive him in Sweden. His guard, Corporal Knobloch, who was devoted to him, assisted in this and was prepared to 'disappear' with him. Several members of the conspiracy tried to escape also, but very few succeeded. The arrests continued, touching Bonhoeffer's family, and at last all was ready for his escape in early October, but the arrest of Klaus and others led him to abandon his plan. He did not want to make things more difficult for Klaus or expose his parents and Maria to further dangers. He remained in Tegel, continuing his theological work. And he wrote a new poem: *Jonah*,[3] which began, 'In fear of death they cried aloud'. It is a short, four-stanza poem on the dramatic moment when the fearful seamen agree to throw Jonah overboard once he has confessed his guilt and pleaded with them:

> Behold! I sinned before the Lord of hosts.
> My life is forfeit. Cast me away! My guilt must bear the wrath of God;
> the righteous shall not perish with the sinner!

In his letters too he had raised the question of whether life is worth living. There is little doubt that all those involved in the conspiracy contemplated suicide. None of them knew whether they could stand up to torture and all feared they might betray their friends. In a letter dated 21 August, Bonhoeffer anticipates Bethge's birthday and tells of how the readings and meditations are helping him. The key to all our problems he finds is living 'in Christ'. 'All that we may rightly expect from God, and ask him for, is to be found in Jesus Christ.' Again, 'In Jesus God has said Yes and Amen to it all, and that Yes and Amen is the firm ground on which we stand.'[4]

He admits that when some loved one dies we ask if life is worth living and concludes, 'if this earth was good enough for the man Jesus Christ, if such a man as Jesus lived, then, and only then, has life a meaning for us.' The words, although spoken to himself, are explicitly for Bethge in his separation, his lonely birthday. Bonhoeffer had no doubt about the power of prayer: 'I think I owe it to the prayers of others that I have often been kept in safety.' But soon he returns to the repeated injunctions in the New Testament to us to 'be strong'. He quotes four such verses and then comments: 'Isn't people's weakness (stupidity, lack of independence, forgetfulness, cowardice, vanity, etc) a greater danger than evil? Christ not only makes people "good"; he makes them strong also.'

A day or two later he writes that he is now working on 'A Stocktaking of Christianity'. After admitting that his work depends too much upon having a supply of cigarettes, he comments that he is rather shocked at what he is writing, but takes comfort in the thought that so far he has only done the negative, critical part and will be able to balance and edit the script before publication. There is hope still of that, but during September he becomes anxious, not about his poems and theological work, but lest any remarks might be taken up by the wrong people: 'The only thing to be careful about is that nothing gets into the wrong hands.'

On 22 September the discovery of documents by the Gestapo made the situation dangerous for the Bonhoeffer family. Dietrich gave up his plan for escape and *Jonah* is associated with that. It was probably written about 5 October. On 8 October he was transferred from Tegel to the cellar of the Gestapo prison in Prinz Albrecht Strasse. There he no longer had the freedom to see visitors or write letters to the extent that he had had in Tegel. He was interrogated by the Reich Security Office. At the same time, Klaus Bonhoeffer, Rüdiger Schleicher, and Eberhard Bethge were imprisoned in the Reich Security Office in Lehrter Strasse.

Outline for a Book[5]

Before entering the gloomy portals of Prinz Albrecht Strasse prison, let us step back to August and look at that 'Outline for a Book'. All we have is the

'Outline', notes and comments made in letters. But to that can be added Eberhard Bethge, who was so close to Dietrich and discussed so much with him, that I sometimes feel that he should write and publish that book!

Bonhoeffer's plan was to write quite a short book – not more than 100 pages, with three chapters: 1. A Stocktaking of Christianity; 2. The Real Meaning of Christianity; 3. Conclusions.

Chapter 1 is the part he refers to as rather negative. It is to have four parts:

(a) the coming of age of mankind, in which he develops the thesis that man has insured himself against the menace of nature and environment, but not yet against his own organisation.

(b) the religionlessness of man who has come of age, so that God as a 'working hypothesis' has become superfluous.

(c) the Protestant Church, dealing with pietism as a last attempt to maintain Evangelical Christianity; Lutheran Orthodoxy as an attempt to rescue the Church as an institution for salvation; the Confessing Church with its theology of revelation, standing for the Church's cause, but little personal faith in Christ.

(d) the public morals – as shown by sexual behaviour.

Chapter 2 is divided into five parts and is obviously to be the heart of the book:

(a) God and the secular.

(b) the experience of God, not as a religious relationship, but through Christ, being with God 'for others'.

(c) the interpretation of biblical concepts on this basis – creation, fall, atonement, repentance, faith, the new life, the last things.

(d) the cultus, i.e., liturgical worship and its relation to religion.

(e) What do we really believe? a critical assessment of the inadequacy of the Church and its creeds as means of hiding our own disbelief.

Chapter 3 is not divided up, but continues the discussions in his letters to Bethge. 'The Church is the Church only when it exists for others.' He suggests as a beginning the Church should give away its property to those in need. The clergy should find some secular occupation and otherwise depend upon the collections at Church services. Obviously it must serve those in need and must teach what it means to live in Christ, 'to exist for others'. Of course it must stand for certain values in society, but it should do this more by example than by commandments. It should give up all sense of power over others and become the servant Church. Bonhoeffer would like to revise the creeds, reform the system of training clergy, change both Christian apologetics and the life-style of clerical life. He admits that all this is crude and condensed, but there are things he wants to say quite simply and directly. The Church must be open and honest. What might he have done to the Protestant Churches of Germany and through them the world if he had lived.

His letters now become heavy with news of suicides and arrests all hinted at in coded language. Maria is not well, travel is restricted by the air-raids. But Bethge's arrest brings the correspondence to an end.

His last letter from Tegel to Eberhard is the one talking about his work on the book. Eberhard's last letter to him at Tegel is dated 30 September. He has received the poem, *The Death of Moses*.[6] He finds it different from the other poems, but is deeply moved by it and suggests no improvements. In it Moses accepts his fate which is to die on the mountain:

> To punish sin and to forgiveness you are moved,
> God, this people I have loved.
> That I bore its shame and sacrifices
> And saw its salvation – that suffices.

A few days later he wrote *Jonah*.

Prinz Albrecht Strasse

In the Gestapo cellar there were no privileges. For Christmas and New Year, he was allowed to write a letter to Maria (17 Dec.) and to his mother (28 Dec.). They are letters of love and comfort. To his mother, after assuring her of his love and how much her love has meant to him, he risks a glimmer of hope: 'My wish for you and father and Maria and for us all is that the New Year may bring us at least an occasional glimmer of light, and that we may once again be together.' To Maria, he writes of how her love banishes loneliness: 'Therefore, you must not think I am unhappy. What is happiness and unhappiness? It depends so little on the circumstances: it depends really only on that which happens inside a person. I am grateful every day that I have you, and that makes me happy.'

Fabian von Schlabrendorff

A cousin of Maria was in the Gestapo cellar at the same time as Bonhoeffer. He saw him for the first time at night when, during an air-raid, the prisoners had been taken from their cells to a cement shelter. The Gestapo were anxious that they should not die until they had extracted all the information they could from them. He was comforted by Bonhoeffer's composure and they contrived to meet in the communal shower. Bonhoeffer made quite clear to him 'that he was determined to resist all the efforts of the Gestapo, and to reveal nothing of what our friends' fates made it our duty to keep dark'. It is interesting that one of the reasons Bonhoeffer gave in his *Ethics* for a man honourably to commit suicide is if he thought that under torture he might betray his friends. A little later Bonhoeffer was transferred to a cell which was next to that of Maria's cousin. Through a common wall and during times in the washroom they managed to carry on quite a regular conversation although this was not permitted. The air-raid warnings also provided opportunities for meeting.

A good picture of Bonhoeffer in Prinz Albrecht Strasse comes from this fellow prisoner who found the conversations life-giving:

> Dietrich Bonhoeffer told me of his interrogations: how the very first time they had threatened to apply torture, and with what brutality the proceedings were carried through. He characterised his interrogations with one short word: disgusting. His noble and pure soul must have suffered deeply. But he betrayed no sign of it. He was always good tempered, always of the same kindliness and politeness to everybody, so that to my surprise, within a short time, he had won over the warders.[7]

Bonhoeffer appeared to be fairly optimistic when talking to other prisoners, although he must have known that since the discovery of the papers in the air-raid shelter of the Abwehr at Zossen on 22 September, there was enough known to convict him. After a while, Hans von Dohnanyi was also brought to the Gestapo prison in Prinz Albrecht Strasse and Bonhoeffer was able to get in touch with him. Dohnanyi was very ill by now – lying on a stretcher with both legs paralysed. Bonhoeffer took the opportunity to dive into Dohnanyi's open cell when they were filing back after an air-raid and, after brief conversations to check what each was saying, re-join the column of prisoners without being noticed by the warders! In those short visits he agreed with Dohnanyi upon all the essential points of the witness they would give when on trial. It was not all triumph and at one point he nearly lost heart. He had skilfully avoided giving any important information when the interrogator recognised that he was holding something back. He thereupon threatened Bonhoeffer with the arrest of his fiancée and his aged parents if he did not give a more comprehensive reply. In a way very similar to the account given by Von Moltke in his own letters to his wife, Bonhoeffer found the right moment to express his opposition to National Socialism and explain it on Christian grounds. He was making sure that, if condemned, he would be accused not of high treason, but of being a Christian.

Fabian von Schlabrendorff tells how they shared the few things they were allowed to receive from relatives and friends. And it was an opportunity for Bonhoeffer to talk to Fabian about Maria: 'With shining eyes he told me of the letters from his fiancée and his parents, whose love he felt near him even in the Gestapo prison.' On the morning of the 3 February, a very heavy air-raid reduced parts of Berlin to rubble and the Gestapo prison was hit. The Gestapo headquarters were destroyed, but the prisoners were packed tightly in the shelter, which 'rocked like a ship tossing in the storm', but it held. Bonhoeffer stood quite still, then relaxed as though nothing had happened.

Knowledge of Bonhoeffer's Activities

Bonhoeffer told Fabian that, despite the discoveries at Zossen, the Gestapo had no clue to his real activities. Even his relationship with his brother-in-law, Hans von Dohnanyi, he managed to represent in a plausible way. He thought that in their eyes he was quite unimportant, but they interrogated him to fit one or two minor pieces into the puzzle which would enable them to accuse or even discover others far more involved. He had even explained his visits to Switzerland and Sweden as in the national interest. That seems an optimistic assessment, but it is very difficult to know what the exact situation was. The closely argued and heavily documented seven pages in Bethge's monumental biography on *The Interrogation* leave the reader still uncertain. Eberhard Bethge, when himself interrogated, was read documents containing full confessions by Bonhoeffer which he was sure Dietrich never signed or wrote. They were skilfully compiled, however, containing sections from letters that Bethge had received from him. The mixing of the genuine with the fabricated was a well known trick of interrogation. So for all the documents, we are none the wiser.

There is, however, one document, discovered by Jorgen Glenthoj and published in 1966, which is an official account of an interrogation. Kaltenbrunner wrote to the German Foreign Office on 4 January 1945 and the letter was laid before Ribbentrop. It consists entirely of information obtained from Bonhoeffer. It begins with an account of the visit to Sweden 'by order of the former Admiral Canaris'. It then goes into detail about the nature of Bonhoeffer's discussions with Bishop Bell. They seem wholly to have been in the interest of the Churches' role in peacefully settling Europe after the end of the war. Several British politicians are mentioned, but Bonhoeffer seems to have done nothing subversive and all in the national interest. The main concern appears to be the way in which the Allies would relate to each other. How would they react to a Russian victory, would America destroy England etc.? It certainly looks as though Bonhoeffer was continuing his double game in his interrogations.

When Fabian von Schlabrendorff thought he might be released, Bonhoeffer urged him to seek an interview with Himmler. It is all very confusing and, despite Bethge's brave attempts, the picture is not convincing. Bonhoeffer was trying to make life difficult for the interrogators, that much is clear. And he was not going to say anything that might endanger others. It must have been difficult, but there is just a hint that Bonhoeffer was enjoying the game and entering into it with all his accustomed gusto and with a determination to win. In a brighter moment he could boast that it would take years to put together a case against him.

But we know that he continued his theological work through all this. In his last letter to his parents in January he is still asking for books! However no papers have survived from this last period in prison. We are left to wonder what changes he would have made in the Tegel papers and how far he got with that book. The most obvious impression of his theological work is that it is in process of formation and he did it as though he still had many years ahead of him.

On 7 February 1945, Fabian von Schlabrendorff spoke to him for the last time and that day he was transported to Buchenwald. After telling of Bonhoeffer's end, as far as he knew it, he gives us a paragraph which is a little parable of Bonhoeffer's survival: 'When after several months I returned to my home, which had been destroyed by bombs, I at first saw nothing but rubble. Anything that the bombs had spared had been stolen. Only one book lay undamaged among the bricks and mortar: Dietrich Bonhoeffer's *Cost of Discipleship*.'[8]

Buchenwald

Around noon on 7 February, Bonhoeffer's cell number was called and he was transported to the notorious concentration camp at Buchenwald, near to Weimar, where Goethe had lived and where Germany had made her last attempt to form a democratic government. For Bonhoeffer it must also have held memories of Paul Schneider who was beaten to death there in 1939, the first of many martyrs of the Confessing Church. But Bonhoeffer was regarded as a prominent prisoner, deserving of special attention. He was also due for interrogation in Buchenwald and had to be kept healthy enough to stand up to it. Such prisoners were put in the air-raid shelter cells, which lay beneath houses outside the actual area of the camp. These houses had at one time been built for camp officials, but were later converted into command headquarters and barracks. Some stored ammunition. The cells in the basement were for SS members who had been sentenced to solitary confinement for some misdemeanour. Now one of them provided a cell for Bonhoeffer – damp, cold and without daylight. Captain Payne Best of the British Secret Service, captured in 1939, was brought to Buchenwald on 24 February 1945 and has much to say about his relations with Bonhoeffer during these Buchenwald days. In his book, *The Venlo Incident*,[9] he describes the cells in detail: 'The wide central corridor of the cells was divided into three parallel corridors by two long walls'. There was a communal washroom and next to that the dampest of the cells, No. 1, where Bonhoeffer was placed. Payne Best's cell, No. 11, was directly opposite Bonhoeffer's, but the dividing walls made visibility impossible. He could hear him but not see him, except in the washroom and during exercises which had to be up and down the corridors. The party which came with Payne Best on 24 February included another English officer, Hugh Falconer, a Russian air force officer, Wasiliew Kokorin and General von Rabenau. Von Rabenau joined Bonhoeffer in Cell No. 1. This soldier had retired from active service in 1942 and had been involved in the conspiracy from the beginning. As early as 1940 he had been an intermediary between Beck's centre of resistance and some of the leading generals who were trying to influence Brauchitsch, when he replaced Fritsch as commander-in-chief of the army. After retirement, Von Rabenau had taken a theological degree at Bonn and continued actively in theological studies. This meant that Bonhoeffer had a cell companion with whom to argue about theology. In the next cell was Dr Hermann Pünder, a Catholic politician who survived and tells of how Von Rabenau continued to write his *Memoirs*, but he could not remember if Bonhoeffer did any writing. He *could* remember that they had 'enthusiastic dogmatic discussions that I was able to listen to with great interest'. Payne Best acquired a chess set for the two theologians and Bonhoeffer was delighted. Most of the cells were shared, but Payne Best reports that Bonhoeffer and Von Rabenau were the only ones who really enjoyed one another. When he could Bonhoeffer talked English with the two English officers, particularly Payne Best, who seems to have known nothing about who he was. In *The Venlo Incident*, Payne Best describes his fellow-prisoners – not always kindly! But of Bonhoeffer he wrote:

> Bonhoeffer was all humility and sweetness; he always seemed to diffuse an atmosphere of happiness, of joy in every smallest event in life, and of deep gratitude for the mere fact of being alive. There was something dog-like in the look of fidelity in his eyes and his gladness if you showed that you liked him. He was one of the very few men I ever met to whom his God was real and ever close to him.[10]

Easter Day was on 1 April that year and spirits rose in Buchenwald when they heard the American guns in the basement cells. The Allies were closing in and no one could expect further interrogations or People's Courts. Some escape plans were thought out and given up. Guards said they must be ready to leave on foot – did that mean to be shot in the nearby woods? Heavy lorries were also ready to take the prisoners away from the front, now rapidly advancing from the east. This suggests that an order had come from Berlin to protect the prisoners, for the normal practice would have been to shoot them if the Allies advanced too near. The heavy lorries were to be used to take some prisoners to Flossenbürg and others further south. No one told them this, but gradually as the crowded uncomfortable closed lorry jolted its way south-eastwards, they realised that they must be making for the notorious Flossenbürg concentration camp. Bonhoeffer shared his tobacco – 'he was a good and saintly man', said Payne Best in gratitude!

The Last Days

The next few days were chaotic and uncertain. After leaving Buchenwald they were anxious to know if they were heading for the annihilation camp at Flossenbürg. On the Wednesday they reached Weiden, where Müller and Liedig were called out and Gehre jumped out. All three appeared to be taken off in the direction of Flossenbürg. When the lorry moved off again with the rest of the prisoners it was in another direction and the guards became more friendly. They let the prisoners get out at a farmer's house. They were allowed to go to a pump in the yard and a country woman brought a jug of milk and rye bread. It was a lovely spring day in the Nab Valley. At night they were taken to Regensburg and put into the prison attached to the court house. There were five in a cell, but they could choose their own companions. Bonhoeffer shared his cell with Rabenau, Pünder, Falkenhausen and Hoepner. The kitchens were closed, but the prisoners demanded food and got it from the slightly intimidated guards – vegetable soup with some bread.

Payne Best describes the reunions in the washroom on Thursday morning as more like a reception than a morning in prison. The prisoners were in good heart. Bonhoeffer was able to tell relatives about the people with whom he had been in the Prinz Albrecht Strasse. It must have seemed as though the worst dangers were over and certainly the relations with the guards changed. Early on the Friday they were back in their closed lorry and soon travelling in good spirits along the Danube. The lorry skidded and the steering broke. A replacement van came from the Regensburg police. They were soon on their way again, past the monastery at Metten and into the Bavarian woods. The van was a great deal more comfortable than their old lorry.

When some village girls asked for a lift they were told that the party was a film group. Their destination was Schönberg below Zwiesel, twenty-five miles north of Passau. They were housed in a school. The unloading began and Payne Best observed that Bonhoeffer still had some books with him. The group of 'special cases' were taken to the first floor, a large classroom with views over the lovely green mountain valley. Bonhoeffer sat at the window in the warm sunshine, sunning himself and chatting with Pünder and learning Russian from Kokorin. There were proper beds with coloured blankets, although, of course, the door was locked. Bonhoeffer's bed was next to that of Kokorin, whom he discovered was a nephew of Molotov. They talked of Bonhoeffer visiting Moscow. Hugh Falconer, writing to Sabine a few months later, gives a picture of this relationship: 'He (Bonhoeffer) did a great deal to keep some of the weaker brethren from depression and anxiety. He spent a good deal of time with Wasiliew Kokorin, Molotov's nephew, who was a delightful young man although an atheist. I think your brother divided his time with him between instilling the foundations of Christianity and learning Russian.' Payne Best produced an electric razor from his luggage and it was plugged in to the classroom point for all to use. Everyone was confident of survival.

Quasimodo Sunday 1945

They were still in the comparative comfort of the classroom in Schönberg when the Sunday after Easter dawned. Low Sunday is the usual name in England, but in Germany it is known as Quasimodo Sunday. He was asked to conduct a service for them all. They were a mixed group of Protestants and Catholics, but that hardly mattered any more. They had lived through such times as made Confessional differences peripheral. There was only one difficulty – Wasiliew Kokorin. He was an atheist and a loyal communist. Bonhoeffer could not tolerate the thought that any of their number be separated from them at such a service. Although he must have longed to conduct the service he refused because their solidarity was more important than a religious service. It was only when Kokorin asked him and wanted to be included that he agreed. I don't think Bonhoeffer's theological arguments had convinced him, but he too saw that their solidarity was more important than their theological differences.

The texts for the day were: 'And with his stripes we are healed' (Isa. 53:5); and 'Blessed be the God and Father of our Lord Jesus Christ! By his great mercy we have been born anew to a living hope through the resurrection of Jesus Christ from the dead' (I Pet. 1:3).

Bonhoeffer explained the texts and applied the message to their condition and destiny – release into a free world, or death. Whichever it may be, the true renewal had already taken place in their hearts. Two things had happened – first, Christ had died for us men and for our salvation. He had suffered and we benefited from his suffering. We live because he died. Then the second – because of this God had renewed us. We were new men, unstained by the past. We do not have the text of that sermon, but one who was there and survived said that, 'he spoke of thoughts and decisions which this captivity had produced in all of us'. Prisoners held in other parts of the school wanted Bonhoeffer to come and conduct services for them too, and even talked of smuggling him over. But there was no time.

Only Plutarch Remains

After the morning service, two civilians entered the room and told Bonhoeffer to collect his belongings and come with them: 'Prisoner

240

Bonhoeffer, get ready and come with us.' He knew what that meant and rapidly said his farewells. First, a book. In his letter to his parents in January (17) he had asked for his copy of *Plutarch* and this was to hand. He wrote his name and address with a blunt pencil on the front, middle and back of the book. It might be picked up by someone trying to trace his movements. One of Goerdeler's sons took the book and gave it to his family years later. Then the Bishop of Chichester. If Payne Best survived he was the most likely to see him – he gave him the task of contacting the bishop and saying: 'that for me it is the end but also the beginning – with him I believe in the principle of our universal Christian brotherhood which rises above all national interests and that our victory is certain – tell him too that I have never forgotten his words at our last meeting.' The importance of the bishop for Bonhoeffer can hardly be measured. At this tragic moment he felt once again the deep love he had expressed in Sweden, which he expressed in a final letter, 1 June 1942:

> Let me express my deep and sincere gratitude for the hours you have spent with me. It will seem to me like a dream to have seen you, to have spoken to you, to have heard your voice. I think these days will remain in my memory as some of the greatest of my life. This spirit of fellowship and of Christian brotherliness will carry me through the darkest hour, and even if things go worse than we hope and expect, the light of these few days will never extinguish in my heart.[11]

It was that he remembered when he sent his greetings to Bishop Bell. That Sunday, he journeyed through the day to Flossenbürg where he was taken before a summary court. Canaris, Oster, Strünk, Gehre and finally Bonhoeffer were examined separately and then confronted with each other before they were executed.

A Report from Flossenbürg

Dietrich was hanged in the early hours of Monday morning, 9 April 1945. Only one eye witness has told the story of that last hour. No story of his life is complete without this last witness of Bonhoeffer to a man who knew nothing about him and who would never understand his theology. He was the camp doctor and, writing ten years after the event, he could not forget it:

> On the morning of that day between five and six o'clock the prisoners, among them Admiral Canaris, General Oster, General Thomas and Councillor of the German Supreme Court Sack, were taken from their cells, and the verdicts of the court martial read out to them. Through the half-open door

in one room of the huts I saw Pastor Bonhoeffer, before taking off his prison garb, kneeling on the floor praying fervently to God. I was most deeply moved by the way this lovable man prayed, so devout and so certain that God heard his prayer. At the place of execution, he again said a short prayer and then climbed the steps to the gallows, brave and composed. His death ensued after a few seconds. In the almost fifty years that I worked as a doctor, I have hardly ever seen a man die so entirely submissive to the will of God.[12]

SIXTEEN

Postlude

The continuous interest in Bonhoeffer over the sixty years since his execution is due largely to his penetrating analysis of the issues of his generation and the questions he raised about the future, particularly the future of his church. His questions remain relevant to each successive generation. For example, his deep concern with the question, 'Who is Jesus Christ for us today?' will not go away. The failure of his church in the crisis of Nazism, when examined with his honesty, reveals doubts about the integrity of every church in the world. Which church can say that, when the world was in crisis, it was not 'concerned primarily with its own self-preservation, as though that were a thing in itself'.

When *The Shame and the Sacrifice* was published in 1987, attention was turning towards his unfinished and fragmentary work on *Ethics*. Even the arrangements of the fragments were much in doubt. How did he begin this work which he regarded as his most important?

We had accepted that it began with a paragraph on Christian ethics: 'The knowledge of good and evil seems to be the aim of all ethical reflection. The first task of *Christian* ethics is to invalidate this knowledge. In launching this attack on the underlying assumptions of other ethics, Christian ethics stands so completely alone that it becomes questionable whether there is any purpose in speaking of Christian ethics at all.' But if one does, 'Christian ethics . . . Professes to be a critique of all ethics simply as ethics'. Or, as the now accepted arrangement has it:

> There is an unprecedented demand which must be confronted by everyone who wishes to take up the problem of a Christian ethics. The demand is that he must from the outset discard as irrelevant the two questions which generally lead him to pursue the problem of ethics: 'How can I be good?' and 'How can I do good?' Instead of these he must pose a question wholly other and totally different from these two, a question about the will of God.

As Ann I. Nickson points out, 'In earlier editions [of *Ethik*] the force of this radical challenge, which defines Bonhoeffer's ethical agenda with startling clarity, had been softened by its placement midway through the volume.'

This is the kind of decision which made it important to work on the order of the fragments, which dominated much of the International Bonhoeffer Conference in Amsterdam in 1988.

The Amsterdam Conference of 1988

The central place given to Bonhoeffer's *Ethik* led to a discussion of political issues of the time. The keynote speaker was Alan Boesak from South Africa. He asked the question, 'When is it responsible to challenge the State?' In an attempt to answer that question by comparing and contrasting the two different situations - Nazi Germany and Apartheid South Africa - he found much relevance, despite the differences, and he made special reference to the poem *Freedom*, the second stanza of which he quoted in his own translation:

> Step out of your anxious hesitation
> into the storm of life,
> carried only by God's word and your faith,
> and freedom will receive your spirit with joy.

It was also becoming clear that the *Prison Poems* were being studied very closely in several of the countries represented at the conference. New translations were needed – they carried the heart of Bonhoeffer's message to the future. The years that followed in South Africa, with the liberation of Nelson Mandela and the black people of that country, recalled Alan Boesak's prophetic words and Bonhoeffer's, which he summed up with,

> It never occurred to Bonhoeffer that he could claim *not* to be responsible for the deeds of Hitler or that he could avoid guilt by *not* sharing in the plot, which suggested to me his readiness to accept responsibility for what was happening in Germany. He accepted the guilt. He took steps that were necessary to bring about the change that he believed must come.

Alan Boesak added:

> That decision [to involve himself in the conspiracy] and that responsibility alone places him in a category of theologians that almost does not exist today.

Alan Boesak was not the first South African to make that point. John de Gruchy, in 1974 when he wrote the Introductory essay to Eberhard Bethge's *Bonhoeffer: Exile and Martyr*, related Bonhoeffer's action and responsibility to the failure of the South African churches: 'The Church in

South Africa needs to acknowledge clearly and honestly that it is guilty and responsible for a great deal that is wrong, and that it shares deeply in the total guilt of the nation.

Bonhoeffer's persistent voice on this issue could not be silenced.

The poem most relevant to this acknowledgement of guilt is the long meditation through the night in his prison bed, *Night Voices in Tegel*, particularly the lines:

> At peace and firm, we stand man to man,
> as the accused, we accuse.
> Only before thee, maker of all,
> Before thee alone are we sinners

These lines in the poem are preceded by Bonhoeffer's sense of the darkness,

> You, night, full of horror and evil,
> make yourself known to me!

and then the concluding lines,

> Silence, deep and long,
> then I hear the night, as it comes down to me:
> I am not dark, the darkness is your guilt!

Bonhoeffer realised his guilt before God, but not before those who had driven him to it.

In contrast to this, De Gruchy wrote: 'Our tendency to justify ourselves before others is beginning to look like an attempt to justify ourselves before God.'

But not only in South Africa. At that conference, in Amsterdam, in 1988, Hiroshi Murakami told of a confession of guilt by the Japanese churches. He called his paper, 'Confessions of Guilt by Today's Japanese Church'. It began with the question, 'What have the Japanese churches learnt from Dietrich Bonhoeffer?' and gave the immediate answer, "The Japanese Church is guilty".

During the Nazi period, the so – called Free Churches, especially the Baptists and Methodists, had given strong support to Hitler. In Amsterdam in 1988, two representatives of the Free Churches in England and in South Africa (Keith Clements and John de Gruchy) spoke on what they had learnt from Bonhoeffer about real freedom. They made the point that the Free Churches had tended to perceive themselves as gathered apart from the world, but were again beginning to understand the greater freedom of participating in the sufferings of the world. Bonhoeffer learnt the advantage of seeing 'world events from below'. Clements and De Gruchy both saw Bonhoeffer's influence as the challenge to their churches to participate in the struggle for justice and liberation in society, if needs be in resistance to the State".

Keith Clements

Although the bulk of literature in the English language on Bonhoeffer has been from America, one of the most influential of the Bonhoeffer scholars in England is Keith Clements. Two books by him have shown the relevance of Bonhoeffer in world affairs outside the usual activity of the churches. The first was in reaction to the Falklands War. Clements had been surprised, like many others in Britain, by the upsurge of so-called 'patriotism' a jingoistic fever, which swept over Britain. In 1984 he published *A Patriotism for Today*, with the subtitle, 'Love of Country in Dialogue with the witness of Dietrich Bonhoeffer'. Several writers on Bonhoeffer have used the word 'Patriotism' in the title of their books. These writers asserted, against the official German view, that Bonhoeffer was not a traitor because of his involvement in the 20 July plot. It was, in fact, not until 1996 that a Berlin court decision confirmed a Bavarian court decision 'invalidating the treason verdict against Bonhoeffer and other conspirators'.

Clements attacks the patriotism he saw in England as the very opposite of 'true patriotism' which can well show love of country, by opposing the legitimate government when it is wrong – even working against it as Bonhoeffer did. That was 1984/1986. His second book published in 1990 was on 'Freedom'. There he asked, 'What Freedom?' He went back to an answer given by Bonhoeffer in 1932 (aged 20):

> To be free is to be in love, is to be in the truth of God. The one who loves, because made free by the truth of God, is the most revolutionary person on earth . . . Upsetting all values, the dynamite of human society . . . The most dangerous of people.

Clements usually argues from a knowledge of the totality of Bonhoeffer's writing. This was very clear in the earlier book. In the later book he points out the importance of the prison writings, including the drafts for a novel, a short story and the poems. Dealing with perspectives of liberation he refers to the poem, *Night Voices in Tege*.This poem has since undergone several retranslations and does in fact show some of Bonhoeffer's ideas of freedom most profoundly. There is much work yet to be done on it.

Ann Nickson's *Bonhoeffer on Freedom* is a more thorough exploration of this theme and she makes use of two poems – obviously, *Stages on the Way to Freedom*, but also *The Friend*.

The American writing, particularly that of Geffrey Kelly has consistently dealt with the totality of Bonhoeffer's writing – as available. The amount of material grows.

The Availability of New Material

Since the publication of *The Shame and the Sacrifice* three major events have occurred which provided substantial new material.

(a) At the 6th International Bonhoeffer Conference, held in New York in 1992. Ruth-Alice Wedemeyer-Bismarck, the sister of Bonhoeffer's fiancée, read a selection of the letters which passed between the two betrothed while he was in prison. Maria had kept most of them from publication until after her death. Maria was now dead and Ruth – Alice felt able to make them public. They show Bonhoeffer in a new light, but still consistent with the man we know from other sources. They throw a new light on some of the poems, particularly *Vergangenheit*, written after she had visited him in prison for the last time. Her footsteps dying away remained in his memory and pervade the poem. All the available letters were published and by 1994 translated into English. The letters are revealing of the very human side of Dietrich Bonhoeffer and the depth of his love for Maria.

When the young man of 20 wrote, 'To be free is to be in love, is to be in the truth of God', he did not know how far these words would be tested. But in 1944, a prisoner who had little contact with his beloved could write:

> My dear, dear Maria,
>
> It's no use, I have to write to you at last and talk to you with no one else listening. I have to let you see into my heart without someone else, whom it doesn't concern, looking on. I have to talk to you about that which belongs to no one else in the world but us, and which becomes desecrated when exposed to the hearing of an outsider. I refuse to let anyone else share what belongs to you alone; I think that would be impermissible, unwholesome, uninhibited, and devoid of dignity, from your point of view. The thing that draws and binds me to you in my unspoken thoughts and dreams cannot be revealed, dearest Maria, until I'm able to fold you in my arms. That time will come, and it will be all the more blissful and genuine the less we seek to anticipate it and the more faithfully and genuinely we wait for each other.

This is a side to Bonhoeffer that we could not have known without these letters. The contrast with the letters to Eberhard Bethge, which were also very personal, helps us to see the rounded man. He writes of his longing for marriage and a family. In exchanges of letters they plan their home together, even to the point of discussing the furniture. On her part, she tells of chalking out on the floor of her room, the size and shape of his cell in order to live in as confined a space as he was.

In *The Cost of Moral Leadership* (2002), Kelly and Burton Nelson comment:

> In considering the spiritual life of Bonhoeffer, we need this touching portrait of a man in love alongside those of the scholar who wrote *Act and Being*, the seminary director who impacted over one hundred and fifty students, the double agent who sought to stay one step ahead of the Gestapo, and the prisoner who beckoned the contemporary church to ponder the meaning of 'nonreligious Christianity' and 'The World Come of Age'.

(b) The publication in the 1990s of 17 volumes of the *Works of Dietrich Bonhoeffer* included many letters and statements of significance, previously unknown and enabled us to see his works in totality.

(c) The publication in the year 2000 of a thoroughly revised edition of Eberhard Bethge's definitive *Biography of Dietrich Bonhoeffer* in English opened up a much clearer view of the man and his thought. This *Biography*, first published in 1961 had been severely edited and cut. Limitations, imposed by the publisher, meant that the English edition contained little material about his background and family. It also left out other passages which were important. However, in the year 2000, much more was known about Bonhoeffer and readers were anxious to have the whole story. Victoria Barnett not only restored these cuts but also revised the translation in the light of greater knowledge of the circumstances of Bonhoeffer's life. There was, of course, far more interest in Bonhoeffer, at least in America in 2000 than in 1967. As it now stands, the book is a remarkable resource for the study of Bonhoeffer's life and thought. Unfortunately, it has not found a publisher in the UK.

As a result of this extended knowledge of Bonhoeffer's writing and activity many of the earlier opinions about him have changed. This is a continuing process and like his theology is affected by events and the need to interpret them. Eberhard Bethge, on his visit to South Africa in 1973, illustrated this process of understanding and influence by describing the different developments in the two parts of a divided Germany.

'For many in the West', he said, 'Bonhoeffer is a menace to Christian identity and a destroyer of the Lutheran doctrine of the two separate kingdoms of Church and State. His 'non-religious interpretation' is looked upon as one of the causes of a dangerous second 'Enlightenment', and his underground activities against Hitler as overstepping the legitimate boundaries of the Church's domain.'

That was a Church still enjoying privileges. But in the East, 'There, Bonhoeffer's death, and his fragmentary notes from Tegel prison mark, not only the end of an epoch in secular and church history, but the beginning of a new one.'

When the reunion came, the two separate Bonhoeffer Societies in Germany were amalgamated. The mix was not entirely happy. The West had so many resources that they saw themselves as liberators. It took a very long time, even in the Bonhoeffer Society, to hear what the East had to say about the liberating value of Bonhoeffer studies when they were still an unprivileged body.

The Bonhoeffer Archives

(a) The International Bonhoeffer Society, housed in Düsseldorf, preserves the documents and follows the writings about Bonhoeffer in German. An important part of its ongoing activity is the publication of a *Rundbrief* – a circular letter, which was first issued in 1975 as a cyclostyled few sheets, but from 1984 has been circulated as a booklet of 60–70 pages. It includes details of events, lists of publications, articles and scripts of addresses given at Bonhoeffer functions. Over a period of 20 years and in 75 issues it traces the changes in Bonhoeffer studies and publishes newly discovered documents. The editor is Professor Christian Gremmels, who is the president of the Society, assisted by the vice-president, Professor Dr Martin Nüneke.

The issue for November 2004 included an article by Bernd Vogel setting the scene for celebrations in 2005 (60 years after Bonhoeffer's execution) and 2006 (centenary of his birth). These will centre on questions about the future. Those who have responded to Bonhoeffer in their work will ask the question: 'What must be our "yes" and our "no" to Dietrich? Bonhoeffer?' This will mean asking frankly, was he wrong about 'religionlessness'? Can we learn anything from Bonhoeffer's Christian peace ethic today? In fact, what does his *Ethik* hold for the Church or for the State today? Those who have learnt to face the future in our present society from Bonhoeffer's incisive questioning are now beginning to ask how far his answers are still relevant. Society has greatly changed. Sexual ethics, for example, is totally different from that accepted in Bonhoeffer's day. While it is right to continue to listen to this seminal thinker, it is wise to remember that he was not always right. Even when he was for his generation, how much was specific to that time and situation? All these contributions, when applied to the issues of our day, will need some modification if not rebuttal. The major question now seems to be the question of relevance. The German Section is well aware of the need to re-examine as well as to search out new documents. Sometimes this takes the form of looking more closely at some of his writings which have been known but not always taken into account. The two areas of main development have been a closer study of his preaching and the poems he wrote in prison.

(b) The English-speaking Section of the International Bonhoeffer Society is housed in America. Geffrey Kelly has been secretary of this English language Section and for two terms its president; Burton Nelson was vice – president. Both have been assiduous Bonhoeffer scholars and have published, both jointly and separately.

In 1984, Geffrey Kelly published, *Liberating Faith*. Eberhard Bethge wrote an Introduction in which he said, 'We have now before us the first book by an American that combines accurate analysis with the creation of valuable guidelines for future discussion of the critical implications of Bonhoeffer's life and theology.' One of the many issues he tackles afresh in the book is the way in which Bonhoeffer's theology encouraged the Liberation Theology of Latin America. This was certainly true and much work has since been done to develop that relationship. One of the tendencies in Bonhoeffer studies today is that of developing new ways of thinking, often more revolutionary than he would approve.

Almost two decades later, in 2003, these two – Burton Nelson (who has since died) and Geffrey Kelly wrote one of the most important books so far published on Bonhoeffer, under the title *The Cost of Moral Leadership*. All the emerging issues are dealt with and much of the work of former scholars discussed and incorporated in this most readable book. The life of Bonhoeffer is retold, taking into account the latest publications.

They state their conviction that the legacy of Bonhoeffer's life 'will indisputably affect the course of Christianity for decades to come.' The rest of the book supports that assertion. While much of the book contains material which is familiar to those who read Bonhoeffer literature, the greater part indicates the direction studies of Bonhoeffer's life and thought have proved relevant in a number of different political situations. After the terrorist attack on the American centres of trade and government in New York and Washington on 11 September 2001, there was much discussion about an American response. Burton and Kelly compare that issue with Bonhoeffer deciding to leave the pacifist position and support the conspiracy. In view of the suffering of Jews and others who were powerless, Bonhoeffer was prepared to seek the defeat of his country, knowing that many innocent people would be killed. The attack on Afghanistan, in response to 9/11 was to unseat the Taliban. This they claim can be justified on Bonhoeffer's arguments in *Ethics*. This killing 'could be countenanced morally only in order to protect the lives of the nation's innocent civilian population including the victims of systematic genocidal terror'. But Bonhoeffer writes convincingly that, 'the sparing of life has an incomparably higher claim than killing can ever have'. When he wrote as he did about war, he had in mind the Nazi attempt to destroy the helpless and powerless who were economically of no value to the building of a pure race. For him, it is the duty of the moral leader as well as the strong and those hailed 'socially valuable' to defend even those whom 'class conscious societies' have labeled 'less valuable'. His authority for saying this is the right to life of all those created by their Father God to be brothers and sisters of Jesus Christ'. If that took war, then so be it. Much has been written on Bonhoeffer's pacifism in view of his later activities. This preoccupies many Bonhoeffer scholars still. Emphasis is moving away from studying Bonhoeffer's minutiae in theology, even disputes over texts, towards the relevance of his life and thought in today's world. Afghanistan, Iraq, Sudan and many other ethically confusing problems have been faced with his help. Although a man of strong ideas, Bonhoeffer was, to the end, not bound by his earlier convictions. His previous pacifism, for example, seemed no longer realistic enough in the changing context of Nazi terror. He does not solve problems, but he indicates the way in which the solving process may go. We have grown used to the phrase 'peace process' rather than the simplistic idea that peace comes by words.

The Modern Martyrs in Westminster Abbey

On 9 July 1998, the stone statues of ten modern martyrs were unveiled on the West Front of Westminster Abbey and a memorial service was held with great splendour. The ten included Martin Luther King, Archbishop Romero and Dietrich Bonhoeffer. The title 'marty' means simply, 'one who witnesses' and a Christian martyr is only who witnesses to his faith in Jesus Christ. It has come to be used as 'one who witnesses unto death'. And that is the sense in which these 'martyrs' of Westminster – Abbey were chosen – one from each section of the Christian Church, and from each continent . . . For a Lutheran of Europe, the choice of Germany was natural, but why Bonhoeffer? Like Martin Luther King, and Archbishop Romero, he was not put to death for being a Christian or even for his Christian preaching. In fact, part of his defence before the interrogation in prison was that the Gestapo had never denounced him for any sermon that he had preached. None of these three fit the traditional view of a Christian martyr. But all three by defending the underprivileged – the black people, the poor of El Salvador and the Jews of Germany – lived out their faith in Jesus Christ and their conviction that such were brothers and sisters. To use his language in the circular he wrote just before his arrest, *Ten Years After* (i.e. after 1933): 'We have for once learnt to see the great events of world history from below, from the perspective of the outcast, the suspects, the maltreated, the powerless, the oppressed, the reviled - in short, from the perspective of those who suffer.'

An article in *The Times* on the day following the unveiling listed the ten "Westminster Abbey Modern Martyrs" and recalled Bonhoeffer's words in a sermon as early as 1932: "We must not be surprised if also for our Church there will be times again when the blood of martyrs will be called for'. He added, '. . . but it will not be innocent blood'.

The Sermons

Apart from a few sermons which seemed topically relevant, most had been neglected until Otto Dudzus published them in their entirety in two volumes (1985). His introduction and editing made clear what Eberhard Bethge had indicated in his *Biography*, that these sermons showed another side to Bonhoeffer. Since then they have been translated and studied. Coming from *Letters and Papers from Prison*, the English language reader can be excused for finding a puzzling contrast. Although Bonhoeffer was well aware of the scholarly work done in higher criticism of the books of the Bible, he seems to take up a very conservative attitude to the text when preaching. There is room in the lecture room for careful study of the background to the books of the Bible and reasonable discussion about authorship and dates, but in preaching, Bonhoeffer is anxious to let the text speak for itself. The most detailed and honest criticism of the text must never prevent the Word from proclaiming in powerful terms the message of the Bible. When dealing with the Psalms he is prepared to let David be considered the author if that is what the Psalm requires. His sermons illustrate what he taught at Finkenwalde. He himself practised daily meditations on a Scripture passage, letting the text speak to him by reading, even short passages, again and again. He differentiated clearly between the uses of the Bible in the pulpit, in the study and in private prayer. Bethge tells how he listened carefully to his students when they were preaching in the setting of worship, never criticising or analysing them. He listened reverently and with attention to sermons which were often very poorly structured. He regarded the sermon as God's word to him individually, as to others of the worshipping community.

For Bonhoeffer, preaching was above all proclamation, not exegesis. He would preach upon the prophetic texts which have been used to predict the coming of the Christ, without reference to their original objective in history. The ancient prophets proclaimed the Word of God over the manger in Bethlehem. 'For to us a child is born, to us a son is given', is ascribed without discussion to the Christ child born in Bethlehem. Even those great claims, 'And he will be called Wonderful Counsellor, Mighty God, Everlasting Father, Prince of Peace' are without reservation individually explained as the attributes of the Christ. Above all, the Word of God must be heard and proclaimed.

The place for study was in the classroom or alone with the commentaries in the study. Once in the pulpit, the Word must be handled with confidence and care. This made his sermons enormously relevant and direct. He was not a political preacher, but he allowed the Word to have freedom. Some of the sermons are the most incisive and relevant of all his writings. When he preached to his Confirmation Class at their confirmation, on Jacob wrestling with the angel at Jabbok, then going on to meet his brother whom he had wronged, he did not have to press the point that Jacob looked at Esau and 'his face was as the face of God'.

The more intensive study of the Psalms has shown us Bonhoeffer as the biblical preacher, proclaiming the Word with power. No 'Evangelical' could ask more, but he does not subscribe to 'Fundamentalism'.

The Poems

The poems which Bonhoeffer wrote towards the end of his prison years have received new attention since *The Shame and the Sacrifice* was published. They were always popular and well received in their early English translation. They contributed to the publication by Collins of most of his works over several years and to the English translation of Bethge's *Biography*. *Von Guten Mächten* found its way into many hymnbooks in several languages, including English. Others too became favourites. But the translation into English, at least, did not convey the full force of what Bonhoeffer was agonising to say. He had tried prose and drama, but turned to poetry because it was the only medium in which he could express his deepest thoughts in the dying months of his life.

His longest poem, *The Death of Moses* was not at first included in Bethge's list. He thought it too long and not a very good poem. For some time it was neglected. The theme of the poem was the subject of one of his early sermons, preached in Cuba during his time in New York's Union Theological Seminary. In that sermon he asked why Moses was not allowed to enter the Promised Land. Now, in Tegel, he knew that his vision for the future of Germany and the Church would eventually be 'marching free into the Promised Land', but he would not be with them.

Another poem which has attracted attention is *Glück und Unglück,* at first translated as *Joy and Sorrow*. A careful examination in the way that Bonhoeffer uses these words in his attempt at a novel raises questions about the translation. The poem was written while he was anxiously waiting for news of the attempt to assassinate Adolf Hitler, planned for 20 July 1944. Its theme is that 'Glück' and 'Unglück' are not so clearly separated. They both have their effect and one is not quite sure which is to be preferred. He was in doubt about the plot and uncertain whether he would welcome its success. The poem recognises that while Glück and Unglück are opposites, they can be almost indistinguishable. It points out the arbitrariness of the two and how they are outside our control. Either one can take hold of us and destroy us. When at last we know that what looks like success has been revealed in its true outlines as failure, then only steadfast love can transform that failure into true success. The poem will attract many more interpretations yet as we ponder the inexplicable nature of Glück and Unglück.

The Cost of Moral Leadership

Under this title, Geffrey Kelly and Burton Nelson have produced the most important book on Bonhoeffer to appear for many years. Its theme is 'The Spirituality of Dietrich Bonhoeffer' and it sets the agenda for Bonhoeffer studies for years to come. The Appendix to the main text of the book contains, 'Questions for Discussion', chapter by chapter. Many of these are questions still to be satisfactorily answered.

Each chapter has ten extended questions. Here are three from those questioning paragraphs:

1. How would we describe our relationship with Jesus Christ in the light of Bonhoeffer's contention that Christ 'asks us for help in the form of a beggar, the form of a ruined human being in torn clothing'?
2. What is a servant church?
3. How do Bonhoeffer's comments on the biblical story of Gideon apply to the moral leadership that should be exercised in both church and secular government? How does the faith demanded of Gideon correlate with the practical, complex tasks of administering the day-to-day affairs of an institution?

That last question has added to it a direct question to the United States, but in some measure is relevant to all nations:

'does the United States rely too much on its weapons arsenal and too little on what God has mandated of leaders through the biblical Word?'

There are a hundred such questioning paragraphs in this Appendix, but these three will occupy many minds and consciences for some time to come.

Notes

Key to the abbreviations

Bethge, D.B.	*Dietrich Bonhoeffer: a Biography by Eberhard Bethge*, E.T., Collins, 1970.
I.K.D.B.	*I Knew Dietrich Bonhoeffer*, ed. Wolf-Dieter Zimmermann, E.T., Collins, 1966.
N.R.S.	*No Rusty Swords*, ed. Edwin H. Robertson, E.T., Collins 1965.
T.W.F.	*The Way to Freedom*, ed. Edwin H. Robertson, E.T., Collins 1966.
T.P.	*True Patriotism*, ed. Edwin H. Robertson, E.T., Collins, 1973.
Predigten	Otto Dudzus, *Dietrich Bonhoeffer: Predigten, Auslegungen. Meditationen* Vol. 1, 1984; Vol. 2, 1985. Chr, Kaiser Verlag. München (German text).
Leibholz	Sabine Leibholz, *The Bonhoeffers*, E.T., Sidgwick & Jackson, 1971.
C.A.H.	*Christians against Hitler* by Edwin Robertson, SCM Press, 1962.
Ethics	*Ethics*, by Dietrich Bonhoeffer, E.T., SCM Press, 1963 edn.
C.D.	*The Cost of Discipleship*, by Dietrich Bonhoeffer, E.T., SCM Press 1959 edn.
L.P.P.	*Letters and Papers from Prison*, by Dietrich Bonhoeffer E.T., SCM Press, 1971 edn.
G.S.	*Gesammelte Schriften*, Vols. 1–5. Chr, Kaiser Verlag, München, 1958–72.

Chapter One

1   Bethge, D.B. p. 6
2   Bethge, D.B. p. 9
3   Bethge, D.B. p. 24, cf. Sabine Leibholz, in I.K.D.B. pp. 23–4
4   Bethge, D.B. pp. 25–6
5   Emmi Bonhoeffer, in I.K.D.B., p. 37

Chapter Two

1   N. R. S. p. 76
2   N.R.S. pp. 75–6
3   N.R.S. pp. 77–8

Chapter Three

1   The Rome Diary, quoted by Bethge, D.B. p. 39
2   E.T., Collins, 1963
3   Bethge, D.B. pp. 50, 51
4   Predigten, I. p. 96
5   Bethge, D.B.
6   Predigten, I. pp. 207–8
7   Predigten, I. pp. 208–9
8   Predigten, I. p. 213
9   E.T., Collins 1962
10   Full text of the inaugural lecture, N.R.S. pp. 46–65

Chapter Four

1   N.R.S., pp. 107–9
2   Predigten, I. pp. 220–6
3   Text of the whole letter in English, N.R.S., pp. 67–72
4   Leibholz, p. 76
5   Leibholz, p. 81
6   Burton Nelson, Bonhoeffer Conference, Forest Hill, 1985
7   Paul Lehmann, in I.K.D.B., p. 45
8   Burton Nelson
9   Bethge, D.B. pp. 117–18
10   N.R.S., p. 101

Chapter Five

1   N.R.S., pp. 131–5
2   N.R.S., p. 116
3   N.R.S., p. 119
4   The whole letter is in N.R.S., pp. 135–7; a further letter to Sutz
     on the Confirmation Class is on pp. 145–8
5   Predigten, I. pp. 263–70
6   N.R.S., pp. 149–53
7   N.R.S., pp. 153–69
8   N.R.S., pp. 178–84

9   Bethge, D.B. p. 188
10   Predigten, I. pp. 328–36
11   Predigten, I. pp. 337–9
12   Predigten, I. pp. 340–9

Chapter Six

1   Bethge, D.B. p. 191
2   N.R.S., pp. 186–200
3 & 4 C.A.H., p.18
5   Full text in English of this 'Platform of the German Christians' is in Appendix A to 'The German Phoenix', by Franklin Littell, pp. 180–3
6   C.A.H., pp. 28–32
7   C. A. H., p. 29
8   N. R. S., p. 217
9   Bethge, D.B. p. 202
10   G. van Norden, 'The Church in the Crisis of 1933', p. 57
11   N.R.S., pp. 203–5
12   N.R.S., pp. 212–13: the whole sermon pp. 208–3
13   N.R.S., pp. 217–18
14   N.R.S., pp. 226–7
15   N.R.S., pp. 230–3
16   N.R.S., pp. 223–36

Chapter Seven

1   N.R.S., pp. 249–50
2   I.K.D.B., pp. 77–8
3   Lawrence B. Whitburn, in I.K.D.B., pp. 79–81
4   Predigten, I. pp. 380–501
5   Ethics, p. 147
6   Predigten, I. pp. 425–30
7   N.R.S., pp. 250–1
8   N.R.S., p. 252
9   N.R.S., pp. 252–3
10   This was a major German Christian Rally at which an extremely pro-Nazi statement had been made – see, Bethge, D.B. p. 263
11   Full text of the statement in N.R.S., pp. 257-8
12   N.R.S., pp. 260–1
13   N.R.S., pp. 265–6
14   The Times, 4 June 1934 – reproduced in C.A.H., pp. 48–52
15   Bethge, D.B. p. 299

16   Stephen Neill & Ruth Rouse, 'A History of the Ecumenical Movement: 1917–1954', p. 58

17   N.R.S., pp. 284–7

Chapter Eight

1   Bethge, D.B. p. 334

2   Wolf-Dieter Zimmermann in I. K. D. B., p. 108

3   I.K.D.B., p. 109

4   E.T., SCM Press, 1954

5   E.T., SCM Press, 1959

6   N.R.S., pp. 292–3

7   N.R.S., pp. 293–6

8   N.R.S., pp. 293–6

9   Bethge, D.B. pp. 395–6

10   N.R.S., pp. 321–39

11   'The Visible Church in the New Testament' – full text in English in T.W.F., pp. 42–51

12   T.W.F., pp. 69–70

13   T.W.F., p. 73

14   T.W.F., pp. 122–8

15   Predigten, II. pp. 64-71(E.T., T.W.F., pp. 137–43)

16   T.W.F., pp. 147–9

17   T.W.F., pp. 149–60

18   Correspondence of Bishop Bell in Lambeth Library, 3 July 1937

Chapter Nine

1   'Paul Schneider: Pastor of Buchenwald', SCM Press, 1956, pp. 69–73

2   Life Together, SCM Press, 1954, pp. 100–12

3   C.D., pp. 115–16

4   C.D., p. 117

5   T.W.F., pp. 164–72

6   I.K.D.B., pp. 126–9

7   Bethge, D.B. p. 497

8   N.R.S., p. 221

9   Bethge, D.B. p. 237

10   Bethge, D.B. p. 236

Chapter Ten

1   T.W.F., pp. 204–6
2   13 April 1939. T.W.F., p. 210
3   Bethge, D.B., p. 549
4   Bethge, D.B., p. 547, the correspondence with Hodgson in Oxford is reproduced in T.W.F., pp. 206–10
5   Bethge, D.B. p. 552
6   T.W.F., pp. 222 and 226
7   The American Diary is reproduced in English in T.W.F., pp. 227–42
8   T.W.F., p. 246

Chapter Eleven

1   Mary Bosanquet, 'The Life and Death of Dietrich Bonhoeffer', Hodder & Stoughton, 1968, p. 219
2   T.W.F., pp. 224–6
3   L.P.P., p. 16
4   T.W.F., p. 249
5   T.W.F., p. 251
6   'Ethics', pp. 59–66
7   'Ethics', pp. 98–160
8   T.P., pp. 38–43
9   T.P., pp. 57–62
10   Bethge, D.B. p. 591
11   T.P., pp. 64–7
12   Bethge, D. B. pp. 587–8
13   '*Ethics*', pp. 56–9
14   T.P., p. 70
15   T.P., pp. 71–2
16   T.P., p. 72
17   T.P., p. 73
18   T.P., pp. 74–5
19   Predigten, II. pp. 335-43, cf. his Advent Letter to the Brethren, T.P., pp. 77–81
20   I.K.D.B., pp. 193–5

Chapter Twelve

1   Ethics, p. 91
2   'To Kill Hitler' by Constantine Fitzgibbon, 1972, p. 61
3   T.P., p. 98

4	T.P., p. 99
5	T.P., p. 103
6	T.P., pp. 116–17
7	T.P., p. 131
8	Leibholz, p. 107
9	Leibholz, pp. 160–1
10	C.A.H., p. 95
11	C.A.H., p. 100
12	G.S., II. pp. 433–7
13	G.S.,I. p. 50 (quoted by Bethge, p. 647)
14	Bethge, D.B. pp. 393–4

Chapter Thirteen

1	L.P.P., pp. 24–5
2	L.P. P., p. 17 from 'After Ten Years', a reckoning made at New Year 1943
3	L.P.P., pp. 56–61
4	L.P.P., pp. 61–9
5	L.P.P., pp. 41–7
6	L.P.P., p. 415, from an Appendix to L.P.P., headed, 'The Other Letters from Prison'.
7	L.P.P., p. 416, cf. the letter to his parents, 17 December 1943, pp. 165–6
8	L.P.P., pp. 347–8
9	L.P.P., p. 418
10	L.P.P., pp. 147–50

Chapter Fourteen

1	L.P.P., pp. 248–52
2	L.P.P., p. 278
3	L.P.P., p. 280
4	L.P.P., p. 280
5	L.P.P., p. 282 – cf. 'Christology', SCM
6	L.P.P., p. 282
7	L.P.P., pp. 294–300
8	L.P.P., pp. 311–12
9	L.P.P., pp. 319–20 – the poem is on pp. 320–3
10	L.P.P., p. 327
11	G.S., IV. pp. 597–612
12	L.P.P., pp. 340–1
13	L.P.P., pp. 344–6

14   L.P.P., pp. 349–56
15   L.P.P., pp. 357–61
16   L.P.P., pp. 360–1

Chapter Fifteen

1   Bethge, D.B. p. 730
2   'Ethics', p. xvii
3   L.P.P., pp. 398–9
4   L.P.P., pp. 391–2
5   L.P.P., pp. 380–3
6   Bethge, D.B. p. 791
7   Fabian von Schlabrendorff, in I.K.D.B., pp. 226–31
8   I.K.D.B., p. 231
9   Captain Payne Best, 'The Venlo Incident', pp. 171ff
10   Bethge, D.B. p. 823
11   T.P., p. 180
12   I.K.D.B., p. 232

Index

I Stand at the Door

The Advent Sermons of Dietrich Bonhoeffer

Edited and translated by Edwin Robertson

'And then, Advent comes,' wrote Dietrich Bonhoeffer. 'So many beautiful memories we share of that season . . . A prison cell is like our situation in Advent: one waits, hopes, does this and that, meaningless acts, but the door is locked and can only be opened from the outside. That is how I feel just now.'

Preaching was the essence of Bonhoeffer's witness and no season was more important to him than the Advent season, leading up to Christmas. One story he told to Sunday school children in his first pastorate was to be repeated and expanded many times. Its essence was of an old woman shut out in the cold on a snowy night, with the door locked against her. He used this theme repeatedly to illustrate the Advent message of the locked door – to keep the Saviour out – or to keep the Christian waiting inside.

It was however in the afterglow of Easter that the door opened for him on 9th April 1945, when he walked naked to his cruel execution, with his last words, 'This is the end – but for me the beginning of life.'

This collection is a moving compilation of Bonhoeffer's Advent sermons from 1929 to 1944.

Eagle
ISBN 0 86347 572 8

My Soul Finds Rest in God Alone

Reflections on the Psalms by Dietrich Bonhoeffer

Edited and translated by Edwin Robertson

'The only way to understand the Psalms,' wrote Dietrich Bonhoeffer, 'is on your knees, the whole congregation praying the words of the Psalms with all its strength.'

By the time he was executed by the Nazi government in 1945, Bonhoeffer had established himself as one of the leading theologians of his day – not only in his native Germany, but also around the world.

During the years 1935 to 1937 he gave a series of lectures and sermons on the Psalms, describing the incredible range of the various psalmists writings as '. . . a strange journey of ups and downs, falling and rising, despair and exhilaration . . . which is the experience of all those who pray their way through the Psalms, one after the other.'

This book also includes material preached during the war, ultimately to fellow-prisoners awaiting their fate.

Eagle
ISBN 0 86347 401 2

Voices in the Night

The Prison Poems of Dietrich Bonhoeffer

Edited and translated by Edwin Robertson

'By kindly powers protected wonderfully,
confident, we wait for come what may,
Night and morning, God is by us, faithfully
And surely at each new born day.'

The final verse of the last poem written by Dietrich Bonhoeffer

On the 9th April, within earshot of the guns of the approaching American army, the German theologian Dietrich Bonhoeffer was executed for treason. He had been in prison for two years, firstly at military interrogation prisons in Berlin, then in the notorious detention cellar in Prinz Albert Strasse and finally in the concentration camps of Buckenwald and Flossenburg.

During his time in prison he wrote many poems to his family and friends. From these can be detected a subtle change of mood as his knowledge both of his church and of himself grew and as his prison conditions worsened. The importance of these poems lies in their attempt to express his deepest feelings about himself, his friends, his church and the future of Germany.

This new translation, bearing on Edwin Robertson's intimate knowledge of Bonhoeffer's work since 1945 is the result of many years of careful work. The depth, immediacy, poignancy and relevance of Bonhoeffer's poetry will strike the reader afresh. Some are well known, others such as *The Death of Moses*, appear in English for the first time.

Eagle
0 86347 576 0